T0324738

Enacting Research Methods in Information Systems:
Volume 2

Enacting Research Methods in Information Systems: Volume 2

Edited by

Leslie P. Willcocks
London School of Economics and Political Science, UK

Chris Sauer
Oxford University, UK

and

Mary C. Lacity
University of Missouri-St Louis, USA

Editors
Leslie P. Willcocks
London School of Economics and
Political Science, London, UK

Chris Sauer
Oxford University
Oxford, UK

Mary C. Lacity
University of Missouri-St Louis
St Louis, Missouri, USA

ISBN: 978-3-319-29268-7 (hardback)   ISBN: 978-3-319-29269-4 (eBook)
DOI: 10.1007/978-3-319-29269-4

Printed on acid-free paper

This Palgrave Macmillan imprint is published by Springer Nature
The registered company is Springer International Publishing AG Switzerland

Contents

List of Figures and Tables

Figures

Tables

Introduction

Leslie P. Willcocks, Chris Sauer and Mary C. Lacity

Overview

Volume 2 of the Enacting Research Methods in Information Systems (IS) series collects compelling articles from the *Journal of Information Technology* (JIT) pertaining to *interpretive* and *action research approaches*.

Interpretive research approaches assume that meaning is socially constructed and temporally fluid. Interpretive researchers are concerned with understanding what is specific, interesting, and unique about social phenomena and how such understanding is bounded by time, context, and culture (Dudovskiy 2015; Walsham 1993). With interpretive approaches, researchers engage closely and naturalistically with "participants" to collaboratively co-construct meaning. Interpretive researchers treat research participants as contributors to the sense-making process of inquiry; they are not passive "subjects" to be remotely observed and analyzed. Furthermore, the researcher is not presumed to be an objective witness. Because the researcher–participant relationship takes on the form of an exchange relation (Evans 2012), a researcher will feel he or she "owes" something to the participants, which can influence interpretation and what researchers write (Denzin 1994). The researcher must therefore securitize his or her biases and consider how these biases might influence interpretation (Lacity and Jansen 1994). The notion that interpreters' biases must also be considered before understanding social phenomena is a distinguishing characteristic of interpretive approaches. The same researcher may even ascribe different meanings to the same social phenomena after reconsiderations over time. Thus, multiple interpretations— even by the same researcher—are possible (Wolcott 1990).

There are many *methods* that fall within the broader category of interpretive approaches, including hermeneutics, interpretive case studies, ethnography, phenomenology, and intentional analysis. As a research outlet for interpretive research, JIT is distinguished[1] among top information systems journals: 40 percent of articles published in JIT were based on interpretive approaches during a 10-year period (Chen and Hirschheim 2004). In comparison, only 12 percent of articles in the *European Journal of Information Systems* (EJIS), 9 percent in *MIS Quarterly* (MISQ), and 6 percent in both *Information Systems Research* (ISR) and the *Journal of Management Information Systems* (JMIS) were based on interpretive approaches. In this volume, we are pleased to reprint five interpretive research articles from JIT. Two chapters are based on hermeneutics, one chapter examines the role of research participants in co-creating meaning, and two chapters are examples of interpretive case studies.

Action research approaches place social scientists in the dual roles of researcher and influencer/consultant. The term "action research" was developed by Kurt Lewin in the US and concurrently and independently developed by the Tavistock Clinic in the UK during the 1940s (Baskerville 1999). Action research was evangelized in the strategic management literature three decades later as a way to address the "crisis" in organizational research caused by the disconnect between rigorous research methods and their usefulness for solving practical problems (Susman and Evered 1978). Action research aims to bridge that gap by meeting two goals: (1) to contribute to an immediate practitioner problem and (2) to contribute to the body of knowledge (Myers 1997). As a method, action research approaches have been conceived of as a five-phase process in which the researcher diagnoses a practitioner problem, plans an action to solve the problem, implements the action, evaluates the action, and extracts the learning (Baskerville 1999). Action research approaches are considered "actions" because the researcher implements actual solutions to real organizational problems. Action research approaches are considered "research" because it either yields grounded theory or assesses a prior theory's effectiveness at diagnosing or improving the practitioner situation.

Action research seems particularly applicable to the study of information systems because the discipline is highly applied. As a research outlet for action research approaches, JIT was recognized as a good outlet during the ten-year period from 1991 to 2001 (Chen and Hirschheim 2004). During that time frame, seven percent of JIT's articles used action research approaches compared to two percent in EJIS, one percent in MISQ, and zero percent in both ISR and JMIS during a ten-year period. (Only ISJ had a higher percentage with 12 percent.) Some scholars have recently expressed concern in the reduction of action research papers published over the last few years in top IS journals (Avison et al. 2015). By including three articles that prescribe and describe the use of action research in information systems contexts, we hope to renew the interest in action research approaches. Most notably, **Chapter 16**, "A Critical Perspective on Action Research as a Method for Information Systems Research," by Richard Baskerville and Trevor Wood-Harper has become a classic methods article and it is the most cited article ever published in the 30-year history of the *Journal of Information Technology*, cited over 1,000 times as of 2015.

Introduction to Section IV: Interpretive Research Approaches

Section IV includes five chapters on interpretive research approaches.

Chapters 11 and 12 discuss the application of hermeneutics to the study of information systems. The etymology of the word "hermeneutics" derives from the Greek god Hermes, messengers of the gods. Hermes not only announced the gods' messages verbatim, but also acted as an interpreter to render meaning to their words.

Hermeneutics began as the science of interpretation of sacred or ancient texts; its practical application was exegesis. As a research method, exegesis originated in the seventeenth century when Renaissance scholars sparked renewed interest in early versions of the Bible and in Greek and Roman classics. Its goals were twofold: first, to ascertain the exact translation of a text, and second, to discover the instructions contained in the text. The exegesis method relied on rules that allowed interpreters to identify the intentions of the author and to place his or her meaning within its historical and cultural context. These rules, however, reflected the background of the interpreter, although they are presumed to capture the author's intentions. For example, a biblical interpreter exacts meaning from the Bible allegorically, literally, or liberally, depending on the interpreter's assumptions about the nature of the Bible. Hermeneutics was extended beyond the study of ancient texts to the study of social action (Lacity and Jansen 1994). Social action, like a text, is a meaningful entity to examine, as discussed in the first chapter of this volume (Chapter 11).

In **Chapter 11**, "Towards a Hermeneutic Method for Interpretive Research in Information Systems," Tom Butler aims to make hermeneutics more accessible to information systems researchers. The chapter begins with an overview of four contemporary views on hermeneutics: (1) the conservative (which seeks to discover the author's original intentions), (2) the pragmatic (which seeks to understand the communal effects on interpretation), (3) the critical (which seeks to emancipate), and (4) the radical (which seeks to reveal what is concealed). Butler also provides an exceptional concise and clear overview of Heiddegger's *Being and Time* as the ontological foundation of all four views of contemporary hermeneutics. As human beings, we are thrown into our situations and often act unreflectively based on historical and contextual preunderstanding. We go through much of life unreflective, but when we have a breakdown of understanding, we must interpret phenomena anew through dialectics (Socratic, Hegelian, or Reductionist). This process of interpretation is circular—one's understanding of phenomena as a cohesive whole is established by referencing individual parts and one's understanding of each individual part by referencing back to the whole—the so-called "hermeneutic circle" (Gadamer 1977, 1985). Multiple iterations are needed to understand social phenomena. Once Butler reviews the ontological and philosophical foundations, he offers a short application of hermeneutic principles to the study of an information systems development effort. The author shows five iterations through the hermeneutic process of moving between understanding the whole of the systems development context to its parts. The interesting conclusion is that the research output (e.g., a journal publication) becomes an artifact with its own horizon that requires another cycle of interpretation by readers.

Chapter 12, "Application of Hermeneutics to Studying an Experience Mining Process," by Tanya Linden and Jacob L. Cybulski provides a detailed example of the application of hermeneutics in an information systems study. The authors used hermeneutic principles to study how graphic designers, web developers, and multimedia producers make design decisions about color schemes, menu design, font selection, and other design tasks. The decisions result in a design pattern. The process for elucidating the design pattern is called "pattern mining," thus the title of the chapter. The authors went through several hermeneutic cycles. During the first cycle, they began to understand the domain and its problems. The output of the first cycle was a refined coding scheme to analyze the audio and video data. The subsequent cycles of revising codes and revealing patterns resulted in the identification of nine aspects of the pattern crafting process.

Chapter 13, "Exploring the Role of Informants in Interpretive Case Study Research in IS," by Bendik Bygstad and Bjørn Erik Munkvold examines the role played by informants[2] in interpretive case study research. Their main point is that "informants" play more in the role of interpretive case study research than serving as fact collectors. Rather informants are also key agents in construction and interpretation of the case. This chapter begins by documenting the fact that none of the classic works on case study research both within (e.g., Dubé and Paré 2003; Klein and Myers 1999; Walsham 1995, 2006) and outside (e.g., Yin 1994) the field of information systems address the depth and richness of interactions between informants and researchers. The authors use a longitudinal case study of an internet-based booking system at an international airline to illustrate the value of informants in interpretive case research. The informants played many roles in the research, including providing feedback on the timeline, actors, and events; co-constructing the case narrative; and discussing research implications. Some of this interaction can be quite heated (the authors call it "engaged"). For example, at one point, the authors were told by a participant, *"I do not agree with your interpretation of this event."* One implied takeaway is that researchers should not look upon tough informant criticisms as problems, but as opportunities to improve the research.

Chapters 14 and 15 provide examples of interpretive case studies. In **Chapter 14**, "An Exploration of Information Systems Adoption: Tools and Skills as Cultural Artefacts – the Case of a Management Information System," Deborah Bunker, Karlheinz Kautz, and Anhtai Anhtuan studied two patterns of adoption of a time-keeping application within the IT department of a large Australian company. One pattern was high adoption because the IT subgroup had skills that fitted well with the tool. These skills related to standardization, policy compliance, and performance feedback to employees. In contrast to the high skills match between tool and tool users in the high adoption IT subgroup, the low adoption IT subgroup did not possess high levels of these skills.

In **Chapter 15**, "Institutionalizing Operational Risk Management: An Empirical Study," Carol Hsu, James Backhouse, and Leiser Silva tackled a huge issue prompted by the global financial crisis: how can banks better manage operational risks? They used an interpretive case study of how one bank institutionalized an operational risk management program over a five-year period based on interviews, documents, and observations during site visits. The authors analyzed the data through the three dimensions of structuration theory—signification, domination, and legitimation. They developed three propositions for future research, which is not normally seen in interpretive research, but propositions are positioned as analytical generalizations rather than as predictions. In interpretive studies, analytic generalizations are theoretical generalizations that suggest phenomena from the case may have much wider applicability.

Introduction to Section V: Action Research Approaches

Section V includes three chapters on action research approaches.

In the application of action research to the study of information systems, Richard Baskerville and Trevor Wood-Harper are luminaries (e.g., Baskerville 1997; 1999; Baskerville and Myers 2004; Baskerville and Pries-Heje 1999; Baskerville and Wood-Harper 1998; Kock et al. 1999; Shah et al. 2007). Thus, we are most pleased to reproduce in this collection, **Chapter 16**, "A Critical Perspective on Action Research as a Method for Information Systems Research," by Richard Baskerville and A. Trevor Wood-Harper. In this chapter, the authors describe the philosophical foundation of action research as post-positivist because action research is empirical yet interpretive, experimental yet multivariate, and observational yet interventionist. In their review of the history of action research in other disciplines, the authors warn, *"This is not a main stream social science technique being applied in the new field of IS. Rather, it is an obscure, contentious method found on the periphery of main stream social science being transported into the IS field"* (p. 174). The authors describe the five phases of the action research method in some detail and its main benefits of rigorous intervention and relevance. They also identify the method's main criticisms of "research impartiality," "consulting masquerading as research," and "lack of generalizability." They offer advice as to how action researchers can address the criticisms as they seek grants and publications.

Chapter 17, "The Rise of the Phoenix: Methodological Innovation as a Discourse of Renewal," by David G. Wastell, Tom McMaster, and Peter Kawalek provides an excellent example of the application of action research to study and influence practice. All the phases of "ideal" action research methods described by Baskerville and Wood-Harper in the previous chapter are evident in this work. The authors helped the Salford City Council, a local government agency in Northwest England, diagnose a prior failed implementation of a system development method. The authors helped the Salford City Council develop and implement a new method, called SPRINT. The authors provide evidence of the intervention's success, including direct quotes from clients. For example, the client lead said, *"SPRINT helped profoundly to re-position IT as a true enabler of business transformation."* The authors then reflected on the case and compared case evidence to prior theories. Of particular interest was their analysis of organizational resilience, the capacity of an organization *"to prevent, minimize, or overcome the damaging effects of adversity."* The authors argue that a new discourse of renewal is required to move an organization from merely *surviving* to actually *thriving* following change.

Chapter 18, "Systems Development as a Research Act," by Jim Hughes and Trevor Wood-Harper provides two more illustrative examples of action research. In this chapter, two action cases are described through the phases of diagnosis, action plan, implementation, assessment outcome (i.e., the action contribution), and research outcome (i.e., the theoretical contribution). The domains of the two cases were very different: one action case involved helping a UK-based veterinary practice identify its information needs; and another action involved in audit of an IS investment strategy for a small manufacturer in Wales. The action research method, the authors argue, helps systems developers to become more critically reflective thinkers.

Notes

1. The *Information Systems Journal* (ISJ) is also distinguished as an outlet with 40 percent of its publications based on interpretive research methods.
2. The authors likely used the term "informant" because the official method is called "key informant interviews," but we much prefer the term "participant". In our research, we have always been concerned about the negative connotations of the term "informant" when asking research participants to review papers. Lay people may associate the word "informant" with "criminal informant," "traitor," or "stool pigeon." We were particularly concerned about using the term "informant" when prisoners, military staff, and veterans participated in our research projects.

References

Avison, D., Davison, R., and Malaurent, J. (2015), "The Decline of Action Research in IS: Diagnosis, Reflections, and Proposed Actions for Change," working paper.

Baskerville, R. (1997). Distinguishing Action Research From Participative Case Studies. *Journal of Systems and Information Technology*, 1(1): 25–45.

Baskerville, R. (1999). Investigating Information Systems with Action Research. *Communications of the Association for Information Systems*, 2(19):1–32.

Baskerville, R. and Myers, M. (2004). Special Issue on Action Research in IS—Forward. *MIS Quarterly*, 28(3): 329–335.

Baskerville, R. and Wood-Harper, A.T. (1998). Diversity in Information Systems Action Research Methods. *European Journal of Information Systems*, 7(2): 90–107.

Baskerville, R. and Pries-Heje, J. (1999). Grounded Action Research: A Method for Understanding IT in Practice. *Accounting, Management and Information Technology*, 9: 1–23.

Chen, W. and Hirschheim, R. (2004), A Paradigmatic and Methodological Examination of Information Systems Research from 1991 to 2001. *Information Systems Journal*, 14: 197–235.

Denzin, N. (1994), The Art and Politics of Interpretation. In N. Denzin and Y. Lincoln (eds), *Handbook of Qualitative Research*, pp. 500–515. Sage Publications, Thousand Oaks.

Dudovskiy, J. (2015). Interpretivism. http://research-methodology.net/research-philosophy/interpretivism/

Dubé, L. and Paré, G. (2003), Rigor in IS Positivist Case Research: Current Practices, Trends, and Recommendations. *MIS Quarterly*, 27: 597–635.

Evans, G. (2012), Practicing Participant Observation: An Anthropologist's Account. *Journal of Organizational Ethnography*, 1: 96–106.

Gadamer, H. (1977). The Scope of Hermeneutic Reflection. In D.E. Linge (ed.), *Philosophical Hermeneutics*, pp. 3–104, University of California, Press Berkeley.

Gadamer, H. (1985). The Historicity of Understanding. In K. Mueller-Vollmer (ed.), *The Hermeneutics Reader: Texts of the German Tradition from the Enlightenment to the Present*, pp. 256–292, Continuum. New York.

Klein, H. and Meyers, M. (1999). A Set of Principles for Evaluating Interpretive Field Studies in Information Systems, *MIS Quarterly*, 23: 67–94.

Kock, N., Avison, D., Baskerville, R., Myers, M., and Wood-Harper, T. (1999). IS action research: can we serve two masters? *International Conference on Information Systems* (ICIS).

Lacity, M. and Janson, M. (1994). Understanding Qualitative Data: A Framework of Text Analysis Methods. *Journal of Management Information Systems*, 11(2): 137–155.

Myers, M., (1997). Qualitative Research in Information Systems. *MIS Quarterly*, 21(2): 241–242.

Shah, H., Eardley, A., and Wood-Harper, T. (2007). ALTAR: Achieving Learning Through Action Research. *European Journal of Information Systems*, 16: 761–770.

Susman, G. and Evered, R. (1978), An Assessment of The Scientific Merits of Action Research. *Administrative Science Quarterly*, 23(4): 582–603.

Walsham, G. (1993). *Interpreting Information Systems in Organizations*. Wiley, Chichester.

Walsham, G. (1995). Interpretive Case Studies in IS Research: Nature and Method. *European Journal of Information Systems*, 4: 74–81.

Walsham, G. (2006). Doing Interpretive Research. *European Journal of Information Systems* 15: 320–330.

Wolcott, H. (1990), Writing Up Qualitative Research. Sage, Beverly Hills.

Yin, R. (1994), *Case Study Research: Design and Methods*. Sage, Thousand Oaks.

Section IV
Interpretive Research Approaches

11

Towards a Hermeneutic Method for Interpretive Research in Information Systems

Tom Butler
Telecommunications Engineer, Telecom Eireann, Cork, Ireland and Lecturer, Department of Accounting, Finance and Information Systems, University College Cork, Ireland

Introduction

Recent studies on information systems (IS) development within organizations have indicated that an interpretivist approach to research on the development process is, perhaps, the most appropriate vehicle for the study of this phenomenon (Kanungo, 1993; Walsham, 1993; Myers, 1995, 1997; Butler and Fitzgerald, 1997a,b; Butler, 1998a,b). However, as Galliers (1985) illustrates, IS researchers may choose from among several interpretive approaches when investigating IS-related phenomena. Boland (1985) was one of the first within the IS field to advocate phenomenological hermeneutics as a valid interpretive approach for research on the phenomenon of information systems development: Visala (1991), Kanungo (1993), Westrup (1994) and Myers (1995) have also recommended that hermeneutic philosophy inform research in this area, while Lee (1993, 1994) has championed the use of hermeneutics in broader research contexts within the field. With some notable exceptions (see Davis *et al.*, 1992 and Lee, 1994) there has been little in the way of guidance or example in the use of the hermeneutic method for research purposes within the IS field: this is also true of research in other disciplines, where the hermeneutic method has been advocated in the study of social phenomena (cf. Guba and Lincoln, 1994). In the absence of a well defined and accepted hermeneutic method for use in the study of social phenomena, the objectives of this paper is to forge a link between hermeneutic concepts and praxis in interpretive studies so as to arrive at a research method that makes explicit its hermeneutic foundation. This paper therefore draws on several concepts and techniques from the related philosophies of phenomenology and hermeneutics, marries them with conventional research approaches, tools and techniques, and presents an empirical example of the resultant method's application in an interpretive case study of the information systems development process.

The first section of this paper provides a short introduction to hermeneutic philosophy. The second outlines the ontological foundations of the hermeneutic method by conducting a phenomenological analysis of the nature of Being. Here, several concepts drawn from the related philosophies of Martin Heidegger and Hans Georg Gadamer are integrated into a conceptual model that helps illustrate the complex nature of Being and understanding. The relevance of hermeneutics for interpreting social action is then discussed and, following this, a set of interpretive principles that act as an interpretive framework for the application of the proposed hermeneutic method is presented. The phenomenological and hermeneutic concepts described herein are applied in conjunction with the aforementioned interpretive principles to inform the hermeneutic research strategy outlined in the penultimate section. Concepts and interpretive principles are then employed in an applied example of the method in a study of the systems development process. In the final section, salient issues arising out of this paper are discussed and conclusions given.

Hermeneutic philosophy or how is understanding possible?

The origin of the term hermeneutics (from the Greek *hermënuetikós*) bears an obvious reference to Hermes, the messenger god of the ancient Greeks. In order to deliver the messages of the gods, Hermes had to be acquainted with their language as well as with that of the mortals for whom the messages were destined. Hence, Hermes had to understand and interpret for himself what the gods wanted to communicate before he could translate, articulate, and explicate this to their mortal subjects (Mueller-Vollmer, 1986). While Hermes had to 'explain' what the Gods' intentions were to mortals, his explanations were clarifications aimed at rendering what was unclear clear in order to allow mortals to make sense of and understand what was being conveyed. Hermeneutic philosophy attempts to foster understanding in this way, as opposed to describing cause and effect when attempting to make sense of and comprehend worldly phenomena (Bauman, 1978)

Hermeneutics is defined as the theory or philosophy of the interpretation of meaning (Bleicher, 1980). As a field of academic endeavour, it was for many centuries a subdiscipline of philology; however, according to Madison (1988, p. 25) hermeneutics is today 'a veritable crossroads where tendencies as diverse as phenomenology and linguistic analysis, semantics and the critique of ideologies, structuralism and conceptual analysis, Marxism and Freudianism come together.' Coyne (1995) argues that contemporary hermeneutics is characterized by at least four distinct perspectives, viz. the conservative, pragmatic, critical, and the radical – these are introduced in Table 11.1. It is evident that the first three perspectives bear a resemblance to Lyytinen and Klein's (1985) depiction of knowledge interests (technical, practical and emancipatory) and their relation to the various branches of science (empirical/ analytic, hermeneutical

Table 11.1 Perspectives in contemporary hermeneutics (adapted from Coyne, 1995)

Perspective	Main theme	Proponents
Conservative	The task is to uncover the original meanings of the action-text as intended by the author. Objective, a-historical, and a-contextual purposeful meanings are secured from the correct and decidable interpretation.	Emilio Betti (1955) and Eric Hirsch (1967), to name but two.
Pragmatic (Constructivist)	Interpretation here involves entering into the interpretative norms of a community; meaning here operates and is to be found within the historical contexts of the interpreter and interpreted.	Hans Georg Gadamer (1975), Ludwig Wittgenstein (1953).
Critical	The purpose of interpretation here is emancipatory; conventional wisdoms within communities are challenged in order to address potential power asymmetries.	Karl-Otto Apel (1980) and Jurgen Habermas (1972, 1980).
Radical (Deconstructionist)	Here texts and social action are treated as an endless play of signs that reveal and conceal knowledge through the play of difference and contradiction.	Jacques Derrida (1970, 1976).

and critical). One may conclude from the different strands of hermeneutic thought presented in this table that there are fundamental differences between the different schools: it is, therefore, important for those advocating hermeneutic approaches to research to clearly identify which perspective is being adopted. What is of note, here, however, is the absence of Martin Heidegger from the taxonomy presented in the table. Coyne (1995) explains this by maintaining that Heidegger's philosophical perspective spans all four in one way or another; but he also maintains that the pragmatic/constructivist perspective best reflects Heidegger's overall philosophical stance (cf. Heckman, 1986; Warnke, 1987).

In presenting his thesis on the design of information technologies, Coyne's (1995) main point of departure is Heidegger's phenomenological hermeneutics. Nevertheless, it was Boland (1985) who first introduced phenomenological hermeneutics as a viable approach to research on information systems (see also Boland and Day, 1989). Edmund Husserls' phenomenological perspective provided Boland with the basis for his phenomenological project; however, Boland also introduced the hermeneutic philosophy of Hans Georg Gadamer to illustrate the importance of interpretation in understanding social phenomena. In subsequent studies, Boland maintained his links with Gadamerian hermeneutics and has broadened it to encompass insights from the constructivist cultural psychology of Jerome Bruner (1990) (see, for example, Boland, 1987; Boland, 1991; Boland *et al.*, 1994; Boland and Tenkasi, 1995). Zuboff (1988) also draws on phenomenology to inform her research; but, again, it appears to owe more to Husserl's perspective, modified as it was within the social sciences by the likes of Alfred Schutz and Talcott Parsons[1], than the strand of post-Husserlian phenomenology advocated by Martin Heidegger. (Bauman, 1978 provides a critical analysis of the related phenomenological perspectives advocated by Husserl, Schutz, and Parsons.) In their treatise on the design of computer technology, Winograd and Flores (1986) explicitly adopt the Heideggerian phenomenological perspective and integrate it with Gadamer's (1975) hermeneutic philosophy in order to enhance the field's understanding of computers and their design. More recently, Introna (1997) provided an analysis of Heideggerian phenomenology and Gadamerian hermeneutics to argue for the utility of hermeneutics in attaining an understanding of information within a managerial context. Indeed, with some exceptions (see for example, Klein and Lyytinen, 1985; Nissen, 1985; Rathswohl, 1991) there is a marked trend within the field of IS to gravitate towards a phenomenological hermeneutic perspective informed by the philosophies of Heidegger and Gadamer (see, for example, Lee, 1993, 1994; Myers, 1995; Butler and Fitzgerald, 1997a,b; Butler, 1998b).

Many prominent social scientists have commented on the merits and relevance of Gadamer's hermeneutics and the related philosophy of Heidegger to the social sciences (Hekman, 1986; Palmer, 1969). Bauman (1978), for example, in his comprehensive study of the relationship between hermeneutics and the social sciences, heavily criticizes the Husserlian perspective that has come to dominate in sociology and elsewhere; instead, he argues for the empirical fidelity of Heidegger's phenomenology and illustrates its contribution to the understanding of social phenomena. As previously indicated, it is evident that the various contributions offered by the hermeneutic philosophers listed in Table 11.1 differ significantly in many respects; indeed, there has been much debate and criticism between the different schools of thought. In her examination of the relationship between hermeneutics and the sociology of knowledge, Hekman (1986), following Rorty (1979), supports what has been described as antifoundational hermeneutic thinkers; that is, philosophers who reject the Enlightenment conception of truth with its a-historical and a-cultural biases, and its objective/subjective dichotomy of knowledge, and emphasize, instead, the primacy of human thought and existence within historical, communal, and cultural contexts. In what is a detailed analysis and critique of contemporary hermeneutic thought, only Heidegger and, particularly, Gadamer emerge unscathed. In one way or another, Derrida excluded, the philosophies of Betti, Hirsch, Ricoeur, Husserl, Habermas, and Apel all are shown to fall into the Enlightenment trap of searching for a stable foundation for knowledge by subscribing to one or other side of the objective/subjective dichotomy (cf. Warnke, 1987). Given the foregoing arguments, it is clear, then, that the related constructivist* philosophies of Martin Heidegger and Hans Georg Gadamer, offer the most suitable foundation on which to build a hermeneutic method for research in IS.

The ontological foundations of the hermeneutic method – a phenomenological analysis of the nature of Being

In *Being and Time*, Heidegger (1976, p. 60) points out that phenomenology is the science of the 'Being of entities'; furthermore, he states that 'only though phenomenology is ontology possible.' Phenomena constitute the 'Being of entities', and it is as such that their meaning, modifications, and derivatives are arrived at. However, Heidegger argues that phenomenology does not have as its object that which is visible and clearly defined; rather, it is those phenomena that remain hidden, 'covered over', or somehow disguised, which are of interest. In essence then, Heidegger's phenomenology provides an ontological description of Being, and attempts to arrive at the primordial foundations and meaning of *Dasein's* 'Being-in-the-world'. (Heidegger (1976) refers to the mode of being that is typical of humans as *Dasein*.)

Heidegger (1976) asserts that the meaning of phenomenological description, as a method, lies in interpretation; consequently, he argues that hermeneutics offers the fundamental ontological insights into human interpretation and understanding. In addition, Heidegger points out that *Dasein's* a 'Being-in-the-world' is, essentially, hermeneutic in character and interpretive in its constitution. All phenomena, be they social, physical, or metaphysical constitute a social actor's 'Being-in-the-world' and are, thereby, the potential subjects of interpretation and understanding – as will be seen later, this also includes phenomena such as the various forms of social action found in organizations. Hence, it is argued that people in everyday settings practise the activity of interpretation; as such, it is an innate characteristic of the human condition (Heidegger, 1976; Ricoeur, 1981). It is Boland (1985; p. 200) who provides a point of departure for this paper's thesis in his observation that phenomenology 'is a way of study that respects the intentionality of actors, the symbolic nature of language, and the universal hermeneutic problem [of understanding].' The following subsections deal comprehensively with these themes.

As indicated previously, the related phenomenological and hermeneutic perspectives of Heidegger and Gadamer underpin the foundations of constructivist thought; the concepts that these philosophers expound are quite detailed and complex and cannot be dealt with comprehensively herein. Nevertheless, what is presented here is a brief integrative overview of the salient tenets of constructivist philosophy based on their work. A phenomenological analysis of the ontology of human Being is undertaken to illustrate these concepts; Figure 11.1 presents a conceptual model based on this.

Throwness and being tuned

To begin, *Dasein's* Being-in-the-world is characterized by its *throwness*; that is, in social situations actors find themselves in many situations where (a) their knowledge and understanding is incomplete; (b) they cannot avoid acting; (c) they have difficulty reflecting on their actions; and (d) they cannot predict the eventual outcomes of their actions. Because social actors are thrown into their 'life-world', their existence has, from the outset, been 'tuned' or 'situated' to be a specific existence with other beings, within a specific tradition, and with a specific history.

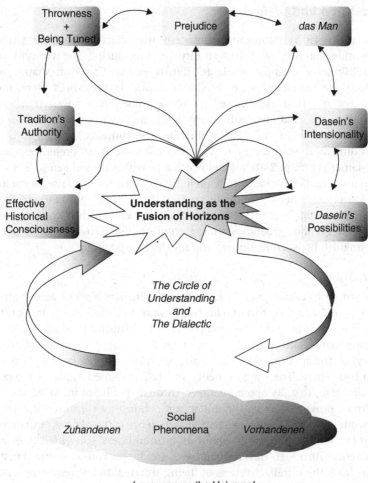

Throwness + Being Tuned

Prejudice

das Man

Tradition's Authority

Dasein's Intensionality

Effective Historical Consciousness

Understanding as the Fusion of Horizons

Dasein's Possibilities

The Circle of Understanding and The Dialectic

Zuhandenen

Social Phenomena

Vorhandenen

Language as the Universal Medium of Being

Legend: The interrelationships between concepts in the upper portion of the model are captured by the double-headed arrows. Here the focal point is the 'fusion of horizons'. Horizons become fused by means of the 'circle of understanding' and the 'dialectic'. Social phenomena consist of those that are ready-to-hand (*Zuhanden*) and present-at-hand (*Vorhanden*); however, it is the *Vorhandenen* that are the object of interpretation and understanding.

Figure 11.1 A conceptual model of the nature of being and understanding

Tradition and prejudice

Gadamer (1975) significantly broadens the concept of Heideggerian 'preunderstanding' and historicality by introducing the concept of Tradition; for example, Gadamer illustrates that Tradition shapes an actor's preunderstanding, or as Gadamer puts it, prejudices. Here, the concept of 'lived experience' Tradition influences a social (*Erlebnis*) describes the relationship between actors and the tradition in which they are embedded; as such, it provides the contexts for their understanding and contributes to the formation of their prejudices. For Gadamer (1975, p. 240) 'a prejudice is a provisional legal verdict before the final verdict is reached.' A prejudice may be true or false, accurate or inaccurate – hence, we might say that there exists legitimate and illegitimate, visible and invisible prejudice. But, as with the 'working out' of Heideggerian 'preunderstanding', 'critical reasoning' is required to distinguish between legitimate and illegitimate prejudice.

Das Man

According to Gadamer (1975), Tradition influences a social actor's attitudes and behaviour through authority, and such authority is transmitted through time and history via cultural mechanisms. Heidegger (1976) argues that it is the quiet authority of *das Man* (roughly translated as 'the they' or 'the anyone') which provides reassurance in the face of existential turbulence. The state of 'being situated' or 'tuned' under the sway of *das Man*, (e.g. as operationalized through public opinion or group norms), provides one with familiar and comforting surroundings; self-reflection precipitated by existential turbulence (a 'breakdown') shatters this tranquillity and brings about an 'unhomliness' (*Unheimlichkeit*) of existence. Although never guaranteed, Heidegger considers the transition from the unreflectiveness of 'being situated' to the reflective state of understanding – the only authentic state of existence – as being achievable by all; an achievement in which the authority of *das Man* and the influence of Tradition are critically scrutinized to verify their authenticity and to overcome such influence if necessary.

Zuhanden versus Vorhanden

In the everyday nature of a social actor's existence, the phenomena that constitute his/her 'life-world' are 'ready-to-hand' (*Zuhanden*) and, as such, are not the object of reflection; the reason for this is that they possess a degree of familiarity that effectively sees them dissolved into an actor's daily existence. From an actor's perspective, such phenomena appear to be perfectly understood, not requiring interpretation as to their ontological status. If, however, an event occurs that constitutes a 'break-down' in understanding, and which challenges the actor's conception of the phenomenon by putting it in a different light, or, indeed, uncovers its ontological status as a phenomenon for the first time, then it will require interpretation so that it may be comprehended. As a consequence of such 'breakdowns', a phenomenon thus becomes the object of 'theoretical' reasoning and acquires the ontological status of being 'present-at-hand' (i.e. a *Vorhanden*). The 'preunderstanding' the actor has of the phenomenon is the starting point from which he will begin his interpretation of the phenomenon. According to Heidegger, this preunderstanding, which is similar to the Gadamerian concept of prejudice, possesses historical and temporal dimensions; consequently, as an anticipatory meaning, it will require 'working out' in terms of the phenomenon itself in order to determine its legitimacy, origin, and validity. This 'working out' is intentional in that the actors will purposefully set about repairing the breakdown and adopt whatever available means to achieve this end.

Dasein's intensionality

Heidegger uses the concept of 'care' to illustrate that social actors will be concerned about their existence and the phenomena that constitute it; they will also be 'involved' in looking after the entities that are of import to them. In this involvement in their 'life-world' actors may, or may not be 'resolute'; by this is meant that they will possess a determination to realize the 'possibilities' they are confronted in their daily round. The whole notion of 'resoluteness' gives rise to the concept of purposeful action and, accordingly, in *Being and Time*, Heidegger (1976, p. 73) argues that 'essentially the person exists only in the performance of intentional acts . . . that are bound together by the unity of meaning.' The everyday Being-in-the-world of *Dasein* is, for Heidegger, teleological in its constitution. According to Heidegger, the Being of *Dasein* is specified in language that consists of terms like 'in-order-to', 'for-the-sake-of', 'for-which' and 'by-means-of'. The social world is therefore constituted by a web or network of relations that are generated by social actors' goals and objectives. Such goals and objectives serve to help actors formulate and realize the possibilities presented to them in the course of their everyday existence.

Dasein's possibilities, effective-historical consciousness and the fusion of horizons

In order to deal with the problems caused by prejudice and the authority of tradition, Gadamer argues that a 'historical consciousness' is vital if misunderstood prejudices are to be understood for what they are. Prejudices need to be isolated; that is, their validity needs to be suspended. This, Gadamer (1975; p. 266) argues, is to be accomplished through the structure of a question: 'The essence of the question is the opening up, and keeping open, of possibilities.' It is here that the issue and importance of the dialectic come into play, an issue that will be addressed presently. However, another concept, that of 'effective-historical consciousness' requires attention. Basically, 'effective-historical consciousness' is the acknowledgement of the fact that the effect of historical events through 'lived experience' influences our interpretation, and hence understanding, of phenomena. The experience of effective-historical understanding is achieved when, in questioning phenomena that are 'present-at-hand', one opens oneself up to tradition and to what the phenomenon has to say, in order to allow its meaning to become evident. In attempting to understand a phenomenon that is 'present-at-hand', a social actor as *Dasein* is confronted with several possibilities of understanding and consequently, for action. In order to ensure an authentic outcome, the actor must enter into a dialectic with the phenomenon and because of his/her 'effective historical consciousness' should be aware of any prejudices at work, will frame his/her questions accordingly, and will be open to what the phenomenon has to say in order to properly apprehend its horizon. A horizon, for Gadamer (1975, p. 269), is simply: 'the range of vision that includes everything that can be seen from a particular vantage point'. Horizons have definite boundaries, and although definable, they are not static. It is the existence of 'historical consciousness' which keeps the horizon in motion; tradition, as the horizon of the past, is constantly in motion with the advance of time. In the 'working out' of prejudices – that is, in interpreting and endeavouring to understand some social phenomenon – horizons are fused: the 'fusion of horizons' is therefore the culmination of the act of understanding between interpreter and interpreted, between researcher and researched.

The central role of the dialectic in hermeneutic thought

Intepretation of social phenomena is never a straight-forward activity: ambiguity and conflict characterize interpretations, such ambiguity and conflict of interpretations can, it is argued, be resolved only through a discursive-dialectic process (Gadamer, 1975; Taylor, 1985). Hermeneutical consciousness, Gadamer (1975) argues, is characterized by the 'logical structure of openness': that is, social actors must remain 'open' to what a phenomenon has to say about itself. As indicated previously, the 'question' is the mechanism that individuals use to open up and keep open the possibilities inherent in Being – possibilities that arise in the existential relationship between the individual and the phenomena that constitute his world. The question, however, must be placed within the context of the dialectic. The term dialectic originates from the Greek expression for the art of conversation. It is accorded several meanings in contemporary philosophy; those that are relevant to the hermeneutical method introduced herein are now outlined and presented in Table 11.2.

The hermeneutic 'circle of understanding'

Perhaps the most fundamental tenet of hermeneutics is that understanding has a circular structure. Because understanding always relates to some phenomenon or other, there is a requirement to posit the basic structure of such phenomena. Gadamer (1975), for example, points out that the 'whole' that is a phenomenon is comprised of the 'parts' or 'details' that constitute it; there is, as Gadamer illustrates, a formal relationship between these 'parts' (component phenomenon), the 'whole' (as constituted by its component phenomena), and what he terms the 'subjective reflex' that an actor adopts towards the phenomenon – that is, the intuitive anticipation of the 'whole' and its subsequent articulation in the 'parts'. Gadamer goes on to stress that the means of apprehending this relationship possesses a circular structure – the 'circle of understanding'. However, the understanding attained in working out this relationship, in negotiating the 'circle', is not in any way perfect; rather, a temporally-based understanding is realized – the so-called 'fusion of horizons'.

Heidegger's view of the hermeneutic 'circle of understanding' posits that in understanding phenomena one remains permanently determined by the anticipatory movement of 'foreunderstanding'. Therefore, commencing with one's 'preunderstanding' or prejudice, the interpretation of a phenomenon (the hermeneutic 'whole') begins by the examination of its component phenomena (the 'parts'). However, understanding the component phenomena can only begin when their relationships to the 'whole' have been determined – the determination of these contextual relationships is itself guided by an expectation of meaning arising from the preceding context (e.g. derived from one's tradition-influenced prejudice). What this means is that when

Table 11.2 A taxonomy of dialectic techniques for hermeneutic research

Type of dialectic	Description
The Socratic dialectic	Gadamer argues that the 'logical structure of openness' is to be found in model of the Platonic dialogue, or, to be more accurate, in the Socratic dialectic of question and answer. In order to effect a 'fusion of horizons' between the horizon of the interpreter and the object of his interpretation, a dialogue takes place between the individual and the phenomenon of interest. However, the interpreter must be aware of his prejudices and recognize that his knowledge is not absolute but incomplete – he must be 'open' to the phenomenon.
The Hegelian dialectic	The Hegelian dialectic comes into play when a particular interpretation or thesis is worked out with a competing interpretation or antithesis so as to arrive at a newer, fuller and more informed interpretation or understanding – the Hegelian synthesis or Gadamarian 'fusion of horizons' results. The Hegelian dialectic involves an interpretive synthesis of expectation or preunderstanding with 'objective' observations in order to make sense of a phenomenon and thus attain an understanding of it (Tarnas, 1991).
Reductionist/ analytical dialectic	The third and final form of dialectic relevant to hermeneutics involves a structural model of dialectic that couples explanation with understanding (Ricoeur, 1981). In subjecting social phenomena to a structural analysis, Ricoeur (1981, p. 220) argues that 'we proceed from naïve interpretations to critical interpretations, from surface interpretations to depth interpretations.' In probing beneath the surface of social phenomena a reductionist/analytical dialectic is employed; this involves the Aristotelian method of division or repeated logical analysis of genera into species or, in hermeneutic terms, of deconstructing the 'whole' into its component 'parts'. It is through the identification and analysis of these 'parts' and their reconstitution into the 'whole' that the structural model of the reductionist/analytic dialectic proceeds. In the social sciences, this approach allows phenomena to be explained in structural terms such that they may be understood. One example of such a technique, employed widely in the IS and management fields, is Rockart's (1979) Critical Success Factors (CSF) Method.

a phenomenon is 'present-at-hand' to an actor, he/she will possess a prejudice-laden preunderstanding of it. Through a dialectic process he/she will identify its 'parts'. Operating from a holistic perspective, each part will be interpreted and its meaning and relationship to the whole consolidated into an emergent understanding of the phenomenon. In cycling through the 'circle of understanding', each 'part' will be consolidated, and in so doing different perspectives will emerge – the horizons of interpreter and phenomenon will gradually fuse; alternatively, one might argue that there will exist as many 'minifusions' as there are component phenomena, the integrative combination of which results in the 'fusion of horizons' that takes place when the phenomenon is fully disclosed. This cycling through the 'circle of understanding' continues until the 'breakdown' has been repaired and the phenomenon achieves the status of a 'ready-to-hand'. It must be noted that, because new questions might arise, or 'facts' emerge, over time, further movements through the circle will be necessary. Thus, as Gadamer (1988, p. 68) points out:

> The movement of understanding always runs from the whole to part and back to the whole. The task is to expand in concentric circles the unity of the understood meaning. Harmonising all the particulars with the whole is at each stage the criterion of correct understanding. Its absence is failure to understand.

In providing an additional insight into the concept of the 'circle of understanding', Ricoeur (1981), too, breaks with the Dilthian dichotomization of understanding and explanation; however he argues that at another level the 'circle of understanding' runs from understanding to explanation and back again. The first part of this movement is congruent with the above description; that is, Ricoeur (1981, p. 211) argues that an understanding of a social phenomenon can only be reached by a dialectic process of narrowing the scope of generic concepts concerning it, and identifying within the 'whole' the 'hierarchy of topics, or primary and subordinate topics' that constitute it – that is, its constituent parts. The second part of this movement, from explanation to understanding, is also dialectical in nature; however, a structural model of explanation is employed (as opposed to the classical Humean causal model) to integrate the 'parts' into the 'whole'. As will be seen, this model relies on some form of structural analysis that provides the explanatory procedure which releases a dynamic meaning and, thus, mediates an understanding of the phenomenon.

Language as the universal medium of understanding

The most fundamental element in Gadamer's (1975, p. 350) onto-logical theory of understanding is, perhaps, language: 'language is the universal medium in which understanding itself is realised. The mode of realisation of understanding is interpretation.' Gadamer's point of departure in his examination of language as the medium of hermeneu-tical experience is that the object of all conversation is understanding. For Gadamer, all understanding is interpretation, and all interpretation takes place in the medium of language – a language that is used to describe phenomena and, yet at the same time, is the interpreter's own language. Beginning from this fundamental insight Gadamer illustrates that the linguistic characteristic of understanding is the 'concretion of effective historical consciousness', and that the shared meaning to be found in the outcome of a dialogue is, in effect, a 'fusion of horizons'. Thus, it is only through language that we can begin to know the world, to possess a community of life and, hence, arrive at a shared common meaning. Language, according to Gadamer, is the universal mode of being and knowledge: it is the middle ground where understanding and agreement takes place between two people concerning the phenomena of interest.

The interpretation of social action as texts

Following Heidegger (1976), Ricoeur (1981) argues that social action and situations can also be understood and read as texts; hence, herme-neutic philosophy and theory may be employed in the social sciences to examine, describe and understand social phenomena (see, for example, Palmer 1969; Bauman, 1978; Hekman, 1986). Social action, like a text, is a meaningful entity that must be construed as a 'whole'; however, an understanding of the 'whole' begins with an interpretive examination of its constituent 'parts' – this again introduces the concept of the circle of understanding. In the context of a hermeneutic study of the systems development process, 'the text [to be interpreted] is social and politi-cal action: case study notes, interviews and documents that record the views of the actors and describe certain events' (Myers, 1995, p. 56). In addition to these 'texts', this study has also included the extant research literature on the phenomenon of interest.

In any attempt at interpreting social action it is important to note that that the meaning of such action is not fixed by the social actors who perform or participate in such action, whatever the ends of these actions may be. This is because they are unanticipated and unintended consequences to all social action; hence, intended ends may not be congruent with the actual ends (Selznick, 1949; Hekman, 1986). Furthermore, as Gadamer (1975) has shown, the tradition, culture or social background in which such actions are embedded has an enormous impact on them. Thomson (1981, p. 247) captures the essence of this predicament: he argues that in order to fully comprehend a subject's actions, the actions must be placed 'within a wider context of institutions and social structure'. This has a corresponding imperative for an interpreter to incorporate these dimensions into an interpretation of social phenomena so that the actions and interpretations of social actors can be comprehended (cf. Kling and Scacchi, 1982; Kling and Iacono, 1989).

The ontological foundations of the hermeneutic method proposed in this paper have been described, so have the epistemological implications for the method. The following section presents a set of interpretive principles for the application of the method within research contexts.

Interpretive principles of the hermeneutic method

Madison (1988) draws on Ricoeur's phenomenological hermeneutics and presents a set of normative methodological principles to guide praxis. Method in the normative sense does not supplant personal, subjective judgement, nor eliminate the need for it, because Madison (1988, p. 28) believes it is meant as an aid to good judgment . . . (it) ensures that the judgments or conclusions arrived at are not gratuitous or the result of subjective whim.' The principles represented in Table 11.3 were proposed by Madison with the interpretation of texts in mind: it has already been seen that text-analogues such as a social actor's behaviour can be interpreted in much the same way as a text, and the wording of the principles has been altered to reflect this.

The need for such principles is indicated by Walsham (1995, p. 77), who reports that 'interpretive researchers are attempting the difficult task of accessing other people's interpretations, filtering them through their own conceptual apparatus, and feeding a version of events back to others, including in some cases, both interviewees and other audiences. In carrying out this work it is important that interpretive researchers have a view of their own role in this complex process.' Thus, Madison's (1988) principles challenge researchers to question their interpretation, especially given that the collection and analysis of data involves the researcher's own subjectivity. These principles were employed

Table 11.3   Methodological principles for the interpretive process (adapted from Madison, 1988)

	Methodological principles for the interpretive process
Coherence	The interpretation of a text or phenomenon/actor's 'thought' must present a unified picture and not be contradictory.
Comprehensiveness	Interpreting a text or an actor's perspective on an issue must take note of the author's/social actor's 'thoughts' as a whole, and not ignore other relevant 'thoughts'.
Penetration	A good interpretation should be 'penetrating' in that it brings out a guiding and underlying intention in an author's/actor's actions and statements: this is indicative of a teleological dimension to the hermeneutic method.
Thoroughness	A good interpretation must attempt to answer or deal with all the questions it poses to the interpreted phenomenon, or those that the phenomenon/social actor poses to the researcher.
Appropriateness	To be considered a good interpretation, the questions the interpretation deals with must be ones that the text/phenomenon itself raises.
Contextuality	The text/phenomenon/actor's thoughts must not be read out of context, i.e. without due regard to its historical and cultural context.
Agreement (1)	An interpretation must agree with what the text/actor actually says, that is, one must not, or normally not, say that the 'real' meaning of what an text/actor says is something quite other than what it/he actually says.
Agreement (2)	A given interpretation should normally be in agreement with the traditional and accredited interpretations of a text/phenomenon.
Suggestiveness	A good understanding will be 'suggestive' or fertile in that it raises questions that stimulate further research and interpretation.
Potential	A given interpretation can be judged to be 'true' if, in addition to meeting the above requirements, it is capable of being extended and if the process by which it is reached, and implications it contains unfold themselves harmoniously.

throughout the interpretive process in the example described in the following section as an aid in arriving at a deeper interpretation of the phenomenon and its component parts. Important as these principles are, they do not in themselves constitute the only tools in the interpretivist toolbox: a knowledge of and familiarity with the hermeneutic 'circle of understanding' as the core concept of hermeneutic thought and of the central role of the dialectic is vital for the hermeneutic researcher.

An application of the hermeneutic method in a study of the systems development process

The continued existence of problems associated with the development of information systems, coupled with the failure of such systems, gives support to the contention that the process by which information systems (IS) are developed is not well-understood (Avgerou and Cornford, 1993; Lewis, 1994; Myers, 1995). Hence, it is maintained that a study of the development process can yield great benefits – it can, as some researchers put it, 'help us understand what a realistic development process is' (Prakash *et al.*, 1993, p. 1).

We have seen previously that terms like tradition, prejudice, *Dasein's* 'intensionality', 'effective historical consciousness', 'horizons of understanding' etc., were employed to provide an ontological description of understanding of Being. It follows, then, that these concepts require recognition if a phenomenon such as the systems development process is to be fully understood. What this implies is that the 'world views' of various social actors involved in the development process need to be comprehensively captured and suitably interpreted if the researcher is to fully confront, in its totality, the 'horizon of understanding' of the phenomenon of systems development. Operating from a constructivist perspective, it is clear that each systems development endeavour in an organization will involve different configurations of social actors, technologies and objectives; in effect, the development process will be socially constructed (cf. Boland, 1985). Therefore, in order to offer an understanding of the phenomenon of systems development that operates at the level of the organization, several systems development projects will require investigation. There is, also, a need to capture the 'world views' of relevant social actors from the environments surrounding the projects who are perceived to have a stake in the development process – e.g. actors from the immediate development, organizational, and external environments (cf. Ives *et al.*, 1980). These factors require attention in the development of a constructivist strategy for research on the systems development process: Table 11.4 provides a brief outline of the strategy employed in the application of the hermeneutic method to the case with the aforementioned points in mind.

Table 11.4 A constructivist research strategy for research on the systems development process

Strategy components	Description
Ontological and epistemological stance	In *ontological* terms, the hermeneutic perspective posits that realities are constructed from multiple, intangible mental constructions that are socially and experientially based, local and specific in nature, and dependent on their form and content on the individual persons or groups holding the constructions. In *epistemological* terms the investigator and the object of investigation are, interactively linked so that the 'findings' are literally created as the investigation proceeds (see Guba and Lincoln, 1994).
Methodological perspectives	In *methodological* terms the variable and personal nature of social constructions suggests that individual constructions can be elicited and refined only through interactions between and among investigator and respondents. These constructions are interpreted using hermeneutical principles and concepts that inform conventional qualitative techniques and are compared and contrasted through a dialectical interchange. It is the task of the researcher as *human instrument* to reconstruct the social world of the phenomena under study utilising his/her own idiographically informed interpretations (Lincoln and Guba, 1985).
Type of study	Exploratory, single instrumental case study. An instrumental case study is undertaken to obtain particular insight into an issue or to refine a theory. The case occupies a supportive role and is of secondary interest.
Research method	The hermeneutic method provided the overarching research vehicle, however the critical success factors (CSF) method was employed as an adjunct as it gives explicit recognition to the teleological nature of human action (see Visala, 1991). Also, Ricoeur (1981) posits the use of structural analytic techniques to augment traditional hermeneutic approaches: the CSF method proved to be useful in this regard as it helped identify the phenomenon's component phenomena ('parts') or CSFs – these are the IS development-related actions (means) employed by social actors to achieve development related objectives (ends).
Unit of analysis	Telecom Eireann, Ireland's state-sponsored telecommunications company.

(continued)

Table 11.4 Continued

Strategy components	Description
Embedded units of analysis	Four systems development projects: two operational support systems projects, a data warehouse/DSS project and a marketing and sales information system project.
Sampling strategy	Purposeful sampling was employed throughout (Marshall and Rossman, 1989; Patton, 1990).
Data collection techniques	Semistructured/unstructured interviews (tape recorded) with 10 IS managers and IT professionals in the pilot study and with 38 business and IS function managers, project managers, developers and user representatives (i.e. social actors participating directly and indirectly in the development process) in the main research endeavour; documentary evidence; informal participant observation and interviews also took place.
Data analysis techniques	Content and constant comparative data analysis techniques, meta- and network analysis of qualitative data etc. (see Patton, 1990; Calloway and Ariav, 1991; Miles and Huberman, 1994).

The circle of understanding and the dialectic as applied in research on the systems development process

The concept of the hermeneutical circle of understanding was applied throughout the case study on the information systems development process. Figure 11.2 provides a graphical representation of the hermeneutic research process in terms of the hermeneutic 'circle of understanding', while Table 11.5 presents an overview of the process of negotiating these various 'circles'. The table provides a useful synopsis of the application of the hermeneutic method in the research on the systems development process. It attempts to capture the recursive nature of 'cycling' through the 'circle of understanding' that occurred throughout the research, and also describes the 'fusions of horizons' that resulted from this process.

In this research undertaking the Socratic form of dialectic was used explicitly at the interview stage – that is, in circles B and C – and was tacitly employed during the initial review of the literature (circle A); it was also employed throughout the data analysis phase and write-up of the research (circles D and E). The Hegelian dialectic was also used in these research activities; however, its main role was to facilitate the transition from one level of understanding or expectation to another – that is,

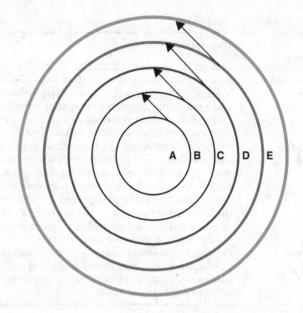

Legend: Gadamer (1988) argues that the unity of understood meaning expands in concentric circles. Figure 11.2 represents this endeavour as it occurred in the present research undertaking. The letters A to E represent the five stages of understanding.

Figure 11.2   The circle of understanding and research on the systems development process

in facilitating a 'fusion of horizons' – and in processing the different sources of research data – that is, in integrating 'parts' into the 'whole'. The reductionist/analytical dialectic was an important mechanism in the identification of the phenomenon's component 'parts' and in integrating these components such that the arc that separates explanation and understanding could be negotiated (see Ricoeur, 1981). The qualitative data analysis techniques of content and constant comparative analysis provided the necessary mechanisms for the required structural analysis – so too did the methods of data reduction and display (Patton, 1990; Calloway and Ariav, 1991; Miles and Huberman, 1994). Also of import in this regard was the application of Rockart's (1979) critical success factors (CSFs) concept and method as per Visala's (1991) recommendations; because of its teleological nature, this helped social actors formally identify the relevant component phenomena or 'parts' of the phenomenon of interest (see Butler and Fitzgerald, 1998). Alternatively put, the CSFs method allowed actors to focus in on phenomena that are at one time or another 'present-at-hand' and are, as a result, the object of some concern and deliberation. Hence, it adequately captures the 'intensionality' of their actions; that is, the means they adopt to fulfil their goals and objectives (in coping with the 'present-at-hand'). It must be pointed out that the three forms of dialectic complemented each other in a synergistic manner, and that the interpretative principles outlined earlier guided the research effort throughout in that they made the researcher's role and judgements 'present-at-hand' to him, and thus the object of question and reflection.

It is outside the scope of this paper to provide a detailed account of the output of the research; the emphasis here was on process not product. Nevertheless, some words on the contribution to the extant understanding of systems development are as follows:

An empirical model of the systems development process

While a full and detailed narrative on the phenomenon of systems development would undoubtedly help researchers and practitioners understand the process, it would obviously be impractical and unwieldy to report on the minutiae of events and practices, many of which would be 'ready-to-hand' to most observers of the phenomenon. Hence, in order to capture the essence of the development process and contribute towards an enhanced understanding of it, those issues and events that were 'present-at-hand' for developers, users, and managers, and which proved to be pivotal in their efforts to develop information systems were focused upon. The CSF concept was employed here for reasons previously outlined and it proved to be quite effective in allowing both researcher and researched to identify salient development-related phenomena that were 'present-at-hand', and that constituted the 'parts' of the 'whole' that is the development process. A descriptive model which attempts to describe the 'whole' of the process in terms of its salient 'parts', and which tend to give definition and shape to it, was constructed: Figure 11.3 presents this model.

As indicated in Table 11.5, the salient 'parts' or component phenomena of the systems development process were first identified from the various narratives and descriptions of the development process provided by social actors. In the context of this study, a CSF is taken to denote a development-related prerequisite, action, or role that is performed in relation to salient endogenous or exogenous factors that constitute, shape and influence the development process and its product – i.e. the 'present-at-hand' of managers, developers and users. Social actors

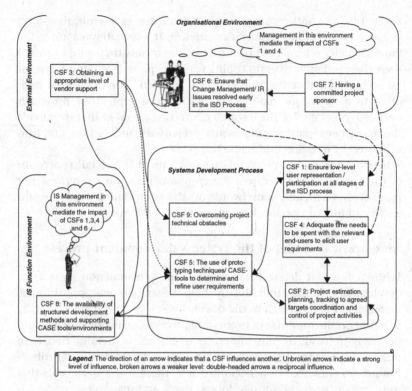

Figure 11.3   An information systems development process model

converged on nine interrelated phenomena that gave definition to the process; these are reported in rank order of 'criticality' in the model. It is clear from the model that these interrelationships are not simple; indeed, the model provides a graphical illustration of the complex web of social conditions and factors that are argued to define the development process and its product (see Kling and Scacchi, 1982). The solid and broken arrowed lines indicate the direction and level of influence that one CSF has on another. Unbroken lines represent strong relationships; broken lines depict weak relationships. It is also evident that several of the phenomena emanate from the environments that surround the development process. The complex network of interrelationships require further explication via integrative narratives (see Butler and Fitzgerald, 1997a, the empirical study on which the example cited in

Table 11.5 The circle of understanding as applied in the case

Circle	Researcher's Horizon	Phenomenon's Horizon	
		Whole	Parts
A.	Preunderstanding of systems development process modulated by the researcher's effective historical consciousness/ prejudice etc.	Systems development process as represented in research literature.	Theories, concepts, themes, findings, etc. in major streams of the literature on systems development–e.g. SDLC / prototyping / evolutionary approach etc.; development methodologies; CASE; user participation; political dimensions; project management and quality-related issues
B.	Fusion of horizons of understanding from the transition through A.	Pilot study of IS functions in Telecom Eireann and its systems-development-related activities.	'World views' of 10 senior IS function managers and IT professionals. These were expressed in their views on IT strategy, current and future development projects, development approaches, use/non-use of methodologies, quality issues etc.
C.	The researcher's horizon is constituted by a fusion of theoretical/ conceptual/empirical perspectives in the literature and the horizon offered by the phenomenon in the pilot study.	Empirical study of the systems development process and its related development, organizational, and external environments.	'World views' and explicit and tacit role-related CSFs of 38 social actors including 7 members of IS function's senior management team, business and IS project managers, developers and user representatives in four development projects. These were expressed in the tape-recorded interview narratives. Additional insights came from documentary evidence and informal sources.
D.	The researcher's horizon now consists of cumulative perspectives resulting in 'fusion of horizons' produced in C.	Accumulated research artefacts on the phenomenon and its environment that describe and give definition to the systems development process.	Interview transcriptions and notes; write up of informal conversations etc. At a more fundamental level, the reductionist/analytical dialectic, as employed by the content and comparative data analysis, revealed the underlying activities/perspectives of the social actors involved in the development process – thus, the parts emerged from the analysis.
E.	The researcher's horizon enncompasses the cumulative fusion of horizons as represented by his understanding of the systems development process resulting from D. The 'fusion-of-horizons' presented in the research artefact itself becomes a phenomenon with its own 'horizon' that requires interpretation by its audience. And so the movement through the circle continues ...	The explanation provided by the research text.	The themes, descriptions, arguments graphical mechanisms, tables, descriptive matrices, contained in various chapters/sections etc. of the text. The complexity of the development process was addressed taking the salient development related activities (the CSFs or, in Heideggerian terrns, those development-related phenomena that were most likely to experience breakdown and thus be 'present-at-hand) and describing them in extended narratives. Discussions and conclusions that coalesce to describe and explain the phenomenon etc.

this paper is based for an example of such, as it is outside the scope of this paper to so do). Such narratives allow the phenomenon and its component phenomena to be described and 'explained' such that an understanding of the systems development process in this organization is arrived at. This understanding can benefit both practitioners and researchers as they can identify with problems and issues that have arisen in their own and other organizations and thereby comprehend 'why' and 'how' they have occurred. This last point received vindication when the empirical research was presented at a recent conference dealing with the phenomenon.

Discussion and conclusions

In the face of a clear paucity of information in the extant literature regarding the use of the hermeneutic method, the objective of this paper has been to provide the necessary philosophical foundations for interpretive researchers who would wish to apply the hermeneutic method for research in the social sciences and, in particular, the IS field. Experienced qualitative researchers will be familiar with many of the research methods, tools and techniques mentioned herein; however, what is important to note here is that the use to which these methods, tools, and techniques are put is very much dependent on the underlying 'world-view' of the researcher. As a constructivist philosophy, phenomenological hermeneutics informs one particular 'worldview' and, as such, it possesses its own unique ontological, epistemological and methodological perspectives. What makes the constructivist approach to research different from that of others is that the constructivist researcher's ontological perspective is informed by a phenomenological ontology and epistemology – notably that of Heidegger's – and a hermeneutic perspective on method. This paper has attempted to forge a link between the insights provided by phenomenological hermeneutics and the practical tasks that researchers must perform in the conduct of their research. This task was accomplished by presenting a phenomenological analysis and conceptual model of Being and by focusing on the key concepts of the 'circle of understanding' and the 'dialectic' in order to illustrate their relevance for the proposed method. A practical example of the application of these concepts was provided to inform and guide future research endeavours.

Researchers may choose from among several interpretive approaches when investigating social phenomena; however, proclaiming oneself as an interpretivist does not go far enough, because of the fact that competing interpretive approaches do not share the same ontological, epistemological or methodological perspectives. There is, therefore, a question mark over studies that identify themselves as interpretivist and who fail to provide clear indication of the philosophical foundations on which their interpretive perspectives are based. The same argument could be levelled against much of what passes for qualitative research in the IS field. Because all human existence is hermeneutic at its essence, it is clear that the act of interpretation is central to the mode of being of all social actors, researchers included. An awareness of this fundamental observation seems to elude those who operate from competing research paradigms and, indeed, some who proclaim to be interpretivists. If socially constructed phenomena, such as the development and use of information systems, are to be comprehensively investigated and understood, there is an imperative for researchers to understand not only the fundamental features of human Being-in-the-world, but also their own existence in their 'life-world'. Hence the importance of the constructivist perspective embodied in phenomenological hermeneutics.

In conclusion, the explication of phenomenological and hermeneutic philosophies delineated herein, coupled with the practical application of related philosophical concepts to accepted qualitative research methods and techniques will, it is hoped, stimulate interest and much needed understanding of interpretivism among the broader research community within the IS field and, also, inform the perspectives of the growing number of interpretive researchers.

Note

1. This is an important umbrella term for the work of many contemporary philosophers and social scientists. Connolly and Keutner (1988) categorize the philosophies of Heidegger and Gadamer as constructivist, while in the social sciences, Guba and Lincoln (1994) – in sociology – and Bruner (1990) – in cultural psychology – also categorize their work as being constructivist.

References

Apel, K.O. (1980) *Toward a Transformation of Philosophy* (Routledge and Kegan Paul, London).
Avgerou, C. and Cornford, T. (1993) A review of the methodologies movement. *Journal of Information Technology*, 8(4), 277–86.
Bauman, Z. (1978) *Hermeneutics and Social Science: Approaches to Understanding*, (Hutchinson and Son, London).
Betti, E. (1955) *Teoria Generale della Interpretatione* (D.A. Giuffe (Ed.), Milano).

Bleicher, J. (1980) *Contemporary Hermeneutics: Hermeneutics as Method, Philosophy and Critique* (Routledge and Kegan Paul, London).

Boland, R. J. (1985) Phenomenology: a preferred approach to research in information systems, in *Research Methods in Information Systems*, Mumford, E., Hirschheim, R., Fitzgerald, G., and Wood-Harper T. (eds) (Elsevier Science Publications B.V., North-Holland) pp. 193–201.

Boland, R.J. (1987) The in-formation of information systems, in *Critical Issues in Information Systems Research*, Boland, R.J. and Hirschheim, R.A. (eds) (John Wiley, Chichester) pp. 362–79.

Boland, R.J. (1991) Information system use as a hermeneutic process, in *Information System Research: Contemporary Approaches and Emergent Traditions* Nissen, H., Klein, H.K. and Hirschheim, R. (eds), (Elsevier Science Publishers B.V., North-Holland) pp. 439–58.

Boland, R.J. (1993) Accounting and the interpretive act. *Accounting, Organisations and Society*, **18**(2/3), 125–46.

Boland, R.J. and Day, W.F. (1989) The experience of system design: a hermeneutic of organisational action. *Scandinavian Journal of Management*, **5**(2), 87–104.

Boland, R.J. and Tenkasi, R.V. (1993) Designing information technology to support distributed cognition. *Organization Science*, **5**(3), pp. 456–75.

Boland, R.J. and Tenkasi, R.V. (1995) Perspective making and perspective taking in communities of knowing. *Organization Science*, **6**(4), 350–72.

Bruner, J. (1990) *Acts of Meaning* (Harvard University Press, Cambridge, MA).

Butler, T. (1998a) Philosophy and method: an empirical application of hermeneutic theory for interpretive research in the social sciences. *Executive Systems Research Centre Working Paper 09/98*, University College Cork, Ireland.

Butler, T. (1998b) Promise and practise: I-CASE and rapid application development in Telecom Eireann. Forthcoming, in *The Proceedings of the British Computer Society 6th Annual Conference on Information Systems Methodologies*, Springer-Verlag, UK.

Butler, T. and Fitzgerald, B. (1997a) An empirical model of the information systems development process, in *Training and Education of Methodology Practitioners and Researchers, BCS Conference Series*, Jaratna, N., Fitzgerald, B., Wood-Harper, T. and Larrasquet, J.-M. (eds) Springer-Verlag, London, UK.

Butler, T. and Fitzgerald, B. (1997b) A case study of user participation in the information systems process, in *Proceedings of the 18th International Conference on Information Systems*, McClean, E.R. and Welke, R.J. (eds), Atlanta, Georgia, pp. 411–26.

Butler, T. and Fitzgerald, B. (1998) New light through old windows: the interpretive foundations of the critical success factor concept and method. Forthcoming in *The Proceedings of the 8th Annual BIT Conference*, Manchester Metropolitan University, Manchester, UK.

Calloway, L.J. and Ariv, G. (1991) Developing and using a qualitative methodology to study relationships among designers and tools, in *Information Systems Research: Contemporary Approaches and Emergent Traditions, Proceedings of the IFIP TC8/WG 8.2 Working Conference*, Nissen, H., Klein, H.K. and Hirschheim, R. (eds) (Elsevier Science Publishers B.V. North-Holland) pp. 175–93.

Conolly, J.M. and Keutner, T. (1988) Introduction, in *Hermeneutics Versus Science? Three German Views*, Conolly, J.M. and Keutner, T. (eds) (University of Notre Dame Press, IN) pp. 1–67.

Coyne, R.M. (1995) *Designing Information Technology in the Postmodern Age: From Method to Metaphor* (The MIT Press, Cambridge, MA).

Davis, G.B., Lee, A.S. Nickles, K.R., Chaterjee, S., Hartung, R. and Wu, Y. (1992) Diagnosis of an information system failure; a framework and interpretive process. *Information Management*, 23(5), 293–318.

Derrida, J. (1970) Structure, sign and play in the discourse of the human sciences, in *The Structuralist Controversy*, Mackesy, R. and Donato, E. (eds) (Johns Hopkins University Press, Baltimore) pp. 246–72.

Derrida, J. (1976) *Of Grammatology*, Translated by Gayatri Spivack (Johns Hopkins University Press, Baltimore).

Gadamer, H.G. (1975) *Truth and Method* (The Seabury Press, NY).

Gadamer, H.G. (1988) On the circle of understanding, in *Hermeneutics Versus Science? Three German Views*, Conolly, J.M. and Keutner, T. (eds) (University of Notre Dame Press, IN) pp. 68–78.

Galliers, R.D. (1985) In search of a paradigm for information systems research, in *Research Methods in Information Systems*, Mumford, E., Hirschheim, R., Fitzgerald, G. and Wood-Harper, T. (eds) (Elsevier Science Publications B.V., North-Holland) pp. 281–97.

Guba, E.G. and Lincoln, Y.S. (1994) Competing paradigms in qualitative research, in *Handbook of Qualitative Research*, Denzin, N.K. and Lincoln, Y.S. (eds) (Sage Publications, CA) pp. 105–17.

Habermas, J. (1972) *Knowledge and Human Interests*. Translated by J.J. Shapiro (Beacon Press, Boston, MA).

Habermas J. (1980) The hermeneutic claim to universality, in *Contemporary, Hermeneutics: Hermeneutics as Method, Philosophy and Critique*, Bleicher, J. (ed) (Routledge and Kegan Paul, London) pp. 181–211

Hekman, S. (1986) *Hermeneutics and the Sociology of Knowledge* (Polity Press, Cambridge, UK).

Heidegger, M. (1976) *Being and Time* (Harper and Row, NY).

Hirsch, E.D. (1967) *Validity in Interpretation* (Yale University Press, New Haven).

Huberman, A.M. and Miles, M.B. (1994) *Qualitative Data Analysis: An Expanded Sourcebook*, Second edn (Sage Publications, CA).

Itrona, L.D. (1997) *Management, Information and Power: A Narrative for the Involved Manager* (Macmillan Press Ltd., London).

Ives, B., Hamilton, S. and Davis, G.B. (1980) A framework for research in computer-based management information systems. *Management Science*, 26(9), 910–34.

Kanungo, S. (1993) Information systems: theoretical development and research approaches. *Information Systems*, 18(8), 609–19.

Klein, H. and Lyytinen, K.J. (1985) The poverty of scientism in information systems, in *Research Methods in Information Systems*, Mumford, E., Hirschheim, R., Fitzgerald, G. and Wood-Harper, T. (eds) (Elsevier Publishers, North Holland) pp. 131–61.

Kling, R. and Scacchi, W. (1982) The web of computing: computing technology as social organisation. In *Advances in Computers*, Yovits, M.C. (ed), vol. 21 (New York, Academic Press) pp. 1–90.

Kling, R. and Iacono, S. (1989) The institutional character of computerized information systems. *Office: Technology and People*, 5 (1), 7–28.

Lee, A.S. (1993) Electronic mail as medium for rich communication: an empirical investigation using hermeneutic interpretation, in *Proceedings of the Fourteenth*

International Conference on Information Systems, DeGross, J.I., Bostrum, R.P. and Robey, D. (eds) Orlando, Florida, pp. 13–21

Lee, A.S. (1994) The hermeneutic circle as a source of emergent richness in the managerial use of electronic mail, in the *Proceedings of the Fifteenth International Conference on Information Systems*, DeGross, J.I., Huff, S.L. and Munro, M.C. (eds), Vancouver, BC pp. 129–40.

Lewis, P.J. (1994) *Information-Systems Development* (Pitman Publishing, London, UK).

Lincoln, Y.S. and Guba, E.G. (1985) *Naturalistic Inquiry* (Sage, Beverly Hills, CA).

Lyytinen, K.J. and Klein, H. (1985) The critical theory of Jurgen Habermas as a basis for a theory of information systems, in *Research Methods in Information Systems* Mumford, E., Hirschheim, R., Fitzgerald, G. and Wood-Harper, T. (eds) (Elsevier Science Publications B.V., North-Holland) pp. 219–36.

Madison, G.B. (1988) *The Hermeneutics of Postmodernity: Figures and Themes* (Indiana University Press, Bloomfield, IND).

Marshall, C. and Rossman, G.B. (1989) *Designing Qualitative Research* (Sage Publications, CA).

Mueller-Vollmer, K. (ed) (1986) *The Hermeneutics Reader: Texts of the German Tradition from the Enlightenment to the Present* (Basil Blackwell, London).

Mumford, E., Hirschheim, R., Fitzgerald, G. and Wood-Harper, T. (eds) (1985) *Research Methods of Information Systems* (Elsevier Science Publications B.V., North-Holland),

Myers, M.D. (1995) Dialectical hermeneutics: a theoretical framework for the implementation of information system. *Information Systems Journal*, 5(1), 51–70.

Myers, M.D. (1997) Qualitative research in information systems, *MIS Quarterly*, 21(2), 221–42.

Nissen, H.E. (1985) Acquiring knowledge of information systems – research in methodology quagmire, in *Research Methods in Information Systems*, Mumford, E., Hirschheim, R., Fitzgerald, G. and Wood-Harper, T. (eds) (Elsevier Science Publications B.V., North-Holland) pp. 39–51.

Palmer, R.E. (1969) *Hermeneutics* (Northwestern University Press, Evanston)

Patton, M.Q. (1990) *Qualitative Evaluation and Research Methods* (Sage Publications Ltd., London).

Prakash, N., Rolland, C. and Pernici, B. (eds) (1993) *Information System Development Process; Proceedings of the IFIP WG 8.1 Working Conference on the Information Systems Development Process* (Elsevier Science Publications, North-Holland).

Rathswohl, E.J. (1991) Applying Don Idhe's phenomenology of instrumentation as framework for designing research in information systems, in *Information Systems Research: Contemporary Approaches and Emergent Traditions*, Nissen, H., Klein, H.K. and Hirschheim, R. (eds) (Elsevier Science Publishers B.V., Amsterdam) pp. 421–38.

Ricoeur, P. (1981) The model of the text: meaningful action considered as a text, in *Hermeneutics and the Human Sciences* Thompson, J.P. (ed) (Cambridge University Press, Cambridge, UK) pp. 197–221.

Rockart, J.F. (1979) Chief executives define their own data needs. *Harvard Business Review*, 57 (2), 81–93.

Rorty, R. (1979) *Philosophy and the Mirror of Nature* (Princeton University Press, Princeton).

Selznick, P. (1949) *TVA and the Grass Roots,* (University of California Press: Berkley and Los Angeles, CA).

Tamas, R. (1991) *The Passion of the Western Mind* (Penguin Books, London).

Taylor, C. (1985) *Philosophy and the Human Sciences* (Cambridge University Press, UK).

Thomson, J.B. (1981) *Critical Hermeneutics: A Study in the Thought of Paul Ricoeur and Furgen Habermas* (Cambridge University Press, Cambridge, UK).

Visala, S. (1991) Broadening the empirical framework of information systems research, in *Information Systems Research: Contemporary Approaches and Emergent Traditions, Proceedings of the IFIP TC8/WG 8.2 Working Conference* Nissen, H., Klein, H.K. and Hirschheim, R. (eds) (Elsevier Science Publishers B.V. North-Holland) pp. 347–64.

Walsham, G. (1993) *Interpreting Information Systems in Organizations* (John Wiley and Sons, Chichester, UK).

Walsham, G. (1995) Interpretative case studies in IS research: nature and method. *European Journal of Information Systems,* **4**(2), 74–81.

Warnke, G. (1987) *Hermeneutics, Tradition and Reason* (Polity Press, Cambridge).

Westrup, C. (1994) Practical understanding: hermeneutics and teaching the management of information systems development using a case study. *Accounting, Management and Information Technology,* **4**(1), 39–58.

Winograd, T. and Flores, F. (1986) *Understanding Computers and Cognition: A New Foundation for Design* (Ablex Publishing Corporation, Norwood, NJ).

Wittgenstein, L. (1953) *Philosophical Investigations* (Macmillan, New York).

Zuboff, S. (1988) *In the Age of the Smart Machine: The Future of Work and Power* (Basic Books, New York, NY).

12

Application of Hermeneutics to Studying an Experience Mining Process

Tanya Linden[1] and Jacob L. Cybulski[2]
[1]*Victoria University, Department of Management and Information Systems, Australia*
[2]*Deakin University, School of Information Systems, Australia*

Introduction

For quite some time, knowledge has been recognised to be an important driver of any present-day organisational process (Drucker, 1995; Lank, 1997; Alavi and Leidner, 2001). Because of its value to business, knowledge ought to be properly managed from the time of its creation, through its structuring and storage, to sharing and dissemination, and its eventual application (Nonaka, 1994).

Organisational knowledge is commonly accessible to employees in the 'canonical' form of business policies and procedures, which help them in establishing useful organisational structures and processes, which assist them in dealing with typical business problems, and which guide them in performing everyday tasks in compliance with the organisation's best practice, laws of the land and management wishes. However, due to the complexity of some of these tasks, the obsolescence and incompleteness of written procedures and instructions, individual workers may need to utilise their own problem-solving intuition, rely on their creativity, and improvise to achieve the desired outcome. Such 'non-canonical' practices (Nissen *et al*, 2000) represent organisational tacit knowledge, which is informal and communicated in the form of 'war stories', is hard to elicit (Orr, 1990) and, in the absence of explicit

Reprinted from "Application of hermeneutics to studying an experience mining process," by T. Linden and J. Cybulski in *Journal of Information Technology*, 24, 2009, pp. 231–250. With kind permission from the Association for Information Technology Trust. All rights reserved.

records, is also vulnerable to loss (O'Leary, 1998a; Rising 1999; Nissen *et al*, 2000). Nevertheless, this living organisational knowledge, stemming from employees' accumulating personal problem-solving experience, is also a valuable business asset, which needs to be protected and cultivated in the fabric of organisational culture.

At the same time, contemporary organisations are set in the global context of international trade, pluralistic management structures and inter-organisational activity; and thus, business knowledge and personal experience need to be shared and disseminated beyond a single organisation, to gain sustainability and resilience across cultural, linguistic, geographic and temporal barriers. This trend alone comprehensively reconfigures business practices to emphasise the need for knowledge management to take place in the complex, diverse and distributed environments (Bender and Fish, 2000). Knowledge management in modern organisations needs, therefore, to facilitate knowledge transfers across organisational boundaries; support collaboration of knowledge workers in joint business transactions; work in inter-related application domains; or merely, pursuing similar professional interests; and yet, being organisationally independent of each other (Stenmark *et al*, 1999).

As Kavan (1998) pointed out, the real value of knowledge acquisition is in the potential for sharing and reusing of this knowledge. As knowledge is normally acquired from multiple sources of incompatible standards and disparate cultures, it is important to represent, formalise and reconcile this knowledge, and then, classify and package it into common knowledge pools (Gaines and Shaw, 1993: 3–4). The main beneficiaries of such packaged knowledge are practitioners, who are 'in the best position to manage this knowledge' (Wenger, 2004: 2), and who apply reusable knowledge in their day to day activities in dealing with their professional issues and in resolving their domain-specific problems. Because of the widespread need for knowledge sharing within professional communities, a number of tools and methods have been developed to support community members in effective communication and dissemination of knowledge (O'Leary, 1998b; Basili *et al*, 1992; Rising, 1999; Kalfoglou, 2000).

As demonstrated by the software development community and its practitioners, individual problem-solving experience can be captured, collected and formalised (in the form of design patterns – Corfman, 1998) and subsequently refined and disseminated across the knowledge domain via workshops and publications (Manns, 2001). Unfortunately, not all domain practitioners actively communicate with each other or participate in knowledge sharing (Rising, 1999). This lack of knowledge sharing eventually leads to losing valuable domain experience (*ibid.*). To prevent such knowledge loss, we have undertaken this research project, which aims to develop an approach to creation, understanding, formalisation, evaluation, sharing and application of practitioners' knowledge across the entire application domain. For the purpose of this study the domain is defined as 'an 'area' of knowledge that needs to be explored and developed', with identified key issues that members need to address (Wenger, 2004: 3).

Background

Practitioners build their knowledge through the problem-solving process. Solving novel problems assists practitioners in identifying gaps in knowledge and facilitates learning new 'models, clues and cues for how to proceed' in dealing with problems at hand (Billett, 2001: 28). Problem-solving knowledge can be very effectively represented in *patterns*, the knowledge format widely recognised as facilitating sharing of problem-solving experience, especially in support of various design tasks (Coplien, 1996; Appleton, 1997). A collection of inter-related patterns is commonly referred to as a *pattern language* (*ibid.*).

A pattern is a description of a successful solution to a problem recurring within a certain context and driven by specific forces. The emphasis here is on the recurring problem. Within a certain context developers encounter similar problems because there exist natural forces and influences that create the problem in the first place. A pattern not only describes the problem and its solution but also specifies consequences (both positive and negative) of applying the solution. Recurrence adds validity to a pattern and certifies the quality of its solution (Corfman, 1998). A collection of inter-related and highly cohesive patterns, which could be collectively used in problem-solving in a given domain, is referred to as a pattern language (in a sense applying several patterns to a single problem is not unlike construction of a meaningful sentence of individual pattern-words).

To make patterns understandable, they are defined using a special literary form that helps non-technically minded problem solvers understand the solution and its consequences. For our study we are using one of the most popular formats depicted in Figure 12.1. However, the adopted format is one of many ways of documenting patterns (Alexander, 1979; Gamma *et al*, 1995; Appleton, 1997; Cybulski and Linden, 2000). The main body of the commonly used pattern structures

---

Name: a word or short phrase
that captures the essence of the pattern.
Collectively pattern names form a vocabulary
that supports better communications.

Problem: a statement of the problem being solved

Context: situations within which the problem
may be expected to occur

Forces: what issues are causing the
problem and how do they interact/conflict
with each other

Solution: how to get the desired
outcome and resolve forces

Resulting context: situation after the solution
has been applied

Consequences of applying the solution
(positive and negative)

Figure 12.1 Pattern format

includes a meaningful name, a clear definition of a problem, a list of situations within which the problem may be expected to occur (context), and finally a specification of the proposed solution with the consequences of its application. In one way or another, patterns always identify the forces causing the problem, the resulting context and relationships with other patterns within the system. Often a pattern's author provides known uses of the pattern as examples illustrating the pattern's application.

Subsequently, patterns can be used by developers in search for the best design practice in common problem solving. However, before applying such a pattern the developer needs to assess whether or not the pattern is related to the experienced problem, and whether the real-life problem and the pattern have the comparable problem context and forces. The developer could then consider the consequences of applying the pattern, usually in terms of developmental benefits and costs, and ultimately, decide on the suitability of the solution prescribed by the pattern.

The process of eliciting a practitioners' experience, representing it in patterns format and evaluating the results is called *pattern mining*.

The pattern mining process commonly involves the following stages (Manns, 2001):

1. *Pattern crafting* – writing the preliminary pattern draft by a practitioner or their cohesive group (e.g. members of the same work team).
2. *Shepherding* – the process of guiding the author(s) in the process of improving their pattern(s). This is usually facilitated by an experienced pattern writer (called a shepherd) who also has some understanding of the domain to which the pattern refers.
3. *Pattern evaluation* at the pattern mining workshop where experienced members of the pattern writing community share their opinions on positive aspects of the pattern and suggestions on how the pattern could be further improved.
4. *Pattern improvement and publication.*

The first stage, while preliminary and leading only to a pattern draft, is one of the more complex, though most rewarding, stages of pattern development. Pattern crafting involves the cooperation of pattern writers and experienced practitioners, who commonly are not adept at pattern writing. The experience to be captured from practitioners is often tacit and largely incomplete. Shared or overlapping, and occasionally conflicting, experiences need to be identified and then reconciled. Boundaries of the problem-solving context could also be ill-defined and thus prevent the effective isolation of experiences related to the technical issues from those of a business, social and personal nature. The complexity and the labour involved in this early, intensely collaborative, stage of pattern development disheartens the majority of active pattern writers, who instead turn to 'mining' their own experience (Manns and Rising, 2002). At the same time, practitioners – the true holders of invaluable and potentially shareable experience – often decline involvement in the process and so their knowledge and their know-how are irretrievably lost to the problem-solving community. The reasons for this situation are many. Firstly, some practitioners simply refuse to share their experience – their main professional asset – with others. Then, some of those few prepared to cede the sole ownership of their expertise, sometimes are not proficient communicators or writers to be effective pattern developers. Still others, busy professionals, cannot afford spending time and effort reflecting on the lessons learnt and on formalising their own experience. As a result of these problems, it has been suggested to employ *ghost writers* – expert pattern writers themselves, also referred to as 'mercenary analysts' (Coplien, 1996), to assist practitioners in the process of pattern creation and formalisation. In such a process, a ghost writer would normally collect practical experience by means of interviews and meetings (Rising, 1999). In addition, those technically-minded practitioners, who indeed are interested in learning pattern writing, may be further assisted by attending pattern writing classes, workshops and by getting involved in teaching pattern writing (*ibid.*).

In practice, however, few practitioners ever participate in the dissemination of their experience and consequently pattern writing has become the domain of a small minority of pattern mining enthusiasts. In response to this problem, Linda Rising (*ibid.*) proposed an informal approach to engaging organisational experts in pattern crafting, which she called 'mining by interviewing', and which she implemented at her organisation. The process included individual interviews and meetings, focused on collecting organisational expertise, translating it into patterns and subsequently refining these patterns. Some of the patterns elicited by her team were later submitted to the standard process of shepherding and workshopping; others were just placed in the form of a problem-solving 'handbook' for internal use.

This process, as described by Linda Rising (*ibid.*), brings a number of clear benefits to the overall process of pattern mining. The major benefit is a direct involvement of practitioners in the process of capturing organisational experience into patterns. Her approach also deals with the ineffectiveness of practitioners as pattern writers, their lack of time to formalise their design experience, and their inability and unwillingness to attend design sharing events outside their normal workplace. However, in spite of these advantages, the patterns and pattern languages produced by her team reflected only the opinions of a relatively small group of people, who were individuals or their cohesive teams in a single organisation. Such a small group of expert problem solvers may indeed represent the organisational best practice but not necessarily the best practice potentially available in the respective problem domain. This issue led us to formulating our research goal, which can be stated as follows.

> To arrive at the process of capturing a domain-wide (and potentially 'best') practices into shareable and reusable experience, in the form of design patterns, with or without practitioners' active pattern-writing cooperation.

This goal, while still elusive, nonetheless provided us with a strong motivation for investigating pattern mining from the vantage point of an entire problem domain. As a consequence, we have undertaken the development of a viable method for domain-wide pattern mining, the effectiveness of which was iteratively improved to the satisfaction of the community of active pattern miners.

Research approach

On reflection, the main problem in the existing approaches to pattern crafting is the significant disparity in the skill sets of domain practitioners and pattern miners. The lack of specific technical proficiency in pattern creation, and for that matter, utilisation of any other form of representing problem-solving experience, prevents practitioners from recording, formalising and packaging their own experience. Our study therefore sets forth the following research aims:

A1. Establish a pattern-crafting process by which practitioners' problem-solving experience can be captured into domain patterns ready for dissemination to the community of practice, in spite of the disparity in the knowledge and skills between domain practitioners and pattern writers.

A2. Evaluate the resulting pattern crafting process through independent examination by the pattern mining community and by comparing it with the existing pattern crafting approaches.

To achieve this research aim, the pattern-crafting process has to:

O1. Provide a method of exploring domain knowledge by pattern-writers. This will enable them to identify and understand issues of concern to domain practitioners.

O2. Identify recurring problem situations as viewed by practitioners; discover the context for these problems and approaches to their resolution. Collecting such problem-solving data will assist in determining common domain experiences.

O3. Facilitate conversion of the collected domain experiences into patterns that are ready for evaluation by practitioners for their content and pattern writers for their form.

To understand the domain of interest and problems routinely solved by practitioners we decided to collect their reflections on experience gained in the project work. In view of this objective, we anticipated the collected data to be qualitative, textual and necessarily very high volume.

The qualitative/interpretive approach to data collection and analysis was therefore deemed most appropriate (Myers, 1997). The pattern crafting process (or the preliminary phases of pattern mining) has not been studied in depth in the past, nor has it been properly formalised (Rising, 1999). Therefore, based on the literature alone it was not possible to propose a significantly improved process of pattern development. However, hermeneutic refinement of such a sub-optimal process – as previously studied in Information Systems (Klein and Myers, 1999) – was deemed as promising in its ability to empirically gather insights into the process, then refine and evaluate both insights and the process iteratively, until convergence of these insights and the simultaneous saturation of empirical results (Drisko, 1997).

Hermeneutics, in general, provides a method of analysing textual data in search of its meaning (Myers, 2004). It can be successfully used in the analysis of text and text 'analogues' (Ricoeur, 1981), i.e. anything that can be described with text (Kvale, 1996; Demeterio, 2001) – in our case, description of the pattern crafting process and its characteristics. The hermeneutic approach, as applied in this study, was based predominantly on the work by Hans-Georg Gadamer (1976), who emphasized the importance of self-reflection and removal of bias, and critical review of collected data and of the methods of data analysis. One of the notions most central to Gadamerian hermeneutics is the concept of a *horizon of understanding*. The notion was first introduced in the 1930s by Husserl (1970) in his phenomenological theory and describes one's vision of the tradition as a historical view of perceived phenomena. The researcher's role is to bring together the possible horizons on the issue at hand at a given time and in a particular place, as well as, their own horizons and pre-understandings. Understanding of concepts, objects and events allows placing them in a larger context and thus making sense of the 'whole'. The process continues in cycles (or circles) (Cole and O'Keefe, 2002) by interpreting parts and their relationships and then moving to a better understanding of the global context, and in turn to an improved understanding of each part. This circular interpretation continues until effective fusion of all horizons (Gadamer, 1979), consequently achieving a complete understanding of the investigated phenomena (Crotty, 1998; Olson and Carlisle, 2001).

Richard Boland is recognised to be one of the first to apply hermeneutics as a research method suitable to studying information systems (Myers, 1997). He (Boland, 1991) proposed to view an information system and its output as text that could be interpreted and analysed by users and which could be assigned meaning by users. Today hermeneutics is a proven research method in Information Systems and has been success-fully used in various research projects, e.g. to design a geographic infor-mation system (Gould, 1994), investigate richness of email exchange in organisational context (Lee, 1994), examine the design of information technologies (Coyne, 1995), analyse IS projects success (Lukaitis and Cybulski, 2004; Myers, 1994), analyse approaches to representation in · design for computer supported collaborative work (Chalmers, 2004), examine Ph.D. educational programs for students with or without prior professional experience (Klein and Rowe, 2007), or to understand infor-mation within a managerial context (Introna, 1997).

The hermeneutic approach was considered the most suitable for the study of a knowledge acquisition process, which itself displays many hermeneutic characteristics, such as

- *Text:* We are studying the pattern crafting process and its outcome which both can be represented with their textual descriptions – the text analogues of the artefacts under investigation.
- *Historicality and context:* The identified issues of importance to prac-titioners have to be studied in the wider context of undertaken pro-jects, conducted at a given point of time, in a particular location and for a specific client.
- *Hermeneutic circle:* As the domain knowledge and practice are broad and not well understood (by researchers) at the time of conduct-ing the study, we therefore aimed at iterative refinement (by means of several cycles) of our understanding of the domain issues and process-related phenomena across the application domain.
- *Horizons of understanding:* The meaning provided by individual prac-titioners will have to be gradually captured, interpreted and repre-sented in a pattern format, thus necessitating 'fusion of horizons' from multiple perspectives.
- *Bias:* Having previous pattern mining and crafting experience and being intimately involved in this research, we had to identify and eliminate our own preconceptions and biases. At the same time, we also dealt with the biases of our subjects.

Information sources in this study were practitioners with various scope of work, selected specifically to meet the requirements of theo-retical sampling (Strauss and Corbin, 1998), as well as, providing the rationale for multiple data sources used in the study triangulation (Fontana and Frey, 2000). We studied practitioners' experience captured as their 'war stories' in audiovisual form and subsequently represented in the text format. Each individual story represented the subject's horizon of understanding, whereas the process of finding shared experience illustrated a fusion of horizons of the subjects and researchers. The collected shared experience was subsequently represented in the pattern format which reflected achieved domain understanding.

The pattern crafting process can be considered hermeneutically as an articulation of the relationship between domain practitioners' personal and socially determined pre-understanding of their practice, and the views of pattern miners on the methods of capturing problem-solving experience. This process does not need to end at this point, as the resulting patterns can be further refined by other practitioners, shepherds and workshop participants to match their pre-understandings of their practice. Thus the pattern crafting and mining process in itself is a specific form of the hermeneutic circle.

The focus of this research is on pattern crafting – the early stage of experience in order to produce patterns. Each round of hermeneutic cycles results in the pattern crafting process refinement and also supports establishing a method of arriving at the process in the domain under investigation.

Domain selection

The multimedia domain was selected because of its fast development pace, high demand for multimedia products, numerous technological and business problems routinely solved in the design process. There have been few prior attempts to cover the domain by pattern mining activities, though as was shown by our study, its problem-solving knowledge has good potential for being represented in a pattern format and subsequent sharing among practitioners.

In technical domains, which are well-covered by patterns and pattern languages, e.g. software analysis, design and development (as discussed above), practitioners commonly understand and use patterns. In such domains, many practitioners are also enthusiastic pattern writers themselves, sharing their own experience with their community of practice. In the multimedia development field, on the other hand, there are few patterns available to practitioners, who are also not aware of their existence, who do not take advantage of experience sharing via patterns, and who do not participate in pattern writing. The evidence from the related development fields, however, gives us confidence that pattern use and mining has strong potential for bringing quality and productivity benefits to multimedia practitioners (Schmidt 1995; Appleton, 1997; Manns, 2001). However, since the multimedia domain is far too big for the purpose of this study, it was hence restricted to the subdomain of front-end multimedia design.

In an effort to develop understanding of multimedia development principles and to explore the suitability of a pattern format to capture experience in multimedia design, a number of multimedia patterns have been crafted and evaluated (Cybulski and Linden, 1998; Linden and Cybulski, 2001). This pilot study helped the researchers gain important insights into the peculiarities of the multimedia domain, the widely used pattern crafting and mining approaches (in other domains) and to discover some deficiencies in this process.

Research design

In accordance with the 'contextualisation' principle of hermeneutics (Klein and Myers, 1999) there is a need to understand the domain under study and to identify areas of practitioners' concerns. This need was set as our first objective. The path towards understanding can be accomplished using various approaches including interviewing, observation and focus groups, to name a few. Hermeneutic studies in Information Systems, which represent contemporary 'lived' phenomena, often employ interviewing for data collection. For example, Butler (1998) used unstructured and semi-structured interviews to collect opinions on IS development processes. Hermeneutics is 'doubly relevant to interview research, first by elucidating the dialogue producing the interview texts to be interpreted, and then by clarifying the subsequent process of interpreting the interview texts produced...' (Kvale, 1996: 46). Interviewing can also be used in pattern crafting. For example, Rising (1999) captured organisational experience via interviews and meetings and recorded it as patterns. Since this research applies hermeneutics to studying the pattern crafting process, interviewing was considered eminently suitable and therefore selected as its main data collection tool, in particular to identify common areas of concern in front-end multimedia development.

In our study, an interview approach to data collection allowed targeting individual subjects from a variety of backgrounds and with a different work scope, to gather a variety of personal views and experiences. Harmer (2003) indicates the importance of providing evidence from multiple sources of data, an important aspect of triangulation (Fontana and Frey, 2000). As hermeneutics focuses on understanding textual descriptions, it does not impose any specific number of sources that need to be consulted in the process. In IS research, as few as four (4) participants (Lee, 1994) have been used in hermeneutic investigations.

In our study, in order to identify common experience across the entire multimedia domain, eight (8) participants from different organisations with various work scopes and working on different projects were interviewed to achieve theoretical saturation (Strauss and Corbin, 1998). Among them were web developers, graphic designers, multimedia designers, etc. Analysis of transcribed interviews led to discovery of individual participants' horizons of understanding, which were then explored in the context of their respective projects, and which eventually merged to reflect on the common experience across the entire domain. The resulting texts had to be interpreted in the historical and project context, since 'a valid interpretation of text without a context is impossible' (Altheide and Johnson, 1998: 306).

In order to find common issues of concern to domain practitioners, this study needed to develop an approach supporting systematic analysis of domain data. There exists a variety of methods that were available to assist this hermeneutic process. For example, in the business context, Ket de Vries and Miller (1987) suggest the use of observations clustering into groups based on common themes. In socially-motivated IS studies, Standing and Standing (1999) recommend theme recognition and the use of keywords in transcripts analysis. However, finding common themes in text by means of coding and indexing has been most widely used in qualitative data analysis (Miles and Huberman, 1994; Kelle, 1997) and supported by modern data analysis software, such as NVivo (Richards and Richards, 1998). This latter approach to qualitative data analysis by computer-assisted text coding has been adopted in our study.

The task of coding the collected experiential data, producing multimedia pattern skeletons and later full patterns was performed by the ghost writer (Rising, 1999). In a typical situation a ghost writer is an experienced pattern writer with some knowledge of the domain under investigation. Being in the unique position of having expertise in both areas, we decided that one of us would take on the role of a ghost writer. This decision was made in the spirit of interpretive research, whereby researchers' impact on their study is unavoidable, and with proper precautions they can become an intrinsic part of the research process (Shanks, 1996; Klein and Myers, 1999). Cole and O'Keefe (2002) further emphasise that hermeneutic studies gain strength from interaction of researchers with their subjects, supporting analysis of data and inducing its rich contextual meaning.

As hermeneutic studies involve iterative discovery of the subject matter, the exact steps and their number are determined based on the insights gained in the process. Therefore, in our hermeneutic research it was impossible to state upfront the sequence and the number of cycles needed to achieve (via theoretical saturation) the goals of this study. Instead, in each hermeneutic cycle we continually reassessed our insights, objectives, methods to be used, and our own prejudices and biases. Having achieved theoretical saturation of findings, in the tradition of Information Systems research, we further decided to conduct an independent evaluation/triangulation of the obtained results (Sarkar and Cybulski, 2004).

Empirical work

This study's main goal was to establish a pattern-crafting process by which practitioners problem-solving experience could be captured into domain patterns ready for dissemination to the community of practice. To achieve this goal, the objectives were to provide a method leading to discovering horizons of domain understanding as held by individual domain practitioners, then to fuse these horizons by finding common issues of concern to practitioners, and finally mapping these commonalities into patterns and pattern languages.

In this empirical work, three (3) hermeneutic cycles were conducted to achieve these objectives. Subsequently these three cycles were found to effectively refine the currently employed pattern crafting process. The three cycles were:

1. *Domain Understanding.* It was important for the researchers to get insights into the domain under study before working on the domain-specific pattern-crafting process. It was also vital for the pattern writers to understand the domain for which they were going to write patterns. The first cycle therefore aimed at developing such understanding by studying domain specific design issues and concerns. Analysis of practitioners' experience resulted in a system of codes – a derivative text that reflected researchers' and pattern writers' horizons of domain understanding.
2. *Extracting Patterns and Pattern Skeletons.* In the second cycle the goal was to identify recurring problem situations by means of coding and categorising collected data. The coding scheme evolved in parallel with domain understanding and was continually adjusted to capture outlines of pattern languages and patterns. This coding scheme represented a rich derivative text reflecting recurring problems in the domain under study, their context and approaches to

their resolution. This text formed the integral part of the researchers' horizons of understanding domain practices.

3. *Pattern Refinement*. The third cycle aimed at refining the previously obtained pattern outlines into full patterns. This step required additional insights into the domain in order to fill in the gaps in patterns. Therefore a mini pattern crafting workshop involving domain practitioners as well as pattern writers was conducted. The text for interpretation was a pattern skeleton that was interpreted by mini-workshop participants and the resulting pattern(s) were the final derivative text that could subsequently be evaluated by practitioners. This cycle illustrates expansion of the researchers' horizon of understanding and its fusion with those of workshop participants.

In this hermeneutic study individual practitioners' reflections on their experiences provided parts that were analysed in the context of the projects and contributed to the understanding of the whole, i.e. the front-end design in the multimedia domain and best practices as viewed by the majority of practitioners.

Throughout the hermeneutics cycles we provided insights into the data analysis, the emerging horizons of understanding and their fusion, and finally the researchers' prejudices and biases and ways of dealing with them.

After the pattern language and patterns had been crafted, the standard pattern mining procedure of shepherding and workshopping the resulting patterns was followed. This part of work did not contribute to the refinement of the pattern crafting process but rather to the evaluation of the patterns quality, which also reflected in the fusion of horizons of understanding as held by domain practitioners and experienced pattern writers.

Domain understanding – first hermeneutic cycle

Domain understanding and studying domain specific design issues and concerns, being the main goal of this first hermeneutic cycle, included the following, more specific, objectives:

- Collecting problem-solving experience of domain practitioners that could become the basis for domain understanding and pattern formation;
- Developing researchers' and ghost writers' basic understanding of the selected domain, i.e. multimedia front-end design;

- Identifying common issues of concern for practitioners – 'fusion of horizons' as seen by the researchers while interpreting practitioners' stories.

Eight (8) practitioners working in front-end multimedia development were interviewed. The subjects were unacquainted with each other, worked for different organisations or were self-employed. To look at the same problems from various perspectives we ensured that all subjects worked in front-end multimedia development, but had a varying work scope, i.e. we interviewed three graphic designers, one multimedia producer, and four web developers. In the semi-structured interviews the practitioners were asked to demonstrate the project of their choice, explaining the design process, discussing different drafts, decisions made and reflecting on their best practices. Some interviewees talked about one project only. Others demonstrated and discussed two or three projects. In total seventeen (17) projects were described.

The data were collected mainly in the form of audio and video recordings, and hard copy notes. McGraw and Harbison-Briggs (1989) report audio and videotaping as highly effective methods especially when combined with selective note taking. These recordings were transcribed because hermeneutics is known to be successfully applied to text analogue with the aim of understanding it (Demeterio, 2001). Screenshots were inserted in the appropriate places in transcribed verbal protocols for illustration purposes.

Analysis of the transcribed data was conducted by themes identification and content indexing, which required defining and structuring of text codes (Huberman and Miles, 1998). We used NVivo for coding our data, however codes were created manually to closely reflect the content of a coded phrase or passage. Such coding approach was very fine-grain and resulted in more than one hundred unique codes. Later these codes were revised to demonstrate commonalities between issues raised and an older version was used as an explanation. Table 12.1 illustrates coding of colour related issues. As it shows codes like 'Grey version – pros and cons', 'Navy blue is too heavy', 'Neutral are to offset bright colours', 'Traditional blue & white', seven in total were replaced by 'Colour-Perception' since at a higher level of abstraction all these codes were referring to the same issue – the perception of colours by viewers. After several rounds of refining the codes, they evolved into a code system of a much higher level of abstraction, and in the end we produced a tree-like structure of codes (see extract in Figure 12.2) where the top level reflected categories of concern common to the interviewed practitioners. For example,

Table 12.1 Examples of color related issues (via coding)

Interview extracts	Code	Explanation
The colours came from their corporate colours	Colour-Corporate	Corporate colours
The colour scheme was taken from the fact that that was their corporate logo and we decided that rather than introducing more colours into it we'd just keep the black and the red then, with white for emphasis, so that the logo stood out.	Colour-Logo	Colours dictated by logo
In this one the client had a great deal to do with the colour schemes involved. She wanted the colours that are used, each section has a different colour associated with it and they're based on, oh what's it, the yogic central, what are they called, the points, the energy points on the body? The colours are significant to the industry that she's in basically and she wanted those colours to be reflected throughout the site. So we put the order of pages in the way that she could keep, the way that the colours go in this particular table, that she got them from, which is why home is at the bottom and timetable is at the top, instead of what you'd expect would be the other way around.	Colour-Context	Colours reflecting yoga body points
I made a number of options in terms of colours	Colour-Choices	Alternative approaches – in terms of colours
The main thing I played with in all of these is colour variations	Colour-Perception	
That's a grey version which	Colour	
I think looks very you know high tech and contemporary but it is a bit too grey for many people's eyes. There was actually a brochure using the Information Division which was a pale green, which again I think is a very contemporary colour scheme, but is definitely a bit more controversial.	Corporate	

(*continued*)

Table 12.1 Continued

Interview extracts	Code	Explanation
That's a grey version which I think looks very you know high tech and contemporary but it is a bit too grey for many people's eyes.	Colour-Perception	Grey version – pros and cons
There was actually a brochure using the Information Division which was a pale green, which again I think is a very contemporary colour scheme, but is definitely a bit more controversial.	Colour-Perception	Pale green version – pros and cons
Navy blue I just think is too heavy to use in light areas, unless it really is a corporate kind page	Colour-Perception	Navy blue is too heavy
When I chose a blue, moved more towards a lilac, because I wanted to use the gold because it offsets the navy blue well but I wanted to push the blue more towards a purple because it's just less oppressive than navy blue.	Colour-Perception	Offsetting the navy blue
I want to have some neutral area to offset the very bright colours	Colour-Perception	Neutral area to offset bright colours
I prefer to use adaptive rather than web, a web palette if I can. Sometimes I work on a project where I'm asked to work in 8-bit colour which means I have to only choose from a very limited palette, but I prefer to use adaptive colours if I can. As a general rule I try and stick with the web safe palette. There are, I think it's 256 colours which can be faithfully reproduced by just about every monitor. Anything else and you're taking chances. It might be reproduced exactly as you saw it on yours, but it might not be. So we tend to just find the closest approximation in web safe, because it's probably safer than finding exactly the right colour on our monitor, but it could look completely different on somebody else's. So if we can at least get something that's close in web safe then that ensures that at least it's consistent.	Colour-Palette Colour-Web	Web palette *vs* adaptive palette

(continued)

Table 12.1 Continued

Interview extracts	Code	Explanation
I suppose this light blue, this choice of the light blue on the white is supposed to be slightly professional, slightly executive. I would say that ' light blue and white is also sort of calm.	Colour-Perception	Blue & white colour scheme
It's very easy to stay in sort of entirely blue or 'blue and white' kind of space because that seems to be one of the generic kind of computer spaces. By looking across these icons here you can see a lot of this blue and white type of style and looking through most of these sort of navigational elements and like in the previous site that I showed you there is a lot of that generic blue and white. And, so I've kind of used that in these GIF images.	Colour-Perception	Traditional blue & white
Because they were setting themselves up to be a prestigious corporate focused company, doing the gold trimmed red buttons on the black background just had this nice, official sort of look to it.	Colour-Corporate Colour-Buttons Colour-Perception	Buttons' colours
She gave me the background that was something that she found and liked the look of and asked if I could work the colour schemes in with the background. So I came up with the idea of picking on the blues and purples from the cloudy sky type image, which I used in the buttons. Playing with colours for the down state made the text look a bit different, tried a few colours and eventually decided that yellow was the most readable and that was the main part of that.	Colour-Background	Colour scheme from background img

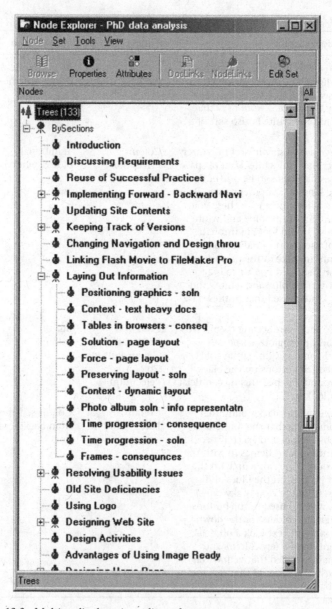

Figure 12.2 Multimedia domain coding scheme

Table 12.2 Common issues of concern to practitioners

Design tasks	WD1	WD2	WD3	WD4	GD1	GD2	GD3	MMP1
Selecting a colour scheme		☑	☑	☑	☑	☑		
Usability issues (screen size, browsers and their versions)	☑	☑	☑		☑	☑		☑
Menu design	☑	☑	☑	☑	☑	☑	☑	
Software applicability for design tasks	☑	☑			☑			☑
Laying out information / Use of templates	☑	☑	☑	☑	☑	☑		☑
Selecting fonts		☑	☑			☑		
Addressing accessibility issues		☑			☑			
Representing timeline								
Working with digital images		☑		☑		☑		
Composing a movie								☑
Communication with the database	☑							☑
Updating site contents by the client	☑							
Keeping track of versions	☑							
Using animations		☑	☑					

(WD – web developer, GD – graphic designer, MMP – multimedia producer)

Table 12.2 demonstrates that categories representing aspects of colour scheme selection, menu design, page layout, and usability issues are important for practitioners across the majority of work scopes.

The hermeneutic analysis of the outcomes resulting from the coding process showed some clear benefits of the adopted fine-grain approach, i.e.

- The process of fine grain coding helped in understanding the studied domain. Researchers' horizons of understanding were represented as a rich textual system of codes which reflected both historicity and context of projects.
- We could identify design issues and areas in the front-end multimedia development process that were important to practitioners. The resulting list of common issues of concern (see Table 12.2) identified horizons of domain practitioners (web developers, graphic designers and multimedia producers).

At this point in time, we also became aware that by gaining a rich understanding of the front-end multimedia design, we introduced the possibility of unwittingly influencing our subsequent work. We recognised it as a threat of possible bias.

This cycle resulted in developing an approach to dealing with the voluminous interview data. In the emerging pattern crafting process a pattern writer could apply our system of codes to categorise practitioners statements, then analyse the interviews for other categories that we may have not discovered since multimedia design is a rapidly developing field and new issues may come to life in the future.

Extracting pattern languages and pattern skeletons – second hermeneutic cycle

The data coding process deployed thus far served the goal of the first hermeneutic cycle, i.e. understanding the domain (objective O1) and identifying common issues of concern for practitioners (objective O2). However, we needed a coding approach that would better support the process of extracting patterns and pattern languages. Therefore, it was deemed that in this cycle the effort should be put into refining the existing coding scheme and that additional data collection was not necessary.

The main objective for this cycle was to develop a coding scheme that could support patterns identification (leading towards objective O3). It is important to note here that it was not expected for the coding scheme to extract complete patterns at this stage, but rather to assist in the production of pattern skeletons with gaps that could be filled in later.

We realised that for pattern languages and patterns to emerge we needed to search within categories of design issues and problems that we identified as common issues of concern for domain practitioners. As a result, broad categories, such as 'Selecting a colour scheme', 'Menu design', 'Laying out information', 'Addressing accessibility issues', etc., were discovered. The quotes below illustrate practitioners' concerns, which under the coding scheme were categorised as 'Laying out information', and which included practitioners' views on the use of tables and frames for the layout purposes (numbers in brackets refer to the coding of nodes in NVIVO):

> **Graphic Designer 2:** 'And it's very important with tables that if you want things to maintain their position you have to be very specific about measurements, the individual cells within the table and overall measurements of the table.' (9.9.6)

> **Web Developer 1:** 'Unfortunately Netscape and Internet Explorer have slightly different ways of rendering frames and they don't line up particularly well.' (9.9.11, 9.17.21)

Web Developer 2: 'I'm fairly ambivalent about frames. They've got their good points which are that, you know, it means that there's parts of the page that don't reload every time and all of that, but frames can get really, really messy.' (9.9.11, 9.17.21)

Some categories had specific aspects associated with them. For example (see Table 12.3), for the 'menu design' task issues such as 'look', 'structure', 'buttons', and 'behaviour', as well as some others, were identified. For each of these task-related issues we also recorded other design aspects, which we found were commonly of concern to multimedia developers, and which we considered good candidates for a potential pattern language (here Menu Design). Reflecting on the effectiveness of identifying pattern languages, we came to the conclusion that initial categories should indeed be based on design tasks and their various aspects.

Further data analysis was expected to help identifying pattern fragments and reconciling them into a small collection of highly focused patterns of experience derived from designers and their project work.

As the intense analysis within each category (i.e. design task) was performed, the analysis process gradually transferred into the next stage – coding within categories which aimed at discovering pattern skeletons. The coding scheme relied on the names of sections of the adopted pattern format (see Figure 12.1), i.e. problem, solution, forces, context and consequences. Disappointingly, application of such a coding scheme failed to induce full patterns in most cases. However, it resulted

Table 12.3 Outline of an emerging pattern language

Design issues	Aspects of design tasks to be considered
Menu Look	• Menu layout
	• Non-ortho linear *vs.* tabular menu items layout
	• Visual representation of menu items
	• Menu context indication
	• Menu persistence during navigation
	• Temporal effects
Menu Buttons	• Tool-specific menu design facilities
	• Creating reusable menu styles
	• Menu image representation (vector *vs.* bitmap)
	• Inter-tool communication and compatibility
Menu Behaviour	• Visual effects (transitions)
	• Navigation behaviour
	• Mouse-click effects
Menu Structure	• Consistency between menu and site/information structure

---

Design Issue - Business Type as Influence on Web Site Design

Name

Problem

Context

> Target audience: with a particular demographic in mind... I was thinking also that a lot of people who visit this site...

Forces

Context – Solution

- (9.13.2) idea of construction being like the arrangement of large objects using really... moving large objects [about large bulky logo falling from the top of the page]. (9.13.3) Perhaps this is like a big thing, which is being sort of dropped down by a crane or something like that

- (9.13.2) if you were to visit the building, if you were to visit the office you would notice that this DE which stands for David Edelman is a pre-existing design feature that has been sort of on their front door and been on their letterhead for quite some time. It was designed by a graphic designer several years ago and that sort of stayed there ever since. [used as a bulky logo falling from the top of the page].

- (9.13.2) This is a more recent site that we did for a blind manufacturer. So we set the site up that the page up to actually look like a blind

- (9.13.2) We did the same thing then in the product directory, we made that look like another set of blinds, the drop down type blinds, which it just kept the theme going through the site.

- (9.13.3) Each section has a different colour associated with it and they're based on, oh what's it, the yogic central, what are they called, the points, the energy points on the body?

- (9.17.5) I looked at the text, I looked at this kind of use of the typography, which is already on their business card

Resulting Context

Consequences

Figure 12.3 A pattern skeleton (with gaps) induced in the second hermeneutic cycle

in outlines of pattern skeletons, such as that in Figure 12.3, of which contents reflected the domain participants' main concerns, and which could be further elaborated by practitioners in the follow-up interviews (see the third hermeneutic cycle).

Our most important finding at the end of this hermeneutic circle was that it is indeed possible to code unstructured and semi-structured interviews with a view to identify important design issues, and then to cast these issues into outlines of pattern languages and pattern skeletons. These design issues can be discovered through coding by categories, which reflect design tasks and their aspects. Coding within categories results in discovering patterns' sections (problem, context, forces, etc) thus producing skeletons with gaps to be filled in the subsequent hermeneutic cycles.

Figure 12.4 illustrates the process we believe could lead to further refinement of patterns. In this figure, the 'Coding by design tasks' box represents the process of merging practitioners' horizons by identifying

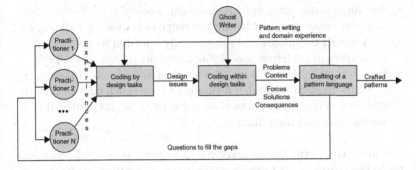

Figure 12.4 Pattern crafting process with coding outcomes noted

common design tasks and issues of concern to them. The 'Coding within design tasks' box reflects the horizon of the researcher(s)/ghost writer(s) and its fusion with the identified practitioners' horizons in the process of representing problem-solving experience as design task related pattern languages and pattern skeletons.

Yet again, the applied process suffered from some bias in the coding and patterns creation due to one of the researchers taking on the role of a ghost writer. As a result, the classification of practitioners' statements into codes (corresponding to the elements of design patterns) was based in its entirety on our subjective decision – the common practice in interpretive studies.

Pattern refinement in the focus group – third hermeneutic cycle

As stated in our objective O3, the purpose of this cycle was to refine the pattern skeletons that emerged in the previous cycle into full patterns. This activity required additional domain knowledge as well as pattern writing skills. Therefore we organised a mini workshop in the form of a focus group session with participants from both backgrounds. It was expected that fusing the horizons of multimedia practitioners with those of pattern writing experts would contribute to better understanding of the pattern crafting process.

The focus group approach was eminently suitable for this cycle for the following reasons:

- The distinguished feature of a focus group is that participants are supposed to be engaged in discussion with each other, the discussion is concentrated on a particular issue or topic and that group dynamics facilitate generating ideas (Frey and Fontana, 1993).

- The focus group environment has been known as facilitating participants interactions, widening the range of responses, building on each other's comments and subsequently releasing forgotten or passive experience (Merton *et al*, 1956; Catterall and Maclaran, 1997).
- For our mini workshop we needed a moderator who would keep participants on track without contributing to the actual pattern crafting process and record the patterns on the whiteboard for participants to see the results of their discussion.

Traditionally focus groups involve 6 to 12 participants and a moderator to keep participants focused; sessions last approximately 2h (Stewart and Shamdasani 1990; Nielsen, 1997). However, there have been studies where the traditional focus group approach has been modified to suit the needs of the research project. For example, Gamson (1992) conducted his 'peer group conversations' in an informal setting, with the minimised intrusion of the moderator and involving only 4–6 participants who discussed issues of invoking media texts on local and national politics. Press and Cole (1999) named their approach 'ethnographic focus groups' to emphasise the deviation from a traditional focus group approach. Their groups had only between 2 and 5 participants who were friends, rather than strangers, due to sensitive emotionally charged topics of discussion. The setting was also informal; to make participants feel comfortable the meeting was arranged in one of the participants' homes.

For this focus group session we could not produce a detailed protocol as it would normally be the case for a traditional focus group since there were no formal questions of discussion. We needed initiative coming from pattern writers who would guide the pattern writing process eliciting knowledge from practitioners as well as sharing their pattern writing skills. The participants of the focus group included two (2) participants with a multimedia background and two (2) participants with good pattern mining skills and some experience in multimedia. Since it is acceptable in qualitative studies for a researcher to facilitate the focus group (Morgan, 1988), one of us moderated the session. The second researcher passively observed the focus group session. The session was audio and video recorded and subsequently the recording was transcribed. The transcript was the fundamental data for further analysis (Morgan, 1988).

The participants' handout included a brief explanation of what patterns are, what pattern format was to be used, description of the issue under investigation – i.e. crafting of patterns by collecting experience across domain, and finally pattern skeletons relating to the design issue 'Business Type and Pre-existing Context as Influence on Web Site Design' (see Figure 12.3). The participants' task was to examine practitioners' concerns related to the specified topic and to attempt producing patterns based on our draft generated from interviews analysis and participants' own experience. The role of practitioners was to provide missing domain information whereas the task of pattern experts was to restructure the emerging patterns according to pattern-writing guidelines.

Only one pattern was produced as a result of this session (see Figure 12.5). However, participants in their discussion pointed out opportunities for more patterns to emerge.

Content coding (Catterall and Maclaran, 1997) was applied to the transcript by clustering sections according to the pattern's sections discussed. This approach is in line with the hermeneutics approach to text analysis (De Vries and Miller, 1987).

At the beginning of the session pattern writers shared their understanding of patterns with domain practitioners. During the session practitioners kept asking for clarification on what level of abstraction patterns should be, how prescriptive or concrete they should be, the role of context and forces in the pattern format, etc.

One of the pattern writers started with expressing her view:

> **Participant 1:** For me, the starting point is the solution. So what is the common theme that's gone through a number of different applications?

And she continued with:

> **Participant 1:** The solution that we're actually talking about is reflect in the web design the actual business type.

The web designer supported this suggestion:

> **Participant 2:** Or at least taking some sort of an inspiration from the business type to get you started on the design. You might end up with something that's a lot more stylised or whatever, but you actually start with the idea of 'let's take something concrete that they do.'

So based on the pattern skeleton in the handout the participants established what issue the pattern should be reflecting and they agreed that it should be related to representation of physical artefacts sold or

Name	Name
Presenting a Product On-line (Presenting a Company On-line)	*Presenting a Product or Service On-line (via Web Site)*
Problem	**Problem**
How to convey to the audience the primary product or service of the company?	**How to convey to the on-line audience the products or services of the company?**
Context	**Context**
• The company manufactures or sells (deals with) tangible products or the company provides services through tangible/physical products.	• The company manufactures or sells tangible products or the company provides services which affect some tangible products.
• Web media are used to reflect type of product.	• A variety of Web media can be used to reflect different types of products and services.
• The company sells limited number of related product types so it is possible to choose primary type or archetype.	• The company sells a limited number of related product types so it is possible to choose primary type or archetype.
• Taking some sort of an inspiration from the business type to get you started on the design.	*(Moved to Solution)*
Forces	**Forces**
• The company is not physically present so the Web site should convey the sense of the company and its products.	• The on-line audience needs to get answers about the company, its products and services; **yet**, Web sites have limited facilities to support interactive communication with the users.
• Target audience are potential buyers, however...	• The on-line audience are potential users of the Web site; **however**, only clients are consulted on its design.
• Clients (company reps) often don't know what they want beyond "I want a web site", however Web designers need more than that as a some kind of a starting point.	• Clients often don't know what they want or what the on-line audience requires; **however**, designers need a starting point, in the form of the Web site requirements or a pilot, to produce its design.
Solution	**Solution**
Reflect in Web design physical artefacts or theme of service associated with the company through the use of colour, layout and graphical elements.	**Design a Web site based on the tangible products or the service theme associated with the company through the use of the appropriate Web media, colour, layout and graphical elements.**
(No explicit reference to forces)	○ The web site should convey a sense of the company and its products, without the need for physical communication between the on-line audience and the company.
	○ Insights into client's business may inspire the initial design, which may help elicit further requirements from the clients and result in refinements to the Web site design.
	○ The pilot version of the Web site provides opportunities to obtain feedback from the on-line audience and to refine the design of the Web site.
Resultin context	**Resultin context**
• It becomes very clear to the audience what the company is providing.	• Through its Web site, the company can effectively communicate its products and services to the on-line audience.
Consequences - Pros	**Consequences - Pros**
• No ambiguity in what the company is providing.	• Elicited client's requirements and the feedback from the on-line audience allow the Web site to clearly convey (by reducing ambiguity) the products or services of the company.
• Gives immediate starting point for the designer.	• Web site design can be initiated before completion of requirements elicitation and can be used for further refinement of requirements.
Consequences-Cons	**Cons**
• If there are several companies providing the same thing, how to convince the audience that this one is the better to deal with?	• The solution does not take into consideration the competing products and services which may be available on the market.

Figure 12.5 The full pattern produced by the focus group on design issue 'Business Type as Influence on Web Site Design' before and after ghost-writer's editing

manufactured by the company ordering the website. However, one of the participants pointed out that example involving yoga body points does not relate to physical artefacts but rather to services. Following some discussion the problem statement was adjusted accordingly. In relation to the established problem the group worked on the wording of the solution.

Participant 3: I think we can actually rephrase a bit. Instead of saying, 'How to reflect', because it looks like it's begging for a solution, what you can say is, 'How to convey to the public the primary product of service'.

Participant 4: But it's more than that. It's the primary product in a graphical form, but in a very simple form. I think it's a pretty basic way to add a product. You could do it in many other ways

After agreeing on the problem-solution pair the participants discussed forces and context. The participants used the pattern skeleton in the handout only as an inspiration for their discussion. Apart from the first few minutes when the theme of the discussion was clearly identified they did not refer back to the handout. All the necessary domain knowledge was provided by the participating practitioners.

Unfortunately due to the time limit, the solution was not refined to resolve all of the identified forces and forces were not properly worded as per recommended norms for wording forces (Appleton, 1997), though traditionally this would have been completed during the session; therefore the ghost-writer had to do a bit of polishing bringing minor modifications into the pattern. The important point regarding modifications is that no domain knowledge was added.

Figure 12.5 illustrates – on a statement by statement basis – the applied changes. The ghost-writer had to re-word the pattern name to reflect not only company products but also services since both appear in the problem and the solution, which was an oversight on the part of participants. The problem statement had the word 'on-line' added to highlight the focus on the web site design. Two out of four context statements were left without change. In one better wording was applied without changing its meaning. The fourth statement was merged into the solution.

Forces were re-worded to follow the guidelines on wording forces, but the actual number and meaning of forces were left as discussed by participants. The solution should show how it resolves the forces, therefore quite often pattern writers specify the main solution statement (in bold) and then elaborate on it. Due to time limitations, the group did not return to the discussion of the solution after finalising forces and therefore this task remained incomplete. The ghost-writer had to fill in this gap based on the focus group discussion. The three bullet points in the solution correspond to the three listed forces and show how the solution balances forces. Also there were minor wording changes made to the Resulting Context and Consequences sections.

Since the ghost-writer had some background knowledge of multimedia which has been enriched in the previous two cycles, she had to control her input into the pattern, i.e. her contribution had to be restricted to editing only with no additional content for the pattern.

There were several points in the discussion where the participants suggested other patterns emerging:

> **Participant 2:** ... That might be another pattern for later, which would be about what happens if they already have a corporate image? What do you do to bring that into the website?

> **Participant 3:** ... As earlier we said that the website could also reflect the philosophy of the company, but that may not be what they're selling directly. But that would be a different pattern.

Thus the focus group discussion is useful not only for producing patterns based on presented material but also may be a good source of additional patterns that were not noted in the first round of data collection and coding or could be missed at the time of coding.

The analysis of the focus group transcript showed that:

- A focus group session is a suitable approach to reproduce a pattern-crafting mini-workshop.
- Focus group participants can cast domain experience into full patterns. Multimedia domain knowledge and pattern writing skills, when put together, add quality to the resulting patterns. These patterns represent text analogue of domain understanding and reflect the fusion of horizons of both domain practitioners and pattern writers.
- In the discussion focus group participants pointed out potential patterns not noted by the ghost writer in the preparatory data analysis.
- Focus group participants used all information contained within the pattern skeletons; however, they ignored the allocation of statements to pattern's sections. As coding within categories proved to be of no value to domain practitioners and pattern writers, it has been

decided that only coding by categories (corresponding to design tasks) should be performed and consequently presented for discussion in a focus group.

- Coding by categories (i.e. design tasks) was found to be very helpful with discovering real issues and clustering designer concerns: it places all quotes from different sources relating to the same issue together for further analysis.
- Knowing that classification during coding by categories reflects the horizon of understanding of the ghost writer, it was no surprise to note that the focus group participants moved statements between pattern skeletons. Fusion of the horizons of understanding of the ghost writer and focus group participants effectively improved the accuracy of both coding and pattern formation.
- Since focus group participants are free to re-arrange the pattern skeleton statements, the ghost writer's bias in coding within categories has less impact on pattern crafting as compared to coding by categories.
- Pattern crafting could possibly further benefit from the ghost writer's active participation in the focus group session; however in our case – to comply with the research design – the ghost writer did not interfere in this process. Her role was just to moderate the workshop and to ensure it meets the objectives of the session. Researcher's bias as a moderator mainly showed in the fact that she was steering the focus group in the direction of filling particular sections of the pattern the participants were working on.
- Participants were quite eager to share their knowledge and as a result multimedia designers obtained some pattern-writing skills. Interestingly, the session demonstrated the process of building a horizon of understanding of pattern crafting for domain practitioners as well as fusion of horizons for people with different backgrounds, i.e. domain practitioners and pattern writers.

Since the group produced a full pattern based on the presented skeleton, the main goal of this cycle was achieved. This resulting pattern illustrated a fusion of horizons of pattern writers and domain practitioners.

Findings and their evaluation

In the course of this study we gained some significant insights into the specifics of the multimedia domain, into the experience of our participants, into the challenges of pattern crafting, and into our own viewpoints on the collected knowledge and attitudes towards the undertaken research process. The issues treated by our research thus spanned four domain-specific (multimedia) dimensions.

- *Domain-specific problem-solving experience*, which we have identified, coded and analysed, and which also provided the context for refining the pattern mining process;
- *Our own prejudices and biases*, which we have formally identified and then dealt with to avoid their interference with the carried out research; and
- *Pattern crafting process*, which we have proposed, iteratively refined and then formalised;
- *Patterns and pattern languages*, which we have developed for the domain under study.

The obtained patterns and pattern languages for the multimedia domain are the tangible outcome of the study. They are shareable and reusable nuggets of multimedia *domain experience* that could be distributed to multimedia developers and applied in multimedia development to enhance their performance and to improve the quality of their products.

The practitioners' experience (coded and analysed) as well as the pattern crafting process are part of the *domain-specific method* of capturing and formalising multimedia problem-solving knowledge. By following the process and reapplying the developed codes (see Table 12.1, Figure 12.2), it is possible to collect experience of as yet unidentified domain practitioners, classifying this experience and casting it into patterns, thus, extending and enriching the shareable domain knowledge.

Identification of our own prejudices and biases in this study provides other hermeneutic researchers with *guidelines* on dealing with the impact of their growing domain understanding, their intimate involvement with the participants, and their subjectivity in data coding and pattern creation.

The *pattern-crafting process* (see Figure 12.6), as revealed to be appropriate for the multimedia domain (and possibly applicable to other domains as well), complements and extends the existing pattern-mining process (Manns, 2001). More specifically, the proposed (induced) process encompasses the following workflow:

- The ghost writer collects practitioners 'war stories' via interviews.
- The ghost writer applies open coding to categorise practitioners' concerns around design tasks. The primary deliverable of this procedure

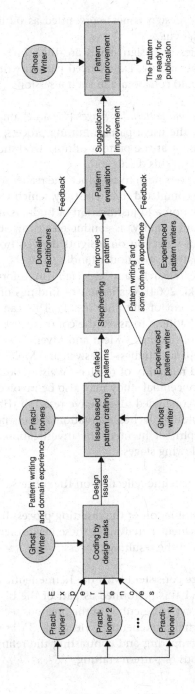

Figure 12.6 Refined pattern mining process

is a collection of design issues represented as outlines of domain-specific pattern languages.

- Selected categories of design issues are then presented to a focus group for pattern crafting. Experienced pattern writers and domain practitioners should collaborate in such a session.

Resulting *patterns and pattern languages* (see an example in the Figure 12.5) are subject to the usual pattern-mining process, including shepherding and discussion at the pattern mining workshop, and patterns improvement based on this discussion.

Qualitative researchers need to convince the readers of the soundness and strength of the completed research study, which requires provision of evidence, explanation and justification of findings and reached conclusions. Hermeneutic inquiry, as conducted in this study, commonly relies on continuous reflection on insights derived from the cycles of data collection, analysis and understanding (Myers, 2004). In other types of qualitative research, and especially in Information Systems (Sarkar and Cybulski, 2004), evaluation of findings often involves an independent assessment of the final results. This can be achieved by applying predefined criteria to assess the contextualisation, abstraction and generalisation of findings – Klein and Myers (1999), triangulation of insights across separate studies – Creswell and Miller (2000), or determining validity and reliability of results – Welsh (2002). Some form of argumentative or conceptual study may also be involved in reassessing the findings of the concluded interpretive research (Harmer, 2003). In view of these possible approaches, evaluation of our study was designed to be within the spirit of hermeneutic investigation, and as such it consisted of the following stages:

1. Continuous hermeneutic reflection on the process and each stage of its refinement.
2. Independent examination of the resulting process by expert pattern miners and hermeneutic analysis of these new insights.
3. Detailed analysis of the resulting process.

Stage 1 and 2 were consistent with the hermeneutic method applied in this study. Stage 1 was performed as part of the hermeneutic circle and mapped on the cycles described in the previous section. Stage 2 was carried out as an extra hermeneutic cycle. Stage 3 was undertaken as a conceptual study comparing and contrasting the refined process with other known methods of pattern crafting.

Independent examination of the resulting process

In this research, hermeneutic evaluation is based on the concept of 'confirmability' (Drisko, 1997) of findings which was adopted from the evaluation framework used by Sarkar and Cybulski (2004). *Confirmability* is similar to the concept of triangulation in case studies research. Triangulation is a multi-method approach that uses 'the strengths of each method to overcome the deficiencies of the other' (Sarantakos, 1996: 155). Confirmability of findings and conclusions are achieved when research results are open to critical examination by other inquirers, who consequently, in respect of a number of predefined criteria, assume understanding of the observed phenomena similar to that of the researcher. Such evaluation, hence, provides evidence as to the research credibility from multiple standpoints, which in this study comprised accounts of practitioners' views collected in interviews and focus group sessions. Sarkar and Cybulski (2004) suggested the following three criteria to be considered as part of this process, i.e. *usefulness, relevance* and *extensibility* of findings, which include domain experience, the refined pattern crafting process, reflection on own prejudices and biases, as well as, patterns and pattern languages. Sarkar and Cybulski (2004) evaluation criteria were adapted to meet the needs of this project. We considered usefulness of the of the pattern crafting process from the perspective of its support for acquisition and formalisation of domain knowledge, we judged the process relevance in relation to the prior experiences of pattern miners, and the process extensibility in terms of its flexibility to accommodate further extensions and enrichments to suit practitioners' needs (also in other domains).

The pattern crafting process was evaluated at a special focus group session at the European pattern mining conference. The process has been examined by deconstructing it and discussing its parts in the focus group attended by eight (8) conference attendees. The discussion lasted 2h and 40 mins. The session was audio recorded and transcribed and the resulting text was hermeneutically analysed in the same manner as that presented in section 4. The three confirmability criteria of usefulness, relevance and extensibility were used as a framework for understanding the discussion of the proposed pattern crafting process by both pattern mining experts and multimedia practitioners.

The analysis of the focus transcript allowed discovering individual horizons of understanding by the session participants (see Table 12.4). Fusion of these horizons highlighted the theoretical saturation of issues where shared understanding emerged. Disagreements point to those

Table 12.4 Evaluation of the pattern crafting process

Aspects of the evaluated pattern crafting process	Usefulness	Relevance	Extensibility
A1 Domain understanding by the ghost writer	☑	☑	
A2 Domain wide pattern crafting	☑	☑	
A3 Source of domain expertise: –domain practitioners –published materials	☑		☑
A4 Ghost writer's sound domain knowledge	☑	☑	
A5 Structured approach to domain understanding	☑	☑	
A6 Need to formalise domain knowledge and the process of pattern crafting	☑	☑	☑
A7 Facilitating iterations in the pattern crafting			☑
A8 Usefulness of domain knowledge for shepherds and workshop participants	☑		☑
A9 Writing patterns by domain practitioners	☑	☑	☑

issues where the convergence of opinions was not reached and the theoretical saturation on these understandings was not possible.

Session participants examined every stage of the proposed pattern crafting process, which included domain understanding, domain-wide experience gathering, knowledge categorisation and further formalisation into a pattern format, and finally proceeding with the standard pattern mining process. The following points summarise some of the aspects discussed by the focus group participants (see indicated Aspects A1–A9 in Table 12.4).

• The participants agreed on the usefulness and relevance of domain understanding (Aspect A1). They emphasised its importance not only as a basis for pattern crafting by a ghost writer (Aspect A4), but also highly desirable in the further stages of pattern mining for shepherds and workshop participants (Aspect A8). While discussing sources for domain knowledge, they saw some room for extension and suggested the use of published materials to complement lived practitioners' experience (Aspect A3). (*Usefulness, Relevance and Extensibility*)

- The focus group participants also explored the nature of the domain-wide experience gathering and knowledge acquisition (Aspect A2). While reaching the consensus on the usefulness of the practice for gaining breadth of domain knowledge they also reflected on the relevance of this practice through their regular consultations with domain practitioners in pattern writing. Some of the participants, however, noted that not all useful domain knowledge could and should be represented in pattern format. (*Usefulness, Relevance and some Reservation*)
- Structuring knowledge before its formalisation has been widely recognised as both important and currently practiced by all our discussants (Aspect A5). While they utilised different forms of knowledge structures – such as word lists, knowledge maps, categories and segments – they all agreed that these techniques assists in dealing with the complexity of domain knowledge and its multiple sources. (*Usefulness and Relevance*)
- The contributors to the evaluation all agreed that patterns are a useful form of knowledge formalisation (Aspect A6). They also shared their experiences in undertaking formal activities required to document insights gained from the domain. At the same time, some of them pointed out difficulties in formalising creative aspects of pattern crafting, which require more flexible and personal approaches to knowledge acquisition and its organisation. To deal with these challenges they suggested that the pattern crafting should incorporate iterations in the process of domain understanding, pattern writing and evaluation (Aspect A7). (*Usefulness, Relevance and Extensibility*)
- Finally, the participants observed that the proposed process not only benefits pattern writers but also domain practitioners because it facilitates their introspection, better organization and formalization of their own knowledge (Aspect A9). Some of the pattern writers who were also experts in their field reflected on the improvement to their domain knowledge and practical skills in the process of pattern writing. (*Usefulness, Relevance and Extensibility*)

The above discussion by the evaluation participants and the hermeneutic analysis of the focus group transcripts *confirmed* the proposed pattern crafting process to be *useful* for the acquisition and formalisation of domain knowledge, *relevant* to their pattern mining practice and *extensible* to capture some of their methods of dealing with the challenges of knowledge capture, processing and complexity.

Detailed analysis of the resulting process

It is worth noting that other methods of pattern crafting are in use by the pattern mining community. As part of the evaluation, we compared the two commonly used methods (Rising, 1999; Manns, 2001) against each other and against our approach in respect of the three criteria that relate to the deficiencies of the current pattern crafting process (see section 2), i.e.:

- reliance of pattern crafting on individual experience instead of broad domain practice;
- ineffectiveness of practitioners in formalisation of their own experience;
- ineffectiveness of communication and dissemination of experience.

Table 12.5 summarises the comparison results. It elaborates each of the listed criteria by identifying several of their aspects, which in turn are used in the detailed comparison.

As depicted in Table 12.5, we contrasted the traditional pattern-crafting method, which is self-motivated by individuals or their cohesive group, with two collaborative processes where participation is facilitated by an experienced ghost writer (as proposed by Rising and us).

The work of Rising was inspired by the fact that practitioners had no time to formally share their experience and the organisation faced the risk of losing knowledge due to staff turnover. Her work in capturing experience and knowledge in the form of patterns was restricted to organisational boundaries. In our process the ghost writer is not restricted by organisational or team boundaries.

All three approaches rely on the active participation of practitioners to provide domain expertise. However, the currently used pattern mining process requires practitioners to also have pattern writing skills, whereas our process and the process used by Rising both employ the services of a ghost-writer skilled in pattern writing. While this approach imposes an additional requirement for the ghost writer to acquire domain knowledge, it does resolve the issue of time-consuming and active participation of practitioners in pattern formalisation, refinement, validation and dissemination, which all occur away from the practitioners' working environment. In the Linda Rising approach, the ghost writer is embedded in the organisation and familiar with the organisational problem domain, whereas in our approach the ghost writer acquires the domain knowledge via hermeneutic analysis of the collected knowledge.

In contrast to the traditional, self-motivated and introspective process of pattern refinement, both Linda Rising and the authors of this paper

Table 12.5 Comparing pattern crafting processes (as embedded in pattern mining)

	Approach	Self-Motivated	Facilitated	Facilitated
		Commonly used process	Linda Rising process	Our proposed process
Dealing with domain experience	Scope of involved practitioners	Cohesive group of people	Organisation	Domain
	Source of domain expertise	Pattern writers must have it	Ghost writer must have both domain knowledge and pattern writing skills	Ghost writer must be domain literate, however, through coding will gain deeper domain knowledge
	Collection of domain experience and knowledge	Mining own experience	Interviewing in meetings	Collecting war stories and recording demonstrations
Dealing with formalisation of experience and knowledge	Source of pattern writing expertise	Participating practitioners must be able to construct patterns	Participating practitioners may not have it, however a ghost writer is primarily responsible for pattern writing	Participating practitioners may not have it, however a ghost writer is primarily responsible for pattern writing
	Analysis of domain knowledge	Informal	Informal	Formal coding and categorisation of domain knowledge
	Approach to pattern refinement	Individual, informal and introspective	Interviews with practitioners – with the purpose of pattern verification	Semi-structured and structured interviews, as well as, focus groups with the purpose of pattern enrichment
Dealing with communication and dissemination of experience	Place and time of experience acquisition	Practitioners are extensively involved in all stages of pattern formalisation and publication, often away from their workplace	Experience transfer occurs as part of normal problem-solving meetings and dedicated interviews in the workplace but pattern formalisation and publication involves only the ghost writer	Experience transfer occurs at dedicated pattern-crafting sessions in the workplace but its formalisation and publication involves only the ghost writer
	Structure of the process	Ad-hoc	Semi-structured iterative process	Hermeneutic meta-process to identify a domain-specific process

promote intensive communication between practitioners and ghost writers to iteratively enrich patterns, which facilitates gradual improvement of the pattern quality as additional sources of expertise become available within an organisation (Rising) or in a domain under study (authors).

The main difference between our proposed approach versus those already practiced in the pattern community is in the structure of the pattern crafting process. While the pattern community does not lay any particular guidelines as to the initial steps in the traditional pattern development, and can be seen as *ad-hoc* or semi-structured at best, our method provides a hermeneutic meta-model for the identification of a domain-specific pattern-crafting process, responsible for construction of patterns and pattern languages. The model offers a variety of data collection methods and formal coding approaches, which could be combined together to form the process appropriate for the domain, and specific in respect of its knowledge and representative experts.

From this comparison we can see that the process proposed in this project most comprehensively addresses the major concerns in the current pattern crafting process.

Summary and conclusions

Pattern crafting – the preliminary stage of pattern mining that focuses on identifying and formalising problem solving knowledge – has not been widely recognised as an important element of pattern mining activities, which could potentially lead to the dissemination of shareable nuggets of knowledge in the form of patterns and pattern languages. However, as has been shown in this paper, pattern crafting provides a number of significant benefits to the process. In particular, it overcomes commonly encountered problems of conventional pattern mining in its (1) reliance on participation of individuals or their cohesive groups rather than a wide spectrum of domain practitioners; (2) difficulties in engaging expert problem-solvers in formalisation of their experience and knowledge; and (3) ineffectiveness of communication between practitioners and pattern writers involved in capturing and dissemination of experience.

Our research goal was to improve the currently used approaches to pattern crafting, so that problem solving experience could be captured across an application domain and resulting patterns would be of high quality and ready for dissemination in the community of practice, despite the disparity in the skills, experience and knowledge of domain practitioners and pattern writers. By employing a hermeneutic meta-process, we have arrived at a method of inducing a domain-specific pattern crafting process that is also capable of capturing domain experience, identifying biases and prejudices of pattern writers, and generating patterns and pattern languages that represent domain practice, its knowledge and experience.

Our proposed pattern crafting process does not engage domain practitioners directly in pattern writing activities but instead focuses on capturing their personal war stories and their experience in dealing with the problems arising in developing specific products and services. The proposed process depends on pattern writers continuing improvement in the understanding of domain knowledge via coding, categorisation, structuring and identifying commonalities in captured domain experiences. It provides a path to knowledge formalisation, starting with informal stories, through the emerging pattern skeletons and the final form of refined and enriched patterns and pattern languages. Domain understanding, knowledge formalisation and enrichment, as present in the proposed pattern crafting process, complement activities commonly employed in existing pattern mining approaches, which also support pattern evaluation, improvement, sharing and application.

Through our research, we have found that hermeneutics is eminently suited to studying and refining a process. By inducing a domain-specific pattern crafting process, we relied on hermeneutics as an instrument for growing comprehension of domain texts, their organisational and technical context, the circular revision and refinement of process understanding, fusion of knowledge horizons representing experience of distinct domain practitioners, and finally dealing with the biases and prejudices of all contributors to this process. In essence, hermeneutics provided a framework for the construction of a meta-process capable of dealing with domain-specific concerns likely to impact the effectiveness of pattern crafting activities. This paper also demonstrated the specifics of applying hermeneutics to studying a body of knowledge, with details that are frequently omitted from publications on hermeneutics.

The proposed process – the crux of our findings – has been thoroughly evaluated. In the spirit of hermeneutic investigation, the emerging insights were continually assessed, documented and reflected upon. The resulting pattern crafting process was then independently examined to determine confirmability of our findings in respect of their usefulness, relevance and extensibility. Finally, detailed comparison of existing pattern mining practice against our resulting process established its strengths and weaknesses.

In conclusion, the application of hermeneutics to studying a process provides investigators with opportunities to shape, form, expand and adjust their understanding of this process. It allows to abstract insights gained about a process into a meta-process that could be reused and applied in other domains. Finally, hermeneutics provides an instrument for managing domain experience, and through the hermeneutic cycles facilitate understanding, formalisation, evaluation, sharing and application of this domain experience.

References

Alavi, M. and Leidner, D.E. (2001). Review: Knowledge management and knowledge management systems: Conceptual foundations and research issues, *MIS Quarterly* **25**(1): 107–136.

Alexander, C. (1979). *The Timeless Way of Building*, Oxford University Press.

Altheide, D.L. and Johnson, J.M. (1998). Criteria for Assessing Interpretive Validity in Qualitative Research, in N.K. Denzin and Y.S. Lincoln (eds.) *Collecting and Interpreting Qualitative Materials*, Thousand Oaks California, USA: Sage Publications, pp. 283–312 (Chapter 10).

Appleton, B. (1997). Patterns and Software: Essential concepts and terminology. Available online http://www.cmcrossroads.com/bradapp/docs/patterns-intro.html (accessed 5th June 2009).

Basili, V.R., Caldiera, G., McGarry, F., Pajerski, R., Page, G. and Waligora, S. (1992). The Software Engineering Laboratory – an Operational Software Experience Factory, in proceedings of 14th International Conference on Software Engineering ICSE. (Melbourne, Australia): ACM Press, 370–381.

Bender, S. and Fish, A. (2000). The Transfer of Knowledge and the Retention of Expertise, *Journal of Knowledge Management* **4**(2): 125–137.

Billett, S. (2001). *Learning in the Workplace: Strategies for Effective Practice*, Crows Nest, NSW, Australia: Allen and Unwin.

Boland, R.J. (1991). Information System Use as a Hermeneutic Process, in H.E. Nissen, H.K. Klein and R.A. Hirschheim (eds.) *Information Systems Research: Contemporary Approaches and Emergent Traditions*, Amsterdam, North-Holland.

Butler, T. (1998). Towards a Hermeneutic Method for Interpretive Research in Information Systems, *Journal of Information Technology* **13**(4): 285–300.

Catterall, M. and Maclaran, P. (1997). Focus Group Data and Qualitative Analysis Programs: Coding the moving picture as well as the snapshots. Available online http://www.socresonline.org.uk/socresonline/2/1/6.html (accessed 5th June 2009).

Chalmers, M. (2004). Hermeneutics, Information and Representation, *European Journal of Information Systems* **13**(3): 210–220.

Cole, M. and O'Keefe, R.M. (2002). Hermeneutic Philosophy and Data Collection: A practical framework, in proceedings of Eighth Americas Conference on Information Systems, pp. 1704–1709.

Coplien, J.O. (1996). *Software Patterns*, New York: SIGS Books & Multimedia.

Corfman, R. (1998). An Overview of Patterns, in L. Rising (ed.) *The Patterns Handbook*, Cambridge England: Cambridge University Press.

Coyne, R. (1995). *Designing Information Technology in the Postmodern Age,* MIT Press.
Creswell, J.W. and Miller, D.L. (2000). Determining Validity in Qualitative Inquiry, *Theory into Practice* 39(3): 124–130.
Crotty, M. (1998). *The Foundations of Social Research,* Crows Nest, NSW: Allen & Unwin.
Cybulski, J.L. and Linden, T. (1998). Composing Multimedia Artefacts for Reuse, in proceedings of Pattern Languages of Programming PLOP'98. (Allerton Park, Illinois, USA).
Cybulski, J.L. and Linden, T. (2000). Composing Multimedia Artefacts for Reuse, in N. Harrison, B. Foote and H. Rohnert (eds.) *Pattern Languages of Program Design,* Reading, MA: Addison-Wesley, pp. 461–488.
De Vries, K. and Miller, F.R. (1987). Interpreting Organizational Texts, *Journal of Management Studies* 24(3): 233–247.
Demeterio, F.P.A. (2001). Introduction to Hermeneutics, *Diwatao* 1(1): 1–9.
Drisko, J.W. (1997). Strengthening Qualitative Studies and Reports: Standards to promote academic integrity, *Journal of Social Work Education* 33(1): 185–198.
Drucker, P.F. (1995). *Managing in a Time of Great Change,* New York, NY: Truman Talley.
Fontana, A. and Frey, J.H. (2000). The Interview. From Structured Questions to Negotiated Text, in N.K. Denzin and Y.S. Lincoln (eds.) *The Handbook of Qualitative Research,* Thousand Oaks, California: Sage Publications, pp. 645–672.
Frey, J.H. and Fontana, A. (1993). The Group Interview in Social Research, in D.L. Morgan (ed.) *Successful Focus Groups: Advancing the State of the Art,* Newbury Park CA: Sage Publications.
Gadamer, H.G. (1976). *Philosophical Hermeneutics,* Berkeley, California: University of California Press.
Gadamer, H.G. (1979). *Truth and Method,* London: Sheed and Ward.
Gaines, B.R. and Shaw, M.L.G. (1993). Eliciting Knowledge and Transferring It Effectively to a Knowledge-Based System, *IEEE Transactions on Knowledge and Data Engineering* 5(1): 4–13.
Gamma, E., Helm, R., Johnson, J. and Vlissides, M. (1995). *Design Patterns: Elements of Reusable Object-Oriented Software,* Reading, MA: Addison-Wesley.
Gamson, W.A. (1992). *Talking Politics,* Cambridge, UK: Cambridge University Press.
Gould, M.D. (1994). GIS Design – A Hermeneutic View, *Photogrammatric Engineering and Remote Sensing* 60(9): 1105–1116.
Harmer, B.M. (2003). Culture at the Edge: An exploration of cultural adaptation and sense-making across workgroup boundaries in complex organizations, in Communications Studies, Wellington: Victoria University of Wellington.
Huberman, A.M. and Miles, M.B. (1998). Data Management and Analysis Methods, in N.K. Denzin and Y.S. Lincoln (eds.) *Collecting and Interpreting Qualitative Materials,* Thousand Oaks California, USA: Sage Publications, pp. 179–210 (Chapter 7).
Husserl, E. (1970). *Logical Investigation,* Atlantic Highlands, NJ: Humanities Press.
Introna, L.D. (1997). *Management, Information and Power: A Narrative of the Involved Manager,* London: MacMillan.
Kalfoglou, Y. (2000). On The Convergence of Core Technologies for Knowledge Management and Organisational Memories: Ontologies and experience factories, in proceedings of ECAI '00 Workshop on Knowledge Management and Organizational Memories (KMOM'00). Berlin, (Germany) 48–55.

Kavan, C.B. (1998). Profit Through Knowledge: The application of academic research to information technology organizations, *Information Resources Management Journal* **11**(1): 17–22.

Kelle, U. (1997). Theory Building in Qualitative Research and Computer Programs for the Management of Textual Data. Available online http://www.socresonline.org.uk/2/2/1.html (accessed 5th June 2009).

Klein, H.K. and Myers, M.D. (1999). A Set of Principles for Conducting and Evaluating Interpretive Field Studies in Information Systems, *MIS Quarterly* **23**(1): 67–93.

Klein, H.K. and Rowe, F. (2007). Marshalling the Professional Experience of Doctoral Students: Towards bridging the gaps between theory and practice, in proceedings of Twenty Eighth International Conference on Information Systems (ICIS 2007). (Montreal, Canada).

Kvale, S. (1996). *InterViews. An Introduction to Qualitative Research Interviewing*, Thousands Oaks, California, USA: Sage Publications.

Lank, E. (1997). Leveraging Invisible Assets: The human factor, *Long Range Planning* **30**(3): 406–412.

Lee, A.S. (1994). Electronic Mail as a Medium for Rich Communication: An empirical investigation using hermeneutic interpretation, *MIS Quarterly* **18**(2): 143–157.

Linden, T. and Cybulski, J.L. (2001). Planning the Process of Multimedia Development, in proceedings of 6th European Conference on Pattern Languages of Programs (EuroPLOP 2001). (Irsee, Germany): UVK Universitatsverlag Konstanz GmbH, 499–510.

Lukaitis, S. and Cybulski, J.L. (2004). A Hermeneutic Analysis of the Denver International Airport Baggage Handling System, in proceedings of Information Systems Foundations Workshop: Constructing and Criticising. (Canberra, Australia).

Manns, M.L. (2001). Patterns: A promising approach to knowledge management, in proceedings of First Annual ABIT Conference (Pittsburgh, Pennsylvania, USA), 31–40.

Manns, M.L. and Rising, L. (2002). What Makes Pattern Languages Work Well, in proceedings of 7th European Conference on Pattern Languages of Programs (EuroPLOP 2002). (Irsee, Germany).

McGraw, K.L. and Harbison-Briggs, K. (1989). *Knowledge Acquisition: Principles and Guidelines*, Englewood Cliffs, NJ: Prentice Hall.

Merton, R.K., Fiske, M. and Kendall, P. (1956). *The Focused Interview: A Manual of Problems & Procedures*, Glencoe, IL: Free Press.

Miles, M.B. and Huberman, A.M. (1994). *Qualitative Data Analysis: An Expanded Sourcebook*, 2nd edn, Thousands Oaks, California: Sage Publications.

Morgan, D.L. (1988). *Focus Groups as Qualitative Research*, Sage Publications, Inc.

Myers, M.D. (1994). A Disaster for Everyone to See: An interpretive analysis of a failed is project, *Accounting, Management and Information Technologies* **4**(4): 185–201.

Myers, M.D. (1997). Qualitative Research in Information Systems, *MIS Quarterly* **21**(2): 241–242.

Myers, M.D. (2004). Hermeneutics in Information Systems Research, in J. Mingers and L.P. Willcocks (eds.) *Social Theory and Philosophy for Information Systems*, Chichester: John Wiley & Sons, pp. 103–128.

Nielsen, J. (1997). The Use and Misuse of Focus Groups, *IEEE Software* **14**(1): 94–95.

Nissen, M.E., Kamel, M. and Sengupta, K. (2000). Integrated Analysis and Design of Knowledge Systems and Processes, *Information Resources Management Journal* 13(1): 24–43.

Nonaka, I. (1994). A Dynamic Theory of Organizational Knowledge Creation, *Organizational Science* 5: 14–37.

O'Leary, D.E. (1998a). Enterprise Knowledge Management, *Computer* 31(3): 54–61.

O'Leary, D.E. (1998b). Using AI in Knowledge Management: Knowledge bases and ontologies, *IEEE Intelligent Systems* 13(3): 34–39.

Olson, D.L. and Carlisle, J. (2001). Hermeneutics in Information Systems, in proceedings of Seventh Americas Conference on Information Systems. (Boston, Massachusetts, USA), 2029–2035.

Orr, J. (1990). Talking About Machines: The ethnography of a modern job, Cornell University.

Press, A.L. and Cole, E.R. (1999). *Speaking of Abortion: Television and Authority in the Lives of Women,* Chicago, IL: The University of Chicago Press.

Richards, T.J. and Richards, L. (1998). Using Computers in Qualitative Research, in N.K. Denzin and Y.S. Lincoln (eds.) *Collecting and Interpreting Qualitative Materials,* Thousand Oaks California, USA: Sage Publications, pp. 211–245 (Chapter 8).

Ricoeur, P. (1981). The Model of the Text: Meaningful action considered as a text, in J.B. Thompson (ed.) *Hermeneutics and the Human Sciences: Essays on Language, Action and Interpretation,* Cambridge, England: Cambridge University Press, pp. 197–221.

Rising, L. (1999). Patterns Mining, in S. Zamir (ed.) *Handbook of Object Technology,* CRC Press, Chapter 38(1): 38–39.

Sarantakos, S. (1996). *Social Research,* Melbourne: MacMillan Education Australia.

Sarkar, P. and Cybulski, J.L. (2004). Evaluation of Phenomenological Findings in IS Research: A study in developing web-based IS, in proceedings of Twelfth European Conference on Information Systems (ECIS 2004). (Turku School of Economics and Business Administration, Turku, Finland).

Schmidt, D.C. (1995). Experience Using Design Patterns to Develop Reusable Object-Oriented Communication Software, *Communications of the ACM (Special Issue on Object-Oriented Experiences)* 38(10): 65–74.

Shanks, G. (1996). *Building and Using Corporate Data Models,* Monash University, p. 426.

Standing, C. and Standing, S. (1999). The Role of Politics in IS Career Progression, *Systems Research and Behavioral Science* 16(6): 519–531.

Stenmark, D., Klang, M. and Olsson, S. (1999). A Critical Look at Knowledge Creation, in proceedings of 22nd Information Systems Research Seminar in Scandinavia (IRIS 22). (Keuruu, Finland).

Stewart, D.W. and Shamdasani, P.N. (1990). *Focus Groups: Theory and Practice,* Vol. 20, Newbury Park, California: Sage Publications.

Strauss, A. and Corbin, J. (1998). *Basics of Qualitative Research. Grounded Theory Procedures and Techniques,* 2nd edn, Thousand Oaks, CA, USA: Sage Publications.

Welsh, E. (2002). Dealing with Data: Using NVivo in the Qualitative Data Analysis Process. Available online http://www.qualitative-research.net/index.php/fqs/article/view/865 (accessed 5th June 2009).

Wenger, E.C. (2004). Knowledge Management as a Doughnut: Shaping your knowledge strategy through communities of practice, *Ivey Business Journal* 68(3): 1–8.

13

Exploring the Role of Informants in Interpretive Case Study Research in IS

Bendik Bygstad[1] and Bjørn Erik Munkvold[2]
[1]*Norwegian School of IT, Norway;*
[2]*University of Agder, Norway*

Introduction

Interpretive case study research constitutes an important and increasing part of the information systems (IS) knowledge base (Walsham, 1993; Myers, 1997; Paré and Elam, 1997; Walsham, 2006). Interpretive case studies can be distinguished from positivist case study research (Benbasat *et al.*, 1987; Lee, 1989; Dubé and Paré, 2003) by the focus on close interaction between researcher and participants throughout the case study process, viewing the case members as active participants in the construction of the case narrative (Boland, 1985; Guba and Lincoln, 1989; Kvale, 2002). However, while the interpretivist perspective ascribes an active role to the case study informants, in practice the extent of this involvement is normally confined to the data collection process and discussion of early versions of the case narrative. In few cases is the involvement of the informants reported to continue further to the final stages of analytical abstraction of the case study data, where the aim is to develop the overall patterns and explanations.

In this paper we explore the question of how the informants may be involved in the co-construction of the case narrative and theory building in interpretive research. The concept of informant is here understood in a broad sense, as a stakeholder that gives qualified information or opinion on a case. As noted by Campbell (1955), 'the anthropological use of the informant is distinguished from the social survey in that the respondents are selected not for their representativeness but rather on the bases of informedness and ability to communicate with the social scientist' (339). We argue that engaging the informants in a discourse on the concepts and patterns of explanation arrived at through the case study may provide an opportunity for mutual reflection and learning on the phenomena studied. Further, it offers a way for the researcher to verify that her interpretation of the phenomenon makes sense to the informants. While this does not necessarily imply a shared interpretation, the informants should at least be able to acknowledge how the researcher has arrived at this interpretation (Schatzman and Strauss, 1973). If not, we argue that there is a risk that the interpretation arrived at by the researcher, however conceptually sophisticated, may be focusing on aspects of the case that are less relevant to the world of practice. Thus, we also argue that a closer involvement of informants in construction of the findings is one way to meet the call for increasing practical relevance of IS research (Benbasat and Zmud, 1999; Rosemann and Vessey, 2008). In that sense, this paper can also be viewed as a response to Van de Ven's (2007) call for re-vitalization of the relationship between research and practice through the concept of *engaged scholarship*, emphasizing research as a collective achievement rather than a solitary exercise: 'Engagement means that scholars step outside of themselves to obtain and be informed by the interpretations of others in performing each step of the research process; problem formulation, theory building, research design and problem solving' (*ibid*, 10).

The question about the role of informants in co-construction of interpretive research entails issues about the epistemological status of the informants' interpretations with respect to the researcher's interpretations. Taken literally, Van de Ven's (2007) bold call for involving practitioners and other stakeholders in all steps of research challenges some of the foundations of the relationship between researcher and practitioner. As pointed out in much methodology literature, negotiating a case construction agreed upon by the researcher and the informants is a risky project that may result in a 'distortion' of the case study findings through mechanisms of post rationalization and underlying power structures framing the informants' views (Silverman, 1993; Klein and Myers, 1999; Walsham, 2006). Addressing these epistemological issues in full breadth is beyond the scope of this paper, and the main focus of our investigation is on the methodological question of how to involve informants in IS case study research. In accordance with the process of engaged scholarship (Van de Ven, 2007), we view the relationship between researchers and informants as involving discussions, mutual

respect and collaboration. However, rather than ascribing equal epistemological status to the interpretations of the researcher and informants,
we discuss how the latter may serve as important sources of data that
may inform the researcher's interpretations.

The research questions framing the discussion in this paper are thus:
*How may an extended role of informants contribute to enhance interpretiv-
ist case study research in IS, and what are the conditions where this type of
approach is appropriate?* To analyze these questions we draw upon literature on qualitative research methods in social sciences and case study
research in IS. Further, as an empirical basis for our discussion, we present experiences from involving the informants in a longitudinal case
study conducted by the first author.

The literature review presents different perspectives on the role of informants in qualitative research, and discusses various forms of feedback from
case study participants. Often referred to as *member validation* or *respondent
validation* (Silverman, 1985; Miles and Huberman, 1994; Yin, 1994) this
may involve different activities conducted throughout the case study process, such as distribution of interview transcripts to informants for verification, presentation of a case study report or summary to key stakeholders for
approval prior to publication and/or group meetings with informants to
discuss different interpretations of the case material. The literature shows
that while using this type of activities for verifying factual information is
common practice, there is more debate on the issue of whether or how to
also involve case informants in co-construction of case narratives (Kvale,
2002; Lincoln and Guba, 2003). Further, our review of case study literature
in IS shows a lack of attention to this debate in IS research.

To illustrate how an extended involvement of case informants may
play an important role in the process of constructing a case narrative,
we present experiences from a longitudinal case study in the airline
industry. During the case study process spanning 18 months, the
researcher engaged the informants in different forms of reflection and
feedback. Through this, both the informants and the researcher shifted
perspectives on aspects of the project studied. We discuss the challenges
experienced by the researcher in this process, where the informants in
several situations voiced strong opinions on both the case study report
and research publications from the case study.

The next sections review former research related to the involvement
of informants in case study research, both in social science research in
general and in IS research. We then present our case study, and describe
how informants were involved in various phases of the study. Then, as
a lense for analyzing our findings, we draw on the ladder-of-abstraction

framework (Carney, 1990). The final sections discuss the findings and implications from the analysis.

The role of informants in case study research

A review of the literature on qualitative research in the social sciences reveals differing perspectives on the role and nature of involving informants in the process of constructing the case narrative. Several terms are used to denote aspects of this process: *member validation* (Yin, 1994; Bloor, 2001), *informants' feedback* (Miles and Huberman, 1994), *respondent validation* (Bloor, 1978; Silverman, 1985; Fielding and Fielding, 1986; Bryman, 1988), *host verification* (Schatzman and Strauss, 1973), *member verification* (Morse *et al.*, 2002), *member checks* (Guba and Lincoln, 1989), *backtalk* (Lanzara, 1991) and *project reviews* (Dubé and Paré, 2003).

Key textbooks of qualitative research recommend that getting feedback from the informants should be incorporated as a part of the research design. Miles and Huberman (1994) refer to this as 'one of the most logical sources of corroboration' yet also 'a venerated, but not always executed, practice in qualitative research' (275). Different techniques for obtaining such feedback include review of draft case study reports by the informants (Yin, 1994), and evaluating the accuracy of 'causal networks with higher-inference findings' (Miles and Huberman, 1994). From a positivist perspective, the involvement of informants should be confined to verifying factual information and assuring that the researcher's understanding of the studied phenomenon as presented in the case report or similar account is correct, in an objective sense, in order to increase validity. As stated by Yin (1994): 'The informants and participants may still disagree with an investigator's conclusions and interpretations, but these reviewers should not disagree over the actual facts of the case' (145). According to this perspective, involving informants implies a potential risk for undue influence on the results and should thus be minimized (Morse *et al.*, 2002).

Several authors present an extended perspective in which feedback from the informants also serves to verify the researcher's understanding of the case study events. For example, using the term 'host verification,' Schatzman and Strauss (1973) discuss how 'credibility may be established with some audiences by showing or simply stating that at least the major propositions were tested or checked against the experiences and understandings of the hosts' (134). Their argument for how this practice may increase validity continues: 'If it was found that the propositions offered to the hosts did not empirically contradict their own understandings of their situation then the researcher may convince audiences that he has a measure of validity – possibly a large measure. This mode of validating one's work does not require that the hosts actually concur in the propositions themselves, but that they recognize rather the validity of the grounds (events) upon which the propositions rest' (134). Similar, in Longitudinal Process Research (LPR) (Pettigrew, 1985; Pettigrew, 1990), member validation plays an important role for ensuring that the case descriptions are meaningful for the practitioners.

In general, phenomenological and interpretive research acknowledges case members as playing a more active role (Boland, 1985): 'When the phenomenologist studies a person, she does not look *at* them, but *with* them in a dialogue searching for understanding. Understanding comes step by step, layer by layer, as preconceptions, prejudices, and assumptions are recognized and seen through' (343). According to this perspective, validity implies a process of social construction (Kvale, 2002). Kvale treats validity as an expression of *craftsmanship*, emphasizing quality of research by checking, questioning and theorizing on the nature of the phenomena investigated. Getting feedback from informants constitutes one of the tactics for checking the credibility of the findings. Further, Kvale discusses the concept of *communicative validity*, testing the validity of knowledge claims through rational discourse between researchers and a set of 'legitimate partners.' The latter may include the subjects interviewed, the scientific community and the general public: 'valid knowledge claims emerge as conflicting interpretations and action possibilities are discussed and negotiated among the members of a community' (Kvale, 1996: 239). According to the constructivist perspective, Guba and Lincoln (1989) define member checks as 'the process of testing hypotheses, data, preliminary categories, and interpretations with members of stakeholder groups from whom the original constructions were collected' (238–239). They regard this as the single most crucial technique for establishing credibility, the constructivist 'parallel criterion' to internal validity. This criterion focuses on establishing the match between the constructed realities of respondents and those realities as represented by the researcher and attributed to various stakeholders. Guba and Lincoln (1989) discuss how member checks can be both formal and informal, and may occur both during the data collection and analysis stage, and when the case narrative is developed. To distinguish member validation from triangulation, they argue that while triangulation is limited to cross-checking factual data, member-checking processes are concerned with verifying that the constructions collected are those that have been offered by the respondents.

Some also argue for an ethical imperative in including informants in the case analysis. For example, Reason and Rowan (1981) argue that refining the tentative results based on the informants' reactions to these is a key characteristic of good research 'at the non-alienating end of the spectrum' (249). They go on asserting that 'instead of a "hit and run" approach which sucks subjects dry and leaves her by the wayside, there needs to be an involvement with the person which enables a process of corrrection of impressions to take place. This should not exclude the possibility of the interviewee doing some theorizing and some checking too. [...] under the right conditions "interviewees" can quite easily turn themselves into co-researchers' (249). The potential role of informants in co-constructing the case narrative is also echoed in Lanzara's (1991) discussion of the concept of *backtalk*. This refers to the process of having the informants 'inspect and test' the researcher's initial interpretation of the data. Through an example from studies of educational practices in a music school, Lanzara describes how this backtalk provided new contextual data that otherwise would not have been readily accessible, leading to a more complex picture of the phenomenon studied. This process also involved extensive discussions with the researcher and the informants, leading to reinterpretation of past events and shifting perspectives of both parties. He also discusses how this process can involve informants producing different descriptions of the same event at different points in time, as the informant shifts his or her perceptions on and cognitions of this event. Reflecting on his role as researcher in this process, Lanzara (1991) states: 'As the actors talked back and told different stories about past events, my job became one of accounting for both the shifting stories and my own evolving understanding of the process, accounts that I then discussed and tested with the actors themselves' (291).

Summing up, our review of key readings on qualitative research in the social sciences has identified several perspectives on the preferred and potential role of informants in case study analysis. This ranges from verifying factual information, through using informant feedback as a source of verifying the researcher's interpretation, to viewing informants as potential co-researchers. While there is general agreement about the importance of verifying factual information and about how informants' feedback may represent a source of additional data and insight (Fielding and Fielding, 1986; Silverman, 1993), the literature review identified conflicting views on the value of involving informants for refining the analysis of the case study. Those expressing caution against involving the informants in constructing the case findings point to potential negative effects such as censorship and defensive reactions from the informants (Bryman, 1988). When reading the interview transcripts or case description the informants may want to justify their actions, thus threatening the integrity of the initial data collection (Bloor, 1978; McDonnell *et al.*, 2000). Further, it has been argued that informants should not be considered as to have a privileged status as commentators on their actions (Fielding and Fielding, 1986; Silverman, 1993).

The discourse surrounding these modes of involvement can be related both to aspects of validity as represented in different research paradigms, and to practical relevance of the research. By focusing on the basic dichotomy between positivist and interpretive research, we have deliberately chosen not to engage in a more refined analysis of possible variations between different forms of interpretivist case studies (e.g., social constructionism, symbolic interactionism and phenomenology), as we do not see this would add significantly to our main argumentation. The same applies with regard to the recent contributions of critical realism in IS research (Smith, 2006), in which the basic epistemological position of critical realism is congruent with interpretivism (Sayer, 2000).

An assessment of IS case study research

In IS research we have found relatively few studies that explicitly address the mutual relationship between researchers and informants in case study analysis. For example, in Walsham's (1995) 'primer' on conducting interpretive case studies in IS, now considered a standard reading for IS Ph.D. students, he discusses how the role of the researcher may vary between that of the outside observer and that of the involved researcher. However, he does not address the potential role of the informants in this type of research. In his follow-up article on conducting interpretive research, Walsham (2006) discusses ethical issues and tensions in the relationship between the researcher and the case informants and their organization, such as how to report bad news uncovered through the field work to the organizational sponsors and whether the case organization ought to be disclosed or not. Yet, the issue of how informants may play a role in interpretation and construction of the case story remains unaddressed.

Several of the principles for conducting and evaluating interpretive field studies in IS defined by Klein and Myers (1999) relate to the issue of informants' feedback, although they do not explicitly discuss this practice. For example, *the principle of interaction between the researchers and the subjects* calls for critical reflection on how the case story was socially constructed through interaction with case actors. Klein and Myers (1999) argue that participants can be seen as interpreters and analysts just as much as the researcher: 'Participants are interpreters as they alter their horizons by the appropriation of concepts used by IS researchers, consultants, vendors and other parties interacting with them, and they are analysts in so far as their actions are altered by their changed horizons' (74). Further, *the principle of suspicion* addresses the problem of 'false consciousness' on the part of the participants; underlying a seemingly unified account of something, the actors may be strongly biased by structures of power. This may produce distorted pictures of reality, which the researcher must see through.

The issue of engaging the informants in a dialogue on the understanding of the case findings also ties into the ongoing debate on how to increase the practical relevance of IS research (Saunders, 1998; Benbasat and Zmud, 1999). Rosemann and Vessey (2008) argue for increasing relevance through an approach they term *applicability checks*, defined as 'evaluations by practice of the theories, models, frameworks, processes, technical artifacts, or other theoretically based IS artifacts that the academic community either uses or produces in its research' (5). This also include research objects resulting from case study research. Through this approach the aim is to ensure the importance of the research to the needs of practice. By being conducted either at the beginning or the end of the research life cycle, the authors state that the approach 'leaves untouched the rigorous methods used to conduct the study, that is, it does not compromise traditional research methods' (1). This implies that the form of informants' involvement focused in our paper is complementary to the applicability checks approach, as the latter does not involve interaction with the informants (or practitioners) related to the data analysis stage.

In empirical IS research, very few studies document in depth the interaction between informants and researchers taking place during the analysis stage of a case study. For example, in a survey of 183 positivist case studies from seven major IS journals, only 15% of the studies explicitly reported any form of feedback session with the case informants (Dubé and Paré, 2003). Building on Yin (1994) and Schatzman and Strauss (1973), Dubé and Paré (2003) define *project reviews* as soliciting research subject or participant views of the credibility of interpretations and findings. On the basis of the results of their survey they argue for wider use of the project review strategy, 'whether under the form of a formal presentation to key actors or a review of the case report itself (...), to corroborate the evidence presented in the case report' (625).

Similarly, in analyzing 22 qualitative studies from four top IS research journals (*MIS Quarterly, Information Systems Research, Journal of AIS* and *Information and Organization*) in the period from 2001–2005, Myers and Newman (2007) found that only six of the studies reported any feedback offered to the companies/subjects. In their discussion on the craft of qualitative interviewing in IS research, presenting findings and results to subjects and organizations is included under the guideline termed 'Ethics of Interviewing': 'it may be advisable sometimes to provide early feedback to subjects and organizations and to check with them about factual matters if needed' (23). The recommendation for this practice is thus rather vague and limited to checking factual matters, not taking into account the potential resource implied in getting feedback from the members.

In the empirical studies where some form of feedback from the informants is reported, this tends to be only briefly mentioned *in passing* to document that standard methodological procedure has been followed but without explaining in detail how the involvement took place or how it possibly did influence on the research outcome. Similar observations have also been made for qualitative organizational studies in general (Locke and Velamuri, 2004). The following examples serve as illustrations of this:

A preliminary draft of the case, in a slightly longer, undisguised version, was circulated to the subjects. This version [the published article] incorporates their comments. In addition, it is disguised at the request of the company and the subjects. (Goldstein, 1990: 259)

Finally, an important guard against an observer effect was the presentation of our findings to Bremerton managers in ways that the findings could be challenged or disconfirmed. The findings presented in this paper incorporate the results of the challenges raised by BI employees. (Levine and Rossmoore, 1993: 63)

While these statements document that the researchers have taken advantage of feedback from the case informants, the reader is not able to learn about the nature of this feedback or how it was incorporated. A somewhat more elaborate description of the feedback process is offered by Nicholson and Sahay (2004) in their study of offshore software development:

A second step in the analysis process was the preparation of management reports that we submitted to the senior managers of both Sierra

England and India. Keeping in mind the readership, this report was quite different in structure and length from our summary document, which was primarily for our internal purposes. In this management report, we tried to concisely identify the problematic issues in the relationship, a description of why we thought it so and our suggestions for action. We submitted two such reports during the course of our research, which helped us not only to maintain our research access, but also served as a vehicle for obtaining multiple perspectives, that of the respondents, on our interpretations. Feedback received from the respondents on our report helped to clarify our own understanding of the issues that we raised, and also identify some other issues that we may have missed out (340–341).

Similarly, Walsham and Sahay (1999) discuss how their role as researchers during a 3-year longitudinal case study gradually evolved from that of independent observer (Walsham, 1995) to 'action résearcher,' with impressions from the first months of field work fed back to the research sites. They reflect on how this had impact on the case, arguing that direct involvement of the researcher is inevitable in longitudinal interpretive case studies. However, apart from a brief mentioning of themes being developed and discussed with informants during the data analysis, they do not report on the process of obtaining feedback from the informants. Another example in the borderline between interpretive research and action research is the *dialogical action research* approach described by Mårtensson and Lee (2004), in which the researcher engaged extensively with practitioners over a long period of time in order to build a mutual understanding of the case organization. Similar to the applicability checks approach suggested by Rosemann and Vessey (2008), dialogical action research aims at 'speaking the practitioner's language' in order to increase IS research relevance.

In summary, there is little IS research that explicitly discusses the practices focused in this paper. With a few exceptions, the discussion on the role of informants in the qualitative research literature is not echoed in the IS literature, and the nature of interaction with informants in IS case study research tends to be underreported. Given the close link between the IS discipline and its vocational nature (Baskerville, 1996; Benbasat and Zmud, 1999), we argue that there is a need for more attention to the question of how involvement of informants in case study research may contribute to enhance practical relevance. To illustrate this, we present a case study example where involvement of the informants contributed to increased mutual learning between informants and the researcher.

Case study

The empirical basis for this paper is a longitudinal case study conducted by the first author, focusing on the challenges of socio-technical integration in IS development projects. The theoretical point of departure was socio-technical research on IS innovation in organizations (Avgerou, 2002) and actor-network theory (Latour, 1987; Hanseth and Monteiro, 1996). This section provides a brief overview of the case and the data collection and analysis, as a basis for the detailed discussion of the informants' involvement process in the next section. A more in-depth presentation of the case study is available in Bygstad (2006) and Bygstad *et al.* (2010).

Case overview

The case organization was an international airline developing an e-business solution. The researcher conducted two workshops and 20 interviews with central stakeholders and IS developers over a period of 18 months, and was given extensive access to project documents. At the outset it was agreed that the project managers (one from the business side and one from IT) should read the draft publications to approve whether the airline could be identified in the publications from the project. As will be explained in the next section, the informants' involvement process resulted in such approval. However, in this paper we have chosen to anonymize the case company, as the focus here is on the interaction with the case informants rather than the actual results of the case study.

In 2000, acknowledging the commercial potential of Internet booking, the airline decided to establish a web-based marketing channel in all important markets, including Europe, Asia and the Americas. To support this new business process, a new content management and publishing solution was needed. A project was initiated, organized with two project managers (one business and one technical), marketing executives from different countries and a team of software developers. The main aim of the project was establishing the new marketing channel. Further goals of the project were to enable the marketing executives with an easy tool to publish materials and campaigns, without the need for using html coding, and to integrate this new system with the airline booking systems.

The development project was structured in five iterations, building on the Rational Unified Process (RUP) (Jacobson *et al.*, 1999). The project was run over 1 year, starting in May 2001, with the system going live in the summer 2002. After two disappointing iterations, in which the developers failed to convince the marketing executives of the need for the system, and the external delivery of central components was seriously delayed, the project was in a state of crisis. In response to this, the project group concentrated successfully on internal technical issues, postponing integration of the e-business solution and the business process. This was addressed in an extended last iteration, in which the social and technical integration challenges were solved by improvisation. After a hectic finish, the system was taken into use by the international airline with relative success.

Data collection and analysis

Data were collected in accordance with the principles of LPR (Pettigrew, 1985; Pettigrew, 1990; Ngwenyama, 1998):

- Engaging with the research site at several times during the study, to collect data reflecting changes over time.
- Participant observation, to understand the actors' language and problem solving, and to make sense of different situations.
- Collecting systematically different types of data, to secure validity.

The informants were two sets of employees in the case organization; the first group was key personnel from the IS department (the developers of the technical solution) and the second group consisted of marketing executives at different geographical locations (the future users of the solution). They were selected based on the following criteria: they were key actors in the e-business project, and they represented both the IT and business side of the project. The researcher was granted permission to interview them at planned intervals during the project, and the key informants (a methodology manager, two project managers and three marketing executives) expressed an initial interest in the research project, in order to give input to the internal improvement process.

The case was researched in four phases, as illustrated in Table 13.1. Data collection included interviews, workshops, project documentation, technical documents, software demos and participant observation from meetings.

The data were coded in an Atlas database. Interview summaries, project documents and technical reports were coded following the guidelines of Miles and Huberman (1994). Then a systematic search

Table 13.1   Data collection in the airline case

Phase	Activities	Documentation
Initial activities	Initial meeting with three managers Document collection	Summary of business and project objectives
Early project phase	A workshop with IT project and business project managers, to get the broad picture Individual interviews	The primary artifact was a graphical illustration of how stakeholders and components were included into the project
Late project phase	Group interviews with project group Individual interviews	Interview summaries
After system in production	Group interviews Individual interviews	Final project reports, user evaluations

for relationships in the data was conducted, based on the following guidelines for data analysis (Pettigrew, 1985; Ngwenyama, 1998):

- Comprehensive analysis; to identify underlying structures and patterns of the organizational process.
- Temporal analysis; to aid in contextualizing findings by placing events and situations in a narrative structure.
- Informants' feedback; to ensure that the case description and researcher's interpretation were considered factually correct and meaningful to the organizational actors.

Data collection and analysis were conducted in an iterative mode; one observation would often trigger a new interpretation, which again could lead to a new question and/or possibly a new stakeholder. The function of informants' involvement in this case was not only to ensure the factual correctness of the case description, it also contributed to the social construction of the case study (Klein and Myers, 1999). The case description was built gradually over time, in a process of learning and discussion between the researcher and the stakeholders. One result of the study was a set of socio-technical integration patterns in IS development projects: big bang, stakeholder integration, technical integration and socio-technical integration (Bygstad and Nielsen, 2003). The paper focused strongly on the practical and managerial implications of the findings.

While informant feedback was conducted in compliance with the longitudinal research method, the practical steps were a combination of planned and improvised action, depending on the practical opportunities and the researcher's initiatives. The next section presents the activities related to the informants' feedback process in the case project.

Informants' feedback in the airline case: correcting, co-constructing and reflecting

As informant feedback was part of the chosen research approach (LPR), the researcher discussed the practicalities of conducting this with key informants at the start of the study. The key informants were all highly educated, with master or bachelor degrees, and many years' experience with large projects in several organizations. From the start of the researcher's engagement they expressed that they would be interested in the researcher's findings, although not necessarily convinced that this research would contribute knowledge new to them.

Informants' feedback in the airline case was carried out in three steps (Table 13.2). First, the documented chronology of events and the illustrated socio-technical network from the workshops were sent to the participants for comments and corrections. Then, at the end of the case study there was a long review session with technical and business stakeholders to discuss the final report. And lastly, the research papers that were published were sent to the two project managers and two business line managers for comments.

The first step was concerned with identifying the time line, and actors and events. The next step was constructing the case description, focusing on relationships and themes. The third step focused on identifying socio-technical process patterns and explanations, with research papers from the case as the main documentation.

Table 13.2 Informants' feedback during three phases

Research project phase	Documentation	Function of informants' feedback
Data collection	A graphical illustration of the actor network plus interview summaries	Correcting errors
Case construction	Case description	Co-constructing the case narrative
Research publishing	Research papers	Discussing implications

Phase 1: Verifying facts

The case was gradually constructed over the whole period of data collection. An early event was a half-day workshop with one group of important stakeholders (the marketing manager, the project manager and the three technical developers), with the aim of establishing a time line for the development project and a model of the socio-technical network. The time line included the activities that initiated the project, the actual project milestones and the iterations. The actor-network model illustrated the step-wise enrollment of stakeholders and technology into the project. Both artifacts were updated throughout the study over 18 months, and were used to structure the findings and analyze changes over time.

The graphical representation was sent to the workshop participants for comments. A number of corrections were given, including for example:

- Corrections to the chronology of events, such as the dates for meetings and workshops.
- Corrections to the persons involved, for example that a vendor was also participating in a meeting.
- Amendments concerning the description of the technical solution, for example that the number of components in the fifth iteration was incorrect, and that a certain component was left out.
- Amendments to lists of relevant documents, for example that a methodology document was produced before the project started.

Summaries of workshops and interviews were commented on much the same way, focusing on factual issues. In addition, there were suggestions for other stakeholders to interview, and other documents to draw upon. The atmosphere of this interaction was generally quite relaxed. Although the graphical actor-network representation was somewhat complex, the comments were all to the point, and errors were easily corrected.

Phase 2: Co-constructing the case description

The case was described in a final case report. It included the timeline and actor-network, but concentrated on interpretations of the case process. Prominent themes were the interaction between the development team and the marketing executives, and also the integration challenges in the project.

The final case report was discussed at a formal review session (suggested by the researcher), in which several stakeholders from both the project and the business organization participated. The discussion focused on interpretations of concepts and events, and the review meeting resulted in a number of changes to the case report. Special care was taken to analyze the instances in which data were contradictory, for example when developers and user representatives had different accounts of what had happened. For example, there was a disagreement about the results of the first two workshops of the project. The project group had followed the plan, involved users and tried to model the use cases graphically, and judged the workshops to be useful. The marketing executives, on the other hand, had felt that the communication between the project and the users was poor, and that the use cases were very theoretical and not related to their work process.

The written project documents supported the developers' view; they had really done what the methodology called for. This was discussed with the marketing executives in a follow-up interview, where they gave two explanations for their negative perception of the workshops. First, they did not really have time to participate, and were not well prepared for the sessions. Second, they were used to another technology (Frontpage), which gave them more freedom in the design, and they regarded the new solution as a step backwards. Both accounts were documented in the revised case report, which was accepted by both sides. This conflict of interpretation became input to a higher level of analysis: enrolling stakeholders from the business process was not successful, in spite of it being done 'by the book', that is by management approval and formal planning. The project group had failed to convince the marketing people of the need for a new solution.

Another issue was a finding that important business needs were not included in the use case requirements. A follow-up e-mail commented:

> You write that important business needs were not part of the requirements. This is not because we did not know, but because of corporate priorities. The number of use cases was reduced after the 9/11 attacks.

The researcher responded by adding a sentence in the case report, to acknowledge this point:

> Of course, the fact that the number of use cases were reduced from 20 to 10 had consequences for the functionality of the system ...

Integration issues included the gradual enrollment of both stakeholders and technology into the project, and the project managers' response to the complexity of the process. An observation was that project managers tended to respond with *project encapsulation*; that is to concentrate on internal project activities instead of addressing external problems. Two case stakeholders had strong objections to this notion of project encapsulation, which they felt was not an accurate description, and also that the notion made the project manager appear somewhat defensive in the situation. In an e-mail response they wrote that what had actually happened was that they were *forced* to postpone some of the technical and stakeholder integration, because of factors they did not control. The alternative would have been to stop the whole project.

The researcher took this into account. But how should it be interpreted? The researcher argued that the event that the plan could not be followed should not be interpreted as an accident or merely as bad luck, but rather as an indication that something was not working properly. Would it be fair to say that the dependency of too many actors *forced* the project into a certain degree of encapsulation? No, the stakeholders replied, because the decision was deliberate, and the risks were assessed. But was encapsulation an unintended *effect* of that decision, then, the researcher asked, and so on.

The atmosphere in the review meeting and the following e-mail exchanges was polite, but quite engaged. E-mails typically started with 'I do not agree with your interpretation of this event ... .' An interesting aspect was that the members started to use the vocabulary introduced in the case report, as the example of *project encapsulation* described above.

Phase 3: Reflecting on the case study implications

The third phase of analysis was concerned with the implications of the case. These implications were discussed in several academic research papers that were written on the basis of the case materials (Bygstad and Nielsen, 2003; Bygstad, 2006). The papers were written in the usual academic style, including research reviews and theoretical discussions. They focused on the more general aspects of socio-technical integration, and used the case as an example of integration patterns.

It had been agreed in advance that all papers should be subject to approval by the airline (represented by the key stakeholders) prior to publication, that is if not approved, the researcher would be asked to anonymize the company in research publications. The papers were sent to the methodology manager, the two project managers and one of the marketing executives. Rather unexpectedly, the papers triggered considerable response from the informants. After receiving the first draft paper, lists of new issues were brought up by three central stakeholders: the two project managers and the methodology manager. The first in a series of e-mails started: *'You cannot be allowed to publish accounts on this company that are not true … .'* The objections included, for example:

(1) My opinion is that we really did aim for socio-technical integration. The reason this was not achieved was that the marketing executives did not prioritize the workshops. This was not a Big Bang pattern project.

(2) You do not seem to realize that a project manager continuously has to balance the risks of such a complex project with many dependencies.

In total, 12 different issues were raised. The researcher wondered why these issues had not been mentioned at the long and quite engaged validation meeting and e-mail exchanges some months earlier. One explanation may be that the theoretical perspectives of the paper had reframed the members' interpretations of their own experience. The concepts of 'socio-technical integration' and 'Big Bang project' had been introduced in the research papers, and they were now used by the members in their arguments.

The objections put the researcher in an interesting but difficult situation, which (it should be admitted) had not been included in the research design. How should they be handled? In responding to them, the researcher was concerned that at this stage of the research the informants' feedback could not be solved by negotiation. Arguably, assessing the implications of a case is a research step in which the researcher must trust his methodology and draw on earlier contributions, in order to arrive at a valid conclusion. On the other hand, it would be contrary to the notion of engaged scholarship to disqualify the objections on principle. But which criteria should guide the response?

The researcher chose to treat the objections in the same way as he would with an academic reviewer, that is at a discursive level. This meant that he would assess the relevance of the objection, and if considered relevant and reasonable, try to address it. Two examples will illustrate this point. In response to objection #1 (above), the researcher acknowledged that the project group indeed had tried to enroll stakeholders early in the process, but that the number of dependencies had made it difficult. This interchange of views became an important input to discuss the forces of the proposed integration patterns, and to propose how they could be managed.

The other objection was different, and expressed a concern that researchers have a limited understanding of the pressures of large IT projects. There might be ample reasons for this belief. Often, university textbooks present relatively simple recipes for handling IT projects, making the (maybe unintended) impression that the main reason for failure is poor project management. In responding, the researcher chose to add a section in the paper, highlighting the increased pressures of large and complex IT projects in a turbulent business context.

The researcher chose to discuss these issues in long emails, in order to invite to a thoughtful and balanced reflection. The final responses from the stakeholders to this were without the tension of the past exchanges, and the new version of the paper was accepted for publication with full disclosure of the company.

Discussion

Our point of departure is the idea that a case narrative is not only a chronology of events, but a medium for sense-making for both the researcher and the informants (Butler, 1998; Wagner, 2003; Czarniawska, 2004). As illustrated by the airline case, the reflexive dialogue between research and informants is both subtle and complex. It blurs the difference between data and interpretations, since the informants may start to use the terms of the researcher, as interpreted within their own frames of understanding. Also, it challenges the traditional role set of researcher and informants, where the informants – within some limits discussed below – actively influence on the interpretation of the case.

The case study shows how the different steps in the informants' feedback process involved different levels of abstraction, and different forms of involvement of the informants. To frame the discussion of these levels, we introduce in the next section a framework by Carney (1990) that defines different levels in the process of analytical abstraction in qualitative research. On the basis of this, we then discuss the findings and implications from our study as related to our initial research questions. Although we do not claim that the case can serve as a methodological model for informants' feedback, we argue that it, through the lens of the framework, serves to highlight that informants' feedback play different roles in the different stages of analysis.

Framework: The ladder of analytical abstraction

As illustrated in Figure 13.1, the framework depicts the construction of a case story as a 'ladder of analytical abstraction' (Carney, 1990; Miles and Huberman, 1994) Starting with the interviews and other textual material, the first level is concerned with summarizing and coding of the data. The next level is focused on identifying themes and trends in

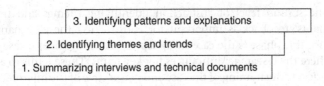

Figure 13.1   Ladder of analytical abstraction, after Carney (1990)

the data, identifying the important concepts and variables. At the third level, the researcher aims at delineating the 'deep structure' of the case, identifying patterns and building explanations.

Climbing this ladder of abstraction is a process of transformation; raw data are transformed to concepts and variables, which again are synthesized to larger explanatory frameworks. For the researcher this is a demanding process, which involves explicating and reflecting upon the views and biases of the different stakeholders and the researcher herself. While the researcher may use established methodological principles for qualitative research (Klein and Myers, 1999) and analytical techniques such as forward-chaining and backward-chaining (Pettigrew, 1985; Pettigrew, 1990), a heavy responsibility resides with the researcher. We will argue that these transformations also represent opportunities for a systematic feedback from the informants.

The ladder of abstraction should not be taken too literally. It may give the misleading impression that case construction is linear, sequential and algorithmic, while it is usually non-linear, iterative and experimental. However, as will be demonstrated in the following sections, the ladder of abstraction as an analytical tool serves to frame our discussion of informants' feedback practice in the case study example.

How may an extended role of informants contribute to enhance interpretivist case study research in IS?

A key observation is that informants' feedback plays an important, but quite different role, at the various levels of abstraction. At the lowest level of abstraction, informants' feedback is important as a means to verify factual information. This typically includes chronology, stakeholders and events. The role of case members here is to correct errors and give additional information. As experienced in our case study, the process may also give important input for data collection, for example by pointing to a new stakeholder. This finding is congruent with earlier studies discussing informants' feedback as an occasion for generating new data (Silverman, 1993; Locke and Velamuri, 2004).

At the second level of abstraction (identifying themes and trends), informants' feedback is important for constructing the case narrative. Focus for this phase is the case study report, which provides a case story, and where the researcher introduces her key terms. These terms to a large extent decide the framing of the case and perspective of the interpretation, and the informants may, or may not, identify with these terms.

While informants' feedback at the first level of abstraction takes the form of factual corrections, the process at the second level may be one of *co-construction*. As the airline case illustrates the understanding of the case events was discussed through the *text*, working on terms and sentences, and discussing nuances and exceptions. This is also exemplified by Locke and Velamuri (2004), referring to a dissertation project in which the Vice President of an Indian case company provided a 36-page response to a case study draft of 42 pages, thus initiating an extensive iterative process of drafts and detailed responses going back and forth over a period of 2 months.

For the researcher, the process of involving the informants in constructing the case report is both interesting and challenging. While some of the informants' views will provide more depth to the narrative, other views may just reflect the informants' wish to justify and defend their own actions. This problem of *distortion* is important, and we will return to it in the next section. But it is a premise for all qualitative researchers that any respondent will provide information from her point of view, whether her intention is to provide as complete a version of the story as possible, or to justify her own views. Neither the researcher nor the informant have access to the God's Eye point of view. When reading and responding to the case description, the respondent may reframe her interpretation of it, and may also give new answers. Our assessment is that this new information is valuable in a double sense; it provides more information on the narrative and it may also reflect the learning and sensemaking process of the informant. The job of the researcher remains the same; to collect the data as faithfully as possible, to document the time and context in which it was produced, and to build on all available sources when constructing the case narrative. Not all evidence may point in the same direction in a complex case. As noted by Van de Ven (2007), triangulation does not always converge into one coherent story.

Thus, we disagree with those who claim that the informants' feedback strategy invalidates the research (McDonnell *et al.*, 2000; Morse *et al.*, 2002). Rather, we argue that if the researcher cannot reach a basic agreement on the case description with key stakeholders, this calls for further analysis and reflection by the researcher on her interpretation of the case. If we accept that stakeholders are co-constructors of the case study, it is unreasonable that their interpretations should not be taken into account as important second-order data. As pointed to by Miles and Huberman (1994) (citing Blumer, 1969), 'an alert and observant actor in the setting is bound to know more than the researcher ever will about the realities under investigation' (275). For how long should this process go on? In principle, it should go on until the researcher believes all relevant information is on the table; in practice it goes on as long as the key informants are willing to respond. We regard this process as steps to increase the internal validity, the credibility, of the case narrative.

At the third and highest level of abstraction the focus is on the *implications* of the case study. The role of the members is now more discursive. While the researcher draws on related research to assess the possible generalization from the case, the case members will draw on their previous experience and on practitioner sources (Mårtensson and Lee, 2004). The examples from the airline case study cited in the previous section illustrate this, as the stakeholders refer to the perceived general conditions of projects and project managers when defending their positions. This contributes to make the discourse informed and balanced, as an opportunity for mutual learning.

In the airline case study, the project members also used terms from the draft papers, such as *socio-technical integration*. This illustrates that in the process of establishing a common ground, the project members were influenced by the researcher's framing of the case. This does not imply that they use the term in the researcher's sense, rather that the new shared ground constitutes a new context, in which also the researcher's terms are appropriated. This phenomenon is also described by Lanzara as 'backtalk,' as discussed in the review section. A similar reflection is made by Walsham and Sahay (1999) in their case study of a Geographical Information System use in Indian district-level administration, where they experienced that the terms of reference for a later phase in the project studied drew heavily from material provided by the researchers in the earlier stages.

Table 13.3 summarizes our argument regarding significance of informants' feedback in the different project phases, and the role of case members in this process.

Overall, we argue that these research activities, used systematically, can also contribute to increase the practical relevance of IS case study research. In the debate on the lack of relevance of IS research, limited exposure to practical contexts (Benbasat and Zmud, 2003) and lack of

Table 13.3   Summary of arguments

Project phase	Level of abstraction	Role of case member	Significance of informants' feedback
Data collection	Low	Verifying facts Generating new data	Increasing factuality
Case study report	Medium	Co-constructing the case narrative	Increasing internal validity
Research publishing	High	Reflecting on implications	Increasing relevance

knowledge transfer between academics and practitioners (Moody, 2000) have been stated to represent parts of the problem. By involving the case informants through practices as described in this paper, the researchers establish an arena for mutual knowledge sharing with practitioners and for testing the perceived practical relevance of their findings. Thus, while informants' feedback at level 2 contributes to increase internal validity, at the discursive level it also contributes to increase external validity, the transferability of findings.

Correspondingly, we propose that *without* informants' feedback the researcher may run the risk of missing important aspects of a case study. In the airline case study the case narrative and also the papers were significantly improved through the process of informants' feedback. In the data collection phase a number of factual corrections were supplied, such as chronology, additional actors and relevant events outside the project. In the case construction phase competing interpretations were offered on several points. In addition to providing more information, these perspectives also challenged the researcher to look for alternative explanations, and to strengthen his own arguments. For example, the identification of one of the generic patterns of integration was done during these discussions. In the paper publishing phase the objections of the informants made the researcher reflect more systematically on competing patterns, and helped to analyze the managerial challenges of each pattern in more depth. All in all, the changes were substantial.

Thus, without informants' feedback, the researcher may lose factual information in the data collection phase. In the construction of the case study report the text may be biased in favor of the perspectives of the researcher, excluding important alternative interpretations from the informants. And in the publishing phase a lack of feedback may lead to reduced practitioner relevance. These potential risks are vividly illustrated by Fitzgerald and Howcroft (1998) in their anecdotal tale of the fictitious researcher Ethna O' Graphy, who in her idealistic attempts to 'always look beyond superficial cause-effect relationships to consider the deeper meaning underpinning all human activity' (315) ends up with losing sight of the practical realities of the research situation. Although clearly representing an extremist position, this caricature underpins well the importance of validating the researcher's interpretation against the informants or stakeholders to be able to produce research of at least some practical relevance. In this sense, our suggested approach also can be seen to extend the applicability check proposed by Rosemann and Vessey (2008). While their approach involves discussion with practitioners *ex-ante* and/or *ex-post* of the case study itself, we argue for engaging in a dialogue with the informants concerning the relevance of the case findings as part of constructing the case narrrative.

What are the conditions in which this type of approach is appropriate?

From what we have written earlier in this paper it is clear that our approach cannot be used as a general strategy in interpretive research, but is applicable in certain conditions. We will focus on four conditions for this approach to be successful.

First, it requires a longitudinal case study design. A reasonable objection to the last suggestion in Table 13.3 is the question of how the researcher can ensure that the member engagement in phase 3 really is informed discourse and not simply *post hoc* rationalization. As shown by Weick (1995), managers tend to make sense of their actions only when they realize the consequences of them. This implies that informants' feedback conducted at a late stage in the analysis may be 'contaminated' by *post hoc* rationalization, and thus actually threaten the credibility of the case. This problem of distortion is an important issue, and our reply is that it must be addressed in the research design. The short answer is that 'truth is the daughter of time.' As pointed out by Van de Ven (2007), engaged scholarship requires multiple iterations between researchers and stakeholders, where they share knowledge, discuss implications and make changes where needed. Our point is that the researcher must be in control of the process. Thus, the three different roles of informants' feedback illustrated in Table 13.3 cannot be chosen arbitrarily. They are mutually dependent parts of a longitudinal study, in which data collection is performed throughout the study. When the researcher gradually constructs and interprets the case, she must keep track of the temporal dimension, in particular the time-stamp of various data. Project members may describe events and issues quite differently during a long project (Lanzara, 1991). When the researcher puts this puzzle together, the phenomenon of *post hoc* rationalization should be known and addressed in the analysis. For example, in the discussions with the stakeholders in the third phase of informants' feedback (as reported in the previous section), the researcher could lean on a substantial amount of materials to assess whether new objections should be addressed or not.

Second, some of the informants must be knowledgeable on how the case connects to other structures. They should be selected in order to ensure that they cover as much of the case and its environments as possible. In this requirement we agree with the critique that has been raised against constructionist approaches, in which the emphasis is mainly on local contexts and situated practice (Kallinikos, 2004). We think it is absolutely essential that – in the actual type of case research – that some (but obviously not all) informants are knowledgeable on not only user aspects, but also on power, organization and technological structures. Without this, knowledge informants would not be able to give informed feedback on suggested patterns and structures, particularly at level 3.

Third, the researcher and the informants should share some basic objectives and terminology. As pointed out by those addressing the relevance problem of IS, one part of the solution lies in the ability of the researcher to 'speak the language of the practitioner' (Benbasat and Zmud, 1999; Hoffman, 2004; Mårtensson and Lee, 2004); to facilitate a dialogue within a terminology familiar to the case informants. The airline case was conducted by a researcher with the explicit aim of contributing to improve socio-technical practices in complex projects. He shared with the key respondents a theoretical and practical knowledge on the development methodology used (RUP), the technology used (web and database technology) and also a more general knowledge on the challenges of large projects, such as risk management. Thus, this case study is representative of a large body of IS research projects that focus on contributing to improve organizational practice through analyzing the development and use of particular IS and related routines and processes. Some examples of domain areas in IS in which this type of research is prevalent are implementation of enterprise systems, software process improvement and IS project management. We argue that in this type of IS research projects, the distance between the researcher and the informants is often smaller than in many other disciplines. In this aspect, our findings contrast earlier findings of how different language styles of researchers and practitioners made informed discourse difficult (Hoffman, 2004; Mårtensson and Lee, 2004). At the same time, we of course acknowledge that IS research also includes other types of projects in which the condition of shared basic objectives and terminology would not be present to a similar degree. Examples of this would include critical research studies on (lack) of end user involvement, and research on power and politics related to IS development and use (Doolin, 1998).

Fourth, the informants need to engage in reflection-in-action. As defined by Schön (1983), reflection-in-action involves thoughtfully considering one's own experiences in applying knowledge to practice: 'When someone reflects-in-action, he becomes a researcher in the practice context. [...]. He reflects on the phenomena before him, and on the prior understandings which have been implicit in his behavior' (Schön, 1983: 68). Through this, 'the practitioner may surface and criticize his initial understanding of the phenomenon' and 'construct a new description of it' (*ibid*, 63). As demonstrated in the study reported in this paper, the approach is dependent on informants that are willing and able to interpret and discuss the case study report and the scientific papers of the researcher, as a basis for challenging both their own and the researcher's understanding.

The informants in our study were highly educated and experienced, and interested in spending their work time (though limited) in reading, discussing and commenting on the researcher's artifacts. We acknowledge that this may yet be unusual in many organizations, but recent developments in education and corporate practices may contribute to change this. One aspect is the increasing level of education of the IS practitioners, in which many IT managers and specialists have been trained in reading scientific papers as part of their Master's degree. Another aspect is the proliferation of improvement programs in the IT industry, such as Capability Maturity Model (Paulk, 1998) and action research (Mathiassen *et al.*, 2001), which encourages systematic learning and reflection.

Practical limitations to informant's feedback practices

In addition to the conditions described above, there are a number of more practical limitations to informants' involvement.

There are practical limitations related to the time frame and scope of the activities of informants' involvement, and the access to different informants and stakeholders. Most often, time is a scarce resource both for the researcher and the case members. Time constraints may thus limit the possibility for the informants to do an in-depth review of the material, and the feedback (if any) may thus be limited to correcting factual errors. As we have experienced in several of our other research projects, the engagement from and interaction with case companies during informants' feedback may therefore often be much less than in the airline case study presented in this paper.

Also, the case company may decide that the informants' feedback is to be handled by the primary contact person thus serving as a gatekeeper in the process of assessing the researcher's interpretation against those of the informants. In such cases, the feedback may run the risk of being overly influenced by concerns for the organization's reputation, rather than the goal of discussing potentially differing perspectives on the case events (Silverman, 1985; Guba and Lincoln, 1989; Locke and Velamuri, 2004; Walsham, 2006). Thus, the opportunity for using informants' feedback as a source of additional data may also be lost.

Conclusion

The point of departure for this paper was the methodological challenges related to the interaction between researcher and informant in interpretive research. As documented in our research review, informants' feedback is a recommended practice in both social science and IS research. The practical research steps involved in this process are, however, not described in much detail. Following Van de Ven's (2007) call for engaged scholarship, our research objective was to explore how, and under which circumstances, the informants could be involved in constructing and interpreting the case narrative.

On the basis of the ladder of analytical abstraction as the conceptual framework, and empirical findings from a longitudinal case study, we find that the role of informants' feedback varies, and should be treated differently, during three steps of analysis. Our findings can be summarized as follows:

- In the data collection phase, informants' feedback can increase the quality of the case documentation through factual verification and the generation of new data. This corresponds to the 'traditional' perspective on informants' feedback.
- In the case study report, informants' feedback may enrich the case narrative and increase the internal validity of the study. In this phase, the role of the informant is to co-construct the case narrative and its interpretation.
- In the dissemination phase, the role of the informants is more discursive, contributing to increase the relevance of findings, the external

validity, by assessing the conclusions and implications of scientific publications in a practitioner context.

Our contribution is practical in nature, intended as an extension to the interpretive case study methodology literature. We argue that informants' involvement, when used systematically, can enhance IS case study research by increasing relevance through mutual learning and reflection. This study illustrates the complexity involved in informants' feedback, which requires careful fieldwork and analysis. We acknowledge that the full scope of this approach is only appropriate under certain circumstances: the research approach should be a longitudinal case study; some of the informants must be knowledgeable on how the case connects to other structures, the researcher and informants should share some aims and related vocabulary, and the informants need to display characteristics of reflective practitioners. We argue that although these conditions are certainly not satisfied in all case settings, they are increasingly common in IS research.

Further research is needed on the practices related to informants' involvement in different forms of qualitative inquiry. This may take the form of both descriptive and/or normative research, and may address in more detail the possible variation in these practices among different qualitative research approaches such as ethnographic studies, action research and critical studies. In particular, we see the need to investigate whether other research designs than the Longitudinal Process Research can benefit from our proposed approach to informants' involvement.

Acknowledgement

We thank Professor Kallinikos and the anonymous reviewers for their constructive and in-depth comments that helped in framing our discussion in this paper.

References

Avgerou, C. (2002). New Socio-Technical Perspectives of IS innovation in Organizations, in C. Avgerou and R.L. LaRovere (eds.) *ICT Innovation: Economic and organizational perspectives*, Cheltenham: Edward Elgar, pp. 141–161.

Baskerville, R. (1996). Deferring Generalizability: Four classes of generalization in social enquiry, *Scandinavian Journal of Information Systems* 8(2): 5–28.

Benbasat, I., Goldstein, D.K. and Mead, M. (1987). The Case Research Strategy in Studies of Information Systems, *MIS Quarterly* 11(3): 369–385.

Benbasat, I. and Zmud, R.W. (1999). Empirical Research in Information Systems: The practice of relevance, *MIS Quarterly* 21(1): 3–16.

Benbasat, I. and Zmud, R.W. (2003). The Identity Crisis within the IS Discipline: Defining and communicating the discipline's core properties, *MIS Quarterly* 27(2): 183–194.

Bloor, M. (1978). On the Analysis of Observational Data: A discussion of the worth and uses of inductive techniques and respondent validation, *Sociology* 12(3): 545–557.

Bloor, M. (2001). Techniques of Validation in Qualitative Research: A critical commentary, in R. Emerson (ed.) *Contemporary Field Research: Perspectives and formulations*, 2nd edn, Long Grove, IL: Waveland Press Inc, pp. 383–395.

Blumer, H. (1969). *Symbolic Interactionism: Perspective and Method*. Englewood Cliffs, NJ: Prentice-Hall.

Boland, R. (1985). Phenomenology: A preferred approach to research on information systems, in E. Mumford (ed.) *Research Methods in Information Systems*, North-Holland: Amsterdam, pp. 181–190.

Bryman, A. (1988). *Quantity and Quality in Social Research*, London: Unwin Hyman.

Butler, T. (1998). Towards a Hermeneutic Method for Interpretive Research in Information Systems, *Journal of Information Technology* 13: 285–300.

Bygstad, B. (2006). Managing Socio-Technical Integration in Iterative Information System Development Projects, *International Journal of Technology and Human Interaction* 2(4): 1–14.

Bygstad, B. and Nielsen, P.A. (2003). The Meeting of Processes, Proceedings of IRIS 26 (Helsinki, Finland).

Bygstad, B., Nielsen, P.A. and Munkvold, B.E. (2010). Four Integration Patterns: A socio-technical approach to integration in IS development projects, *Information Systems Journal* 20(1): 53–80.

Campbell, D.T. (1955). The Informant in Quantitative Research, *The American Journal of Sociology* 60(4): 339–342.

Carney, T.F. (1990). *Collaborative Inquiry Methodology*, Windsor, Ontario, Canada: University of Windsor, Division for Instructional Development.

Czarniawska, B. (2004). *Narratives in Social Science Research*, Thousand Oaks, CA: CA Sage.

Doolin, B. (1998). Information Technology as Disciplinary Technology: Being critical in interpretive research on information systems, *Journal of Information Technology* 13: 301–311.

Dubé, L. and Paré, G. (2003). Rigor in Information Systems Positivist Case Research: Current practices, trends. and recommendations, *MIS Quarterly* 27(4): 597–635.

Fielding, N.G. and Fielding, J.L. (1986). *Linking Data. Qualitative Research Methods Series No 4*, London: Sage.

Fitzgerald, B. and Howcroft, D. (1998). Towards Dissolution of the IS Research Debate: From polarization to polarity, *Journal of Information Technology* 13: 313–326.

Goldstein, D.K. (1990). Information Support for Sales and Marketing. A case study at a small grocery manufacturer, *Information & Management* 19: 257–268.

Guba, E.G. and Lincoln, Y.S. (1989). *Fourth Generation Evaluation*, Newbury Park, CA: Sage Publications.

Hanseth, O. and Monteiro, E. (1996). Inscribing Behaviour in Information Infrastructure Standards, *Accounting, Management and Information Systems* 7(4): 183–211.

Hoffman, A. (2004). Reconsidering the Role of the Practical Theorist: On (re) connecting theory to practice in organization theory, *Strategic Organization* 2(2): 213–222.

Jacobson, I., Booch, G. and Rumbaugh, R. (1999). *The Unified Software Development Process*, 1st edn, Reading, MA: Addison Wesley.

Kallinikos, J. (2004). Farewell to Constructivism: Technology and context-embedded action, in C. Avgerou, C. Ciborra and F. Land (eds.) *The Social Study of Information and Communication Technology*, Oxford: Oxford University Press, pp. 140–161.

Klein, H.K. and Myers, M.D. (1999). A Set of Principles for Conducting and Evaluating Interpretive Field Studies in Information System, *MIS Quarterly* 23(1): 67–94.

Kvale, S. (1996). *InterViews*, Thousand Oaks, CA: Sage Publications.

Kvale, S. (2002). The Social Construction of Validity, in N.K. Denzin and Y.S. Lincoln (eds.) *The Qualitative Inquiry Reader*, Thousand Oaks, CA: Sage Publications, pp. 299–325.

Lanzara, G.F. (1991). Shifting Stories. Learning from a Reflective Experiment in a Design Process, in D.A. Schon (ed.) *The Reflective Turn: Case studies in and on educational practice*, New York: Teachers College Press of Columbia University, pp. 285–320.

Latour, B. (1987). *Science in Action: How to follow scientists and engineers through society*, Cambridge, MA: Harvard University Press.

Lee, A.S. (1989). A Scientific Methodology for MIS Case Studies, *MIS Quarterly* 13(1): 33–52.

Levine, H.G. and Rossmoore, D. (1993). Diagnosing the Human Threats to Information Technology Implementation: A missing factor in system analysis illustrated in a case study, *Journal of Management Information Systems* 10(2): 55–73.

Lincoln, Y.S. and Guba, E.G. (2003). Ethics: The failure of positivist science, in Y.S. Lincoln and N.K. Denzin (eds.) *Turning Points in Qualitative Research: Tying knots in a handkerchief*, Walnut Creek, CA: AltaMira Press, pp. 219–238.

Locke, K.D. and Velamuri, S.R. (2004). Member Checking Challenges, Working paper, Williamsburg, VA, The College of William and Mary.

Mårtensson, P. and Lee, A. (2004). Dialogical Action Research at Omega Corporation, *MIS Quarterly* 28(3): 507–536.

Mathiassen, L., Pries-Heje, J. and Ngwenyama, O. (2001). *Improving Software Organisations*, Boston, MA: Addison-Wesley Professional.

McDonnell, A., Lloyd Jones, M. and Read, S. (2000). Practical Considerations in Case Study Research: The relationship between methodology and process, *Journal of Advanced Nursing* 32(2): 383–390.

Miles, M.B. and Huberman, A.M. (1994). *Qualitative Data Analysis*, 2nd edn, Thousand Oaks, CA: Sage Publications.

Moody, D.L. (2000). Building Links Between IS Research and Professional Practice: Improving the relevance and impact of IS research, in W.J. Orlikowski, P. Weil, S. Ang and H.C. Krcmar (eds.) Proceedings of the Twenty-First International Conference on Information Systems (Brisbane), 351–360.

Morse, J.M., Barrett, M., Mayan, M., Olson, K. and Spiers, J. (2002). Verification Strategies for Establishing Reliability and Validity in Qualitative Research, *International Journal of Qualitative Methods* 1(2): 1–19.

Myers, M.D. (1997). Qualitative Research in Information Systems, *MIS Quarterly* 21(2): 242–242.

Myers, M.D. and Newman, M. (2007). The Qualitative Interview in IS Research: Examining the craft, *Information and Organization* 17: 2–26.

Ngwenyama, O. (1998). Groupware, Social Action and Emergent Organizations: On the process dynamics of computer mediated distributed work, *Accounting, Management and Information Technologies* 8(2–3): 127–146.

Nicholsen, B. and Sahay, S. (2004). Embedded knowledge and offshore software development, *Information and Organization* 14: 329–365.

Pare, G. and Elam, J.J. (1997). Using Case Study Research to Build Theories of IT Implementation, Proceedings of IFIP TC8 WG 8.2, Philadelphia: Chapman & Hall, pp. 542–568.

Paulk, M.C. (1998). Using the Capability Maturity Model for Software to Drive Change, in T.J. Larsen and E. McGuire (eds.) *Information Systems Innovation and Diffusion*, Hershey, PA: Idea Group Publishing, pp. 196–219.

Pettigrew, A.M. (1985). Contextualist Research and the Study of Organizational Change Processes, in E. Mumford, R. Hirschheim, G. Fitgerald and A.T. Wood-Harper (eds.) *Research Methods in Information Systems*, North-Holland: Amsterdam, pp. 53–78.

Pettigrew, A.M. (1990). Longitudinal Field Research on Change Theory and Practice, *Organization Science* 3: 267–292.

Reason, P. and Rowan, J. (1981). Issues of Validity in New Paradigm Research, in P. Reason and J. Rowan (eds.) *Human Inquiry*, Chichester: John Wiley, pp. 239–250.

Rosemann, M. and Vessey, I. (2008). Toward Improving the Relevance of Information Systems Research to Practice: The role of applicability checks, *MIS Quarterly* 32(1): 1–22.

Saunders, C. (1998). Editorial Preface: The role of business in IT research, *Information Resources Management Journal* 11: 4–6.

Sayer, A. (2000). *Realism and Social Science*, London: Sage Publications.

Schatzman, L. and Strauss, A.L. (1973). *Field Research. Strategies for a Natural Sociology*, Englewood Cliffs, NJ: Prentice-Hall.

Schön, D.A. (1983). *The Reflective Practitioner*, New York: Basic Books.

Silverman, D. (1985). *Qualitative Methodology & Sociology*, Brookfield, VT: Gower Publishing.

Silverman, D. (1993). *Interpreting Qualitative Data: Methods for analysing talk, text and interaction*, London: Sage Publications.

Smith, M.L. (2006). Overcoming Theory-Practice Inconsistencies: Critical realism and information systems research, *Information and Organization* 16(3): 191–211.

Van de Ven, A.H. (2007). *Engaged Scholarship*, New York: Oxford University Press.

Wagner, E.L. (2003). (Inter-)Connecting IS Narrative Research: Current status and future opportunities for process-oriented field studies, in E.H. Wynn, E.A. Whitley, M.D. Myers and J.I. DeGross (eds.) *Global and Organizational Discourse About Information Technology*, Boston, MA: Kluwer, pp. 419–436.

Walsham, G. (1993). *Interpreting Information Systems in Organizations*, Chichester: Wiley.

Walsham, G. (1995). Interpretive Case Studies in IS Research: Nature and method, *European Journal of Information Systems* 4: 74–81.

Walsham, G. (2006). Doing Interpretive Research, *European Journal of Information Systems* **15**: 320–330.

Walsham, G. and Sahay, S. (1999). GIS for District-Level Administration in India: Problems and opportunities, *MIS Quarterly* **23**(1): 39–66.

Weick, K. (1995). *Sensemaking in Organizations,* Thousand Oaks, CA: Sage.

Yin, R.K. (1994). *Case Study Research,* Thousand Oaks, CA: Sage.

14

An Exploration of Information Systems Adoption: Tools and Skills as Cultural Artefacts – the Case of a Management Information System

Deborah Bunker[1], Karlheinz Kautz[1,2] and Anhtai Anhtuan[1]
[1]*School of Information Systems, Technology & Management,*
University of New South Wales, Australia;
[2]*Copenhagen Business School, Denmark*

Introduction

Research indicates that many information systems and information technology (IS/IT) implementations are not to the satisfaction of the adopting organisations. Larsen and McGuire (1998) reported that half of all implementations are deemed unsuccessful or inappropriate. Unfortunately, the research into IS diffusion has not yet achieved very fruitful outcomes for the IS community, in academia and industry. Research into this area suffers from weaknesses, including bias and fragmentation (Kautz *et al.*, 2005).

Taking a step back from current research directions, Bunker (2001) explored IS adoption through an anthropological perspective. She argued that IS/IT are tools in context, and are created and used within a cultural framework. Tools inherit the cultural values and assumptions of the creator's culture. As tools and the skills to use them are closely related (Ayres, 1978), the tool's cultural characteristics are manifested in skill sets. Difficulties could thus emerge if the toolmaker's assumptions about the context in which the tool is to be used are not matched by the tool user's actual context. From this background, we outline a skills-focused

Reprinted from "An exploration of information systems adoption: tools and skills as cultural artefacts – the case of a management information system," by D. Bunker, K. Kautz and A. Anhtuan in *Journal of Information Technology*, 23, 2008, pp. 71–78. With kind permission from the Association for Information Technology Trust. All rights reserved.

approach to analyse toolmaker and tool user contextual differences through the comparison of assumed and actual skills, which can assist in anticipating hurdles to successful IS adoption.

This paper examines the validity of the approach by documenting an interpretive field study of an IS adoption in an Australian IT company. In particular, the approach is used to analyse the management control skills required to use a management IS. Three questions guide this research: (1) What is the outcome of a skills match between the set of management control skills assumed by the toolmaker and the skills possessed by the tool user? (2) What factors in the user's process of tool indigenisation appear to contribute to the resulting skills gap, if any? (3) Is the skills-focused approach a valid and effective way of determining the appropriateness of an IS?

The remainder of the paper is organised as follows: The next section provides the theoretical background and introduces the main concepts of the framework. The following section presents the research approach and method. The subsequent section describes the setting of the case study and the penultimate section includes and discusses our findings. We finish the paper with some conclusions in the final section.

Theoretical background and framework

The current fragmented status, and limited value, of IS diffusion and adoption research motivated us to explore alternative models for understanding IS adoption. Scandinavian researchers (Ehn and Kyng, 1984; Kammersgaard, 1988) have suggested a tool perspective on the development and use of computer-based IS. Bunker (1998, 2001) specifically applied this perspective to IS adoption. Based on an anthropological approach to research in IS she developed an argument that views IS as tools that are created in a context, with a particular set of cultural values and assumptions underpinning their creation. These cultural values and assumptions are manifested in skill sets.

Tools, skills and organisational culture as their context

Man is incomplete as a species and without tools (i.e. devices that aid in accomplishing a task or instruments used to perform an operation or necessary in the practice of a vocation or profession) is unsustainable compared to any other species (Stahl, 2002). Technology is a sophisticated type of tool that is able to extend human capacity and even act as a substitution to achieve goals (Stahl, 2002). Tools are created and used in context, and are a reflection of human capacity and human culture (see, e.g., Winner, 1986; Latour, 1987; Winfield, 1991). They inherit the cultural values and assumptions of the toolmaker's culture, and consequently the intent and use of the tool is defined by that culture. It is a challenge for a tool user of a different culture to fully appreciate the original intent and application of the tool.

For any tool the mutual contingency of tools and skills is of importance for an understanding of technology as a function of human behaviour (Ayres, 1978). A tool requires skills not only to use it but also to understand the intent behind it. Ayres argues that technology involves not only the use of tools designed to complete an objective but also the set of skills that accompany tools. There is a natural affinity between tools and skills; '... human skills and the tools by which, and on which, they are exercised are inseparable. Skills *always* employ tools, and tools are such *always* by virtue of being employed in acts of skill by human beings' (*ibid.*). A person's skills set is derived from the culture of which the person is a member (Bunker, 2001). The same cultural derivation applies for tools. Thus, for a tool user to possess the skills to truly understand the intent and use of the tool, the user would have to subscribe to the cultural values and assumptions that are inherent in the tool, that is, assumed by the toolmaker. If tools are a visible manifestation of the assumptions and values that the IS discipline embodies, then IS are those tools.

The term skill is commonly seen as the ability and knowledge used in order to achieve or do something. Skills are goal-directed, well-organised behaviours that are acquired through practice with economy of effort (Proctor and Dutta, 1995). The types of skill can be physical, motoric and partially perceptual or mental, cognitive and perceptual, or a mixture (Jones and Whittaker, 1975). Proctor and Dutta (1995) argue that context partially determines skills acquisition. Skills go beyond their portrayal in the labour process literature as mechanistic and physical; they come as a dual-faceted entity featuring a mechanistic, technical dimension and an organic, cognitive component in which contextual, cultural factors play a role.

Sincoff and Sternberg (1989) report that contextual factors receive significant attention in psychology research. Rosenbaum *et al.* (2001) for instance argue that perceptual-motor skills are affected by context, and that the perceptual, cognitive and motor domains work together to achieve skill acquisition and skilled performance (Jones and Whittaker, 1975; Carlson and Yaure, 1990). Given that skills are defined by mechanistic and organic components, it follows that a person's skills are embedded in the context in which they are learnt. The context shapes the skill through its organic component. This again raises questions about the transferability of skills in other contexts.

In an IS environment skills are critical. Zuboff (1988) talks of the IS environment as a 'computer-mediated' environment where certain realisations about organisations' capabilities must be made. IS are not neutral tools and they embody essential characteristics that are bound to alter the nature of work within our factories and offices, and among workers, professionals, and managers. The profound effect of IS on organisations and the strategy to deal with this relates to the type of skills present in the user organisation. Mastery in a computer-mediated environment depends upon developing intellective skills.

Tools and their associated skills are developed and used in context. Cultural values and assumptions are inherent in tools, and consequently their intent and use is defined by that culture. Organisational cultural theory helps to articulate precisely what is meant by culture and context, and how this impacts on IS adoption. Schein (1984) conceptualises an organisational culture as having three distinct layers. The first layer holds the basic assumptions possessed by all members of that culture. These assumptions concern members' fundamental values regarding reality, human relationships, human nature and the environment. They are taken for granted, subconscious, invisible and most difficult to change. The second layer holds the values to which members subscribe but are espoused, overt and debatable unlike basic assumptions. In the third and most visible cultural layer, labelled artefacts and creations (visual and tangible manifestations of culture) are found, such as technology, art, and visible and audible behaviour patterns.

Management control as a significant dimension of organisational culture

Culture is a multi-faceted, complex phenomenon (Conner *et al.*, 1987). Regrettably, prevailing IS research has taken a rather for-granted view of the concept of culture (Avison and Myers, 1995), which strips away the richness of this socially constructed phenomenon. While our research adopts an anthropological approach to studying IS and organisational culture, it would consume more than one project to conduct complete cultural research. For that reason, this paper's cultural focus is refined to a single yet important dimension of organisational culture, namely that of management control. Rowlinson *et al.* (2007) have elaborated four distinct views of managerialism that align with either mainstream or radical views, from a managerialist or anti-managerialist perspective. They comment on the importance of cultural issues in the 'radical managerialist' perspective of management control, through the works of Hoskin and Macve (1994, 2000), Hofstede (1980, 1991) and MacKinlay (2002). Their Foucaultian approach seeks to promote 'humanism over rationality' and in doing so 'looks for organisational and institutional context' (p. 474). Their definition of radical managerialism focuses on social, organisational and political processes and structures that are manifested in managerial practices. Chenhall and Euske (2007) also highlight the importance of social and contextual issues insofar as they influence management control systems, through the dimensions of: history and external context; integration of change between central and operational sub- units; diffusion and integration of change across the organisation; and gaining employee commitment to change.

Inspired by Hofstede's (1980, 1991) work and using this as a vehicle to focus on dimensions of organisational culture, our analysis of the toolmaker and tool user's contexts has been confined to the culture of management control and the management control skills used with the tool under study, a dimension originally termed the loose *vs* tight control dimension. This was for two reasons. Firstly, in the case study, the management control agenda of the tool user was most pertinent to its decision to adopt a practice management IS. Secondly, there was validity in concentrating on issues of management control because they complement the nature of the tool.

The tool focuses on the time-based accounting of human resources, where standards of performance are monitored, analysed and set. To properly investigate the management control agenda in both the toolmaker's assumed culture and the user's actual culture, we performed a further literature study to unearth common dimensions that could be used to provide specific focus for our investigation. Here, the work of researchers in organisational culture, organisation theory and organisational management was considered. As a result, five dimensions of management control were discovered, namely: standardisation; policy compliance; communication, interaction, behaviour and reporting; group divisions and its formalisation; and attitude towards control. Table 14.1 provides brief details on each of these dimensions, including literary sources and a brief description.

The research approach and method

The study seeks to understand the skills match, resulting skills gap and tool indigenisation efforts between the set of management control skills assumed by the toolmaker and the skills possessed by the tool user.

Table 14.1 The five dimensions of management control

Dimension of management control	Literary sources	Description
Standardisation	Burns and Stalker (1966), Langfield-Smith (1997), Mintzberg (1979), Robbins (1983), Chenhall and Euske (2007)	The implementation of rules, standards, policies of engagement and operation
Policy compliance	Hofstede (1968), Mintzberg (1979), Tricker (1976), Chenhall and Euske (2007)	The measurement of performance and compliance, and the systems in place to motivate performance and compliance
Communication, interaction, behaviour and reporting	Burns and Stalker (1966), Hofstede (1968), Mintzberg (1979), Tricker (1976), Chenhall and Euske (2007)	The nature of the interaction and communication amongst members of all levels within the organisation
Group divisions and its formalisation (structure)	Burns and Stalker (1966), Mintzberg (1979), Robbins (1983), Tricker (1976), Chenhall and Euske (2007)	The formalisation of organisational structure and job roles, the locus of decision-making
Attitude towards control	Langfield-Smith (1997), Mintzberg (1979), Robbins (1983), Wieland and Ullrich (1976), Chenhall and Euske (2007)	Management and employee attitudes to meeting objectives and controlling resources, uncertainty and variability

An understanding of how the skills-focused approach could be a valid and effective way of determining the appropriateness of an IS within an organisation is also an objective of the study.

The research strategy reflects the researchers' relativist and constructionist assumptions. The research questions focus on the exploration and understanding of IS adoption using a skills-focused approach. Thus, the need for contextual respect is an influencing factor on our research strategy. Culture is not something which can exist independently of consciousness and experience (Crotty, 1998). Rather, culture is historically determined, related to anthropological concepts and is socially constructed (Hofstede *et al.*, 1990). Hence, an abductive research strategy is used; its view of a socially constructed reality and use of thick descriptions (Blaikie, 2000) enable the researchers to deal with all three research questions while properly respecting the contextual and cultural aspects of this research.

The strategy of inquiry was a case study featuring a tool user organisation adopting a practice management IS developed by a toolmaker organisation. The research was conducted between the second-half of 2001 and the first-half of 2002. In-depth interviews were performed with four representatives of the toolmaker (mainly consultants), and seven employees of the user organisation (some managers using the information provided through the tool and other employees who as timekeepers were supposed to supply the tool with time information about their work). We gained an understanding of the IS adoption situation in the toolmaker and user organisations by hermeneutically interpreting the text, attempting to make sense of the confused, incomplete, cloudy and contradictory views (Boland Jr., 1991; Myers, 1997) of people through text-analogues in the form of transcriptions of all interviews and documentary texts. Data collected from in-depth interviews took the form of experiences, anecdotes, feelings and statements of respondents. Eventually, following the hermeneutic circle of interpretation led us to a rich understanding of the toolmaker and user contexts, and the IS adoption that took place, and the skills required.

Documentary artefacts also assisted with understanding the issues brought to the surface through the interviews. They were used as a way of triangulating the data, to verify the results. Artefacts included e-mails, memos, minutes of meetings, user manuals, presentations, training guides and product marketing material.

A skills checklist was devised to facilitate the skills matching process. Using the checklist, the tool user's actual skills were checked against the toolmaker's list of assumed skills. The checklist was categorised into the five cultural dimensions of management control.

The case study setting

The tool user

Dataware[1] is a company spanning a number of sectors of the IT industry employing over 1200 employees around Australia. The company had grown significantly from its inception in 1987 and had achieved a solid reputation. Its success in the 1990s attracted a multinational IT company, which bought it in 2001. Along with the purchase came a change in identity and management structure as well as a rationalisation of existing divisions and the creation of new divisions. Every area of the company was affected by the downsizing.

Dataware was an esteemed employer. This was a reflection of the familial culture that existed before the purchase. The culture was reflective of a loosely controlled organisation, where sticking to budget was not a priority. The company was very results-oriented, which contributed to its lack of concern for controlling costs while increasing revenue. Another characteristic of its culture was its enthusiasm for technological innovation. There was no hesitation in adopting new technologies that could assist it in its operations.

The major shake up in the company's size, structure and identity after the purchase changed the organisational culture. The change was evident in the use of words. Rather than describing the culture as 'family' as before, terms such as 'governance' and 'company corporate' were used. There was a profound effect on employee morale after the purchase. With the downsizing continuing, the atmosphere was one of uncertainty. The company's ITS (IT Services) Division was not targeted intensely during the rationalisation. It was responsible for the entire IT infrastructure and covered networking and communications, hardware, operating systems, and system applications for internal use. Staff were segregated into groups according to their function or service: a Project and Development Group managed all IT projects which dealt with the development of system applications for internal use; and a Support Group which had the responsibility of supporting these applications and was in charge of maintaining and enhancing the networking infrastructure, operating systems, and hardware.

The division was mainly made up of system developers, system administrators, IT architecture specialists, project managers, and network engineers. The culture was similar to the rest of the company. The familial culture of optimism lingered for some time after the start of the rationalisation process; however, with the introduction of a new practice management system, the culture was transformed.

The toolmaker

SixSoft is a publicly listed Australian company that has the practice management system called STM as its flagship product. Its services go beyond its systems to the technology, consulting and training domains. The company boasts a global presence of over 1600 employees and a client base of accounting and legal professions, the government sector, small and medium businesses, and large enterprises.

The tool and its adoption

STM was adopted by the commercial areas of Dataware in late 2000 to fulfil its requirements for supporting timekeeping. STM is designed for professional services firms to manage financial administration. It allows firms to record the time their employees spend on client work and subsequently bill the client based on those hours. Although SixSoft proclaimed that the system could be used in any professional services firm, it is interesting to note that it was originally authored as a solution for the legal profession.

During the initial adoption, the ITS Division was not part of the roll-out because it did not charge for work performed for internal customers. In mid-2001, ITS management decided to implement a new version of STM for itself and installed the timekeeping module. It was seen as a way of formally monitoring staff with respect to their time at work. Instinctive and possibly unfounded management perceptions were meant to be replaced by official and factual evidence. The tool required all ITS staff to enter their time spent working.

As a management tool, it would have been expected that ITS management would involve itself heavily with its introduction but in hindsight they realised how little time, management had spent on the project. There was insufficient effort to define precisely what they wanted from the system, and how to go about achieving these objectives. The urgency of a timekeeping solution had put pressure on them to arrive at a resolution on time category definitions. Once STM was operational and staff entered their time into these categories, the definitions were found to cause confusion and subsequently underwent a series of revisions. Our analysis explains the phenomenon in more depth from the tool and skill perspectives.

Findings and discussion

We now present the toolmaker's skill assumptions, as identified through our analysis of our interviews with the four SixSoft consultants, and the user's actual skills as identified from our interviews with the seven employees of Dataware, with regard to the management control dimensions. These are: standardisation, policy compliance, communication, interaction, behaviour and reporting; group division and formalisation (structure) and attitude towards control. We could not, however, identify any common assumptions and skills related to the group division and its formalisation.

Skills assumed by the toolmaker SixSoft

Skills related to standardisation

SixSoft consultants spoke about the need for a standard, accepted basis of roles and responsibilities for recognising business entities and events in order to record, control and measure them properly. It was stressed that performance measures needed to be standardised in two critical aspects: budgeting and human productivity. Based on responses about standardisation, the toolmaker inferred that the user must have the skills to develop clear and uniform measures of performance and decision-making policy.

Skills related to policy compliance

SixSoft consultants assumed that the tool user would have formal programmes that motivate employees to enter their timesheets accurately and expediently. Responses highlighted the need for KPIs to be created to motivate timekeeping that must be applied uniformly to all employees. The assumed policy compliance skill on a divisional level, involved the setting up of motivational programmes for timekeeping.

On the managerial level, SixSoft respondents identified that managers are there to enforce and encourage employees to time-keep accurately. Managers should regularly review their staff's timesheets as the quality of their decisions is contingent on the data derived from their staff, and they should be able to set and track a budget. The budget will determine the scope with which employees can perform work and is a key indicator of the organisation's health. This skill requires managers to act upon the information generated by and for them.

Managers have the need to know what their staff members are doing at all times and constantly monitor and review the projects and jobs that their staff members work on. STM provides managers with the visibility to examine employees' activities in an indirect and less inhibiting way. The constant monitoring and review of employees' work is also performed to detect obstacles that can be detrimental to the goal of productivity or chargeability. Information from STM and other sources should assist managers to foresee obstacles that lay ahead for their staff. The four managerial skills related to policy compliance (as stated by the SixSoft consultants) are to review time sheets, to set and track budgets, to monitor projects and jobs, to detect and clear obstacles to productivity.

Skills related to communication, interaction, behaviour and reporting

SixSoft respondents stated that managers should be coaches and while being in a position of authority they should be in a mentoring role in order to support employees. Managers should be able to provide feedback to employees about their work performance, to take interest in their employees and to help them to improve. Implementing a time accounting system can bring an atmosphere of mutual distrust, if the system and its introduction are not managed carefully and so STM should be made open for all to access. This enhances organisational relationships and facilitates mutual trust. The three SixSoft advocated managerial skills here are being a coach and mentor, providing feedback to employees, and being frank about time accounting performance.

Timekeepers must also recognise the work they performed 'just a minute ago, an hour ago' and break down their day into pieces of work and the amount of time spent on each piece. While the skill of time-keeping appears mechanistic and processual in nature, there is a context in which timekeepers record and enter their time. Timekeepers must understand that timekeeping is both in their own and their organisation's interest. They are accountable to management, the organisation, and to their clients.

Skills related to attitude towards control

Based on the assumption that STM is a tool with information open and visible to everyone, SixSoft consultants advocated that the user should not have any qualms over sharing information among employees. An open culture encourages trust between management and employees and stimulates performance. Related to the user imperative to align revenues and costs closely to budget forecasts in an environment where professionals sell their expertise, the user must be aware of how much revenue is being generated through employees and how much cost is incurred. This information should then be compared with a budget to determine the user's performance. In summary, the tool user must have two attitudinal skills: promoting information visibility and aligning revenues and costs to a budget.

Skills possessed by the tool user Dataware

Our analysis revealed that the ITS Division was split into two different sub-cultures: the Project and Development Group (PDG) and the Support Group (SG). Respondents who worked in the PDG, who performed project work lasting a longer period, saw significant benefit in STM. But respondents in the SG had a consensus that STM's implementation was misguided and not of much value. In terms of management control, differences were discovered between the sub-cultures in every sub-dimension.

Skills related to standardisation

STM was implemented in order to regiment Dataware operations. The ITS division had an image problem for being disorganised and slow to act. This was exacerbated because of the ITS multi-team structure, each with different responsibilities and goals. ITS needed to find common ground for team interaction and organisational unification.

To formalise the processes of the division, the STM implementation was used as a formal standard. Staff were now required to identify pieces of work and classify them appropriately for timekeeping. These new rules proved positive as productivity increased and an organisational appreciation of the division's work developed. Accordingly, ITS appeared to possess skills of developing and disseminating policies, including those on decision-making.

In terms of uniformity in performance measurements, however, ITS differed from SixSoft's assumptions. Common measures of using information from STM across the division were not implemented. The nature of each team's work shaped each manager's idea of performance and only the PDG was concerned with the financial and human aspects of performance. This was indicative in the reports that project managers generated for their use and to show clients.

Overall, the division did not possess the skills of developing uniform standards for performance measurement. The varied nature of its work prevented it from reaching agreement on how performance should be defined. If we look at this situation from the perspective of the two ITS worldviews, only the PDG had its own uniform measures of performance that bear resemblance to SixSoft's assumed ones.

Skills related to policy compliance

ITS used KPIs to motivate employees to time-keep but this approach was fairly simplistic. Management enforced one KPI, which monitored whether each timekeeper submitted weekly timesheets by a certain deadline. This was to ensure that timekeeping was not only observed but also to defuse the initial backlash regarding the 'Big Brother' nature of the tool, and to demonstrate management seriousness regarding timekeeping. The toolmaker's assumption that time capturing is a critical activity was generally not relevant to ITS. The PDG used time as a measure in managing their projects, but to other work timekeeping was secondary. The SG manager stopped recording his time altogether. The division did not have the skills to effectively instil timekeeping in employee's KPIs.

Managers in the PDG were involved in ensuring that their employees complied with timekeeping policy. The information they gained from employees through STM assisted them to manage their projects. One compliance approach was to review the timesheets to check that the allocation of hours was in line with the budget set for each project.

Budgets were crucial to the PDG as they defined the scope with which projects were performed in order to reach the organisation's goals. Managers demonstrated budget tracking skills to check expected project performance; their skills in reviewing timesheets and tracking budgets reflected the discipline of project management. Managers recognised their company and client accountability, and employed their skills as part of efforts to keep themselves and others informed. Hence, managers in the PDG possessed three of the four skills assumed: regularly reviewing staff timesheets, setting and tracking budgets, and monitoring and reviewing projects.

A different picture emerged from the SG. There was no management review of timesheets or monitoring of employees' work on a daily basis. Trust and intuition of employees were the two major values that underpinned this management style. This went against the values of monitoring and reporting, which were manifested in STM. Furthermore, the SG did not charge for work or run explicitly to a budget. The STM implementation had little bearing on SG work. This demonstrates that the SG did not possess the first three assumed managerial skills that were assumed by SixSoft. Their work simply was not congruous with the type of structure and discipline expected.

Only the PDG managers seemed to possess the managerial skill of detecting and clearing obstacles with regard to performance. Staff welfare was managed by using STM to detect possible anomalies in staff productivity patterns as an indication of possible delays to projects. SG managers were also interested in the welfare of their staff; however, the rationale had less to do with maintaining performance and was more related to the camaraderie that existed in the teams. On the whole, the PDG possessed all assumed skills in policy compliance on a managerial level. The SG did not possess any of the assumed skills.

Skills related to communication, interaction, behaviour and reporting

ITS staff did not necessarily require a mentor or coach to guide them. Staff consisted mainly of senior professionals. Team managers promoted autonomy and self-guidance rather than dependence, as managers believed that they and their staff were in teams where support was given to each other. This arrangement appeared to work well for most operations. From a timekeeping perspective, the lack of guidance had a negative impact. The hands-off approach to dealing with staff exacerbated problems with the classification of work in STM, and the managers of both groups did not exhibit the assumed mentoring or coaching skills.

PDG management utilised their policy compliance skills of monitoring, review and budget tracking to provide feedback to employees who were kept up-to-date about their contributions with respect to the progress and performance of projects. On the SG side, STM was not used to prepare feedback for employees and feedback that was given appeared to only recognise workers of long hours. In conclusion, only the PDG possessed SixSoft's assumed skill of providing feedback on performance. The assumed skill of talking openly about performance matters is related to the skill of providing feedback as it presumes that managers access and use STM. Hence, only the PDG managers possessed this skill.

PDG timekeepers recorded (on paper) the amount of time they spent on work in blocks of one-quarter hour. Then, they identified the type of each piece of work, which was one of four standard types of ITS work. Next, they determined how to classify each piece according to the array of projects, clients and codes set up in STM. They also had a common view of the reasons for timekeeping which was focused on management and client expectations. This was what SixSoft assumed.

SG timekeeping behaviour followed a less stringent process. The first step normally saw a rough estimate of time to be spent on the work. The classification of work was then made simple as it was allocated to only two categories, 'support' and 'admin', with an aggregated time for each and no explanatory narrative. Staff controlled how they entered their hours rather than by management prescription. This flexibility in timekeeping was indicative of the assumptions and values underpinning this skill, as SG projects were not financially focused. SG's use of STM was viewed as a tool of scrutiny, which exacerbated feelings of mutual distrust between management and some in the SG. The team was suspicious that management's motives behind STM were for policing purposes.

Timekeepers in the SG were lacking timekeeping skills and despite fulfilling the mechanistic system requirements, their incompatible organic view was at odds with the assumed skill sets for the use of STM.

Skills related to attitude towards control

There was a difference of opinion when the topic of visibility and open culture was raised with some respondents. One PDG manager was convinced that STM made more visible (for everyone) what all staff were actually doing, providing managers appropriately sanctioned access.

It was only the ITS managers who were privy to most of the information. The company's CIO, however, held the inconsistent belief that all information related to time accounting should be made freely available to everyone in the company.

In ITS's implementation of STM, the developer, who was responsible for determining the access list to information, decided on her own to limit access to reports, in spite of a clear mandate from the CIO. The reasoning was that in an open culture, information could be abused. So far, no one has challenged this decision. To see visibility as a negative feature goes against SixSoft's assumption that information openness enhances mutual trust between management and staff. Consequently, ITS failed to possess the skills of promoting visibility and an open culture.

In viewing budgeting and its importance in ITS, the split between the PDG and the SG was clear. Budgeting was a central part of the PDG's mission and performance management, but for the SG project and budget plans were irrelevant to their work and therefore their concerns for these issues were minor. The divide between the two groups on the importance of budgeting highlights another split in skill sets. Only the PDG, motivated by issues that were assumed to drive budgeting, possessed the skill of promoting budget importance.

Conclusions

This study focussed on a number of research questions. How can we understand the alignment of skills assumed by the toolmaker and those apparent in the tool user population, and the ability of the tool user to indigenise the tool to meet any 'skills gap'. Within this study we found that the contrast in the actual skills possessed by the two ITS groups highlights that the tool was only appropriate for one group (PDG) and explains some of the problems accompanying the adoption of this technical innovation. The organisation faced a choice: change the tool to suit the SG or reconfigure the SG to suit the tool.

Beyond this result, and in response to our third research question regarding the relevance of this approach, the study demonstrates that the skills-focused approach is a valid and effective way of exploring IS adoption and it represents a step in a new direction for IS adoption research. Much of the diffusion of innovation (DoI) literature has focussed on the process of, and barriers to, adoption and use of tools by users within their own context (Burns and Stalker, 1966; Tornatzky and Klein 1982; Rogers, 1995; Kautz *et al.*, 2005). There has been very little focus on the tool itself, and the effect of context on the intention of the designer and maker for its use. The concept of skills, as a manifestation of organisational culture, can be effectively used to articulate the differences in toolmaker–tool user contexts, and the effect that this may have on the diffusion of the innovation.

The approach has also favourable consequences for industry. Tool users have an enhanced measure to determine the appropriateness of IS. The assessment could assist them in devising proper indigenisation plans with the intention of eliminating any skill gaps. For management of the potential tool users, the approach could become a tool to assess the organisation's skill sets on varying levels of the organisation, allowing management to be aware of the culture and capabilities that exist in the organisation. This could be of benefit to their decision-making. There are also positive implications for toolmakers. They can become considerate of contextual factors that may inhibit customers' adoption of their products. The approach could arm them with a technique to assess the difference in their customer's skills and context compared to their own assumptions. This could influence how they design and implement the process of transferring their systems.

Our research on the toolmaker side was not directly informed by the actual developers of the tool, but by the consultants responsible for its sales and implementation. Although this resulted in valuable insights about the skill-based assumptions made by the toolmakers, the study might have benefited from the involvement of the actual developers. Another limitation is that the research focused on a single dimension of organisational culture, management control. Expanding the cultural scope, especially with regard to other types of IS, is a task for the future. There are opportunities to study IS adoption that employ different indicators for management control as used in this study. Future research could take on more dimensions of organisational culture. Learning about the impact that other cultural dimensions have on the skills-focused approach would be a constructive contribution to the overall development of the approach.

Note

1. On request to protect any identities, the names for the tool-maker, user and tool have been invented.

References

Avison, D.E. and Myers, M.D. (1995). Information Systems and Anthropology: An anthropological perspective on IT and organizational culture, *Information Technology & People* 8: 43–56.

Ayres, C.E. (1978). *The Theory of Economic Progress: A Study of the Fundamentals of Economic Development and Cultural Change*, Kalamazoo, MI: New Issues Press, Western Michigan University.

Blaikie, N.W.H. (2000). *Designing Social Research: The Logic of Anticipation*, Malden, MA: Polity Press.

Boland Jr., R.J. (1991). Information Systems Use as a Hermeneutic Process, in R. Hirschheim (ed.) *Information Systems Research: Contemporary Approaches & Emergent Traditions*, New York: North-Holland, pp. 439–458.

Bunker, D. (1998). Information Technology and Systems (IT&S) as Tools: Cultural bias and the implications for International Technology Transfer (ITT)? in Proceedings of the 4th Americas Conference on Information Systems (Baltimore, MD, USA, 1998), Baltimore, MD: Association of Information Systems, 818–820.

Bunker, D. (2001). A Philosophy of Information Technology and Systems (IT & S) as Tools: Tool development context, associated skills and the Global Technical Transfer (GTT) process, *Information Systems Frontiers* 3: 185–197.

Burns, T. and Stalker, G.M. (1966). *The Management of Innovation*, London: Tavistock.

Carlson, R.A. and Yaure, R.G. (1990). Practice Schedules and the Use of Component Skills in Problem Solving, *Journal of Experimental Psychology: Learning, Memory and Cognition* 16: 484–496.

Chenhall, R.H. and Euske, K.J. (2007). The Role of Management Control Systems in Planned Organisational Change: An analysis of two organizations, *Accounting, Organisations and Society* 32: 601–637.

Conner, D.R., Fiman, B.G. and Clements, E.E. (1987). Corporate Culture and Its Impact on Strategic Change in Banking, *Journal of Retail Banking* 9: 16–24.

Crotty, M. (1998). *The Foundations of Social Research: Meaning and Perspective in the Research Process*, St Leonards, Sydney: Allen & Unwin.

Ehn, P. and Kyng, M. (1984). A Tool Perspective on Design of Interactive Computer Support for Skilled Workers, in M. Sääksjärvi (ed.) *Report of the Seventh Scandinavian Research Seminar on Systemeering, Helsinki School of Economics. Studies B-74*, Helsinki: Helsinki School of Economics, pp. 211–242.

Hofstede, G.H. (1968). *The Game of Budget Control*, London: Tavistock.

Hofstede, G.H. (1980). *Culture's Consequences: International Differences in Work Related Values*, Beverly Hills, CA: Sage.

Hofstede, G.H. (1991). *Cultures and Organizations: Software of the Mind*, London; New York: McGraw-Hill.

Hofstede, G.H., Neuijen, B., Ohayv, D.D. and Sanders, G. (1990). Measuring Organizational Cultures: A qualitative and quantitative study across twenty cases, *Administrative Science Quarterly* 35: 286–316.

Hoskin, K.W. and Macve R.H. (1994). Reappraising the Genesis of Managerialism: A re-examination of the role of accounting in the Springfield Armory, 1816–1845, *Accounting, Auditing and Accountability Journal* 17: 4–29.

Hoskin, K.W. and Macve, R.H. (2000). Knowing More as Knowing Less? Alternative Histories of Cost and Management Accounting in the US and the UK, *Accounting Historian's Journal* 20(1): 91–150.

Jones, A. and Whittaker, P. (1975). *Testing Industrial Skills*, New York: Wiley.

Kammersgaard, J. (1988). Four Different Perspectives on Human–Computer Interaction, *In International Journal of Man-Machine Studies* 28(4): 343–362.

Kautz, K., Zinner Henriksen, H., Breer-Mortensen, T. and Poulsen, H.H. (2005). IT Diffusion Research – An interim balance, in Proceedings of the IFIP WG 8.6 Working Conference on Business Agility and IT Diffusion (Atlanta, Georgia, USA, 8–11 May 2005) Atlanta Georgia, USA: IFIP WG 8.6.

Langfield-Smith, K. (1997). Management Control Systems and Strategy: A critical review, *Accounting, Organizations and Society* 22: 207–232.

Larsen, T.J. and McGuire, E. (1998). *Information Systems Innovation and Diffusion: Issues and Directions*, Hershey, PA: Idea Group Pub.

Latour, B. (1987). *Science in Action: How to Follow Scientists and Engineers Through Society*, Cambridge, MA: Harvard University Press.

MacKinlay, A. (2002). Dead Selves': The birth of the modern career, *Organisation* 9: 595–615.

Mintzberg, H. (1979). *The Structuring of Organizations: A Synthesis of the Research*, Englewood Cliffs, NJ: Prentice-Hall.

Myers, M.D. (1997). Qualitative Research in Information Systems, *MIS Quarterly* 21: 241–242.

Proctor, R.W. and Dutta, A. (1995). *Skill Acquisition and Human Performance*, Thousand Oaks, CA: Sage Publications.

Robbins, S.P. (1983). *Organization Theory: The Structure and Design of Organizations*, Englewood Cliffs, NJ: Prentice-Hall.

Rogers, E.M. (1995). *Diffusion of Innovation*, 4th edn, New York: Free Press.

Rosenbaum, D.A., Carlson, R.A. and Gilmore, R.O. (2001). Acquisition of Intellectual and Perceptual-Motor Skills, *Annual Review of Psychology* 52: 453–500.

Rowlinson, M., Toms, S. and Wilson, J.F. (2007). Competing Perspectives on the 'Managerial Revolution': From 'managerialist' to 'anti-managerialist', *Business History* 49(4): 464–482.

Schein, E.H. (1984). Coming to a New Awareness of Organizational Culture, *Sloan Management Review* 25: 3–16.

Sincoff, J.B. and Sternberg, R.J. (1989). The Development of Cognitive Skills: An examination of recent theories, in A.M. Colley and J.R. Beech (eds.) *Acquisition and Performance of Cognitive Skills*, Chichester: Wiley, pp. 19–60.

Stahl, B.C. (2002). Information Technology, Responsibility, and Anthropology, in Proceedings of HICSS 35 (Waikoloa, Hawaii, 2002), Washington, USA: IEEE Computer Society.

Tornatzky, L.G. and Klein, K.J. (1982). Innovation Characteristics and Innovation Adoption-Implementation: A meta-analysis of findings, *IEEE Transactions on Engineering Management* EM-29(1): 28–45.

Tricker, R.I. (1976). *Management Information and Control Systems*, London; New York: Wiley.

Wieland, G.F. and Ullrich, R.A. (1976). *Organizations: Behaviour, Design, and Change*, Homewood, IL: R.D. Irwin.

Winfield, I. (1991). *Organisations and Information Technology: Systems, Power and Job Design*, Oxford: Blackwell.

Winner, L. (1986). Do Artifacts Have Politics?, in L. Winner (ed.) *The Whale and the Reactor: A Search for Limits in an Age of High Technology*, Chicago: University of Chicago Press, pp. 19–39.

Zuboff, S. (1988). *In the Age of the Smart Machine: The Future of Work and Power*, New York: Basic Books.

15

Institutionalizing Operational Risk Management: An Empirical Study

Carol Hsu[1], James Backhouse[2] and Leiser Silva[3]
[1]*National Taiwan University, Taiwan;*
[2]*London School of Economics and Political Science, UK;*
[3]*University of Houston, USA*

Introduction

The 2007–2009 crisis was at first seen as a failure of global finance in financial and economic terms but then as a concatenation of operational risk failures triggered first in the mortgage industry and subsequently in all the other financial institutions in asset-backed securities markets (Robertson, 2011; Andersen *et al.*, 2012). Operational risk management (ORM) is a field of knowledge that emerged in the 1990s in a context of mounting losses associated with the misuse of IT-based access privileges and systems failures in the financial industry. As a direct consequence, the Basel Committee (2005: 140) on Banking Supervision began requiring financial institutions to implement arrangements for managing operational risk, which it defined as 'the risk of loss resulting from inadequate or failed internal processes, people, and systems or from external events'.

Although having a key role in mitigating some operational risks (Ciborra, 2006), IT also opens the door to new risks arising from both unintentional and malicious user behaviour. At the time of the 2007–2009 crisis, IT had been widely used in the form of computerized scoring models or automated underwriting systems in the mortgage industry for speeding up the processing of loan applications and avoiding the risk of subjective bias on the part of loan officers. However, as Andersen *et al.* (2012) point out, overconfidence in automated underwriting systems

---

and inappropriate use of scoring models ultimately led to increased operational risk for mortgage brokers and banks. As a result, a wave of failures first hit mortgage underwriters and then engulfed other actors in the mortgage securitization sector, such as investment banks, insurance companies and credit rating agencies. Alleged proximate causes included the digitalization of transactions, the growing interconnectivity and globalization of financial markets that allowed greater access to and trading in these securitized products (Robertson, 2011). The globalization of financial markets also meant that investors in securitized risks had less direct knowledge of the holders of debt. As investors rely on the risk assessment of financial institutions and credit agencies, it could be argued, from a risk management perspective, that the accumulated failures of financial institutions in managing operational risk resulted in a worldwide disaster for the industry.

In this research, we examine the process of implementing ORM in a financial institution before the credit crunch. As indicated earlier, some scholars have traced the causes of this financial crisis back to a collective failure to manage risks properly (Robertson, 2011; Andersen *et al.*, 2012). The financial institution chosen for our empirical case won an industry award for an ORM that helped it to manage the many risks that emerged during the crisis. Our main research objective is to examine and theorize how this particular ORM became institutionalized, that is, how practices become routine, while paying special attention to the role of IT. To achieve this end, we conducted an interpretive case study and adopted structuration theory (ST) as the analytical lens for examining how the organization decided which risk management approach to adopt and how to implement and evaluate it, while assessing the role of IT in this process. To address the research objective we formulate three theoretical propositions in the discussion section.

The paper is organized as follows. In the next section we review the contributions and challenges of the current literature on ORM. We follow this discussion with a summary of ST and how we apply it to interpret our case. After setting out the methodology, we present the narrative and interpretation of the case, exploring a number of themes using the underlying theoretical framework. We conclude by reflecting on the contributions, limitations, further research and implications of our research.

Background literature

The Basel Committee classifies operational risks into seven major types: (1) Internal Fraud; (2) External Fraud; (3) Employment Practices and

Workplace Safety; (4) Clients, Products and Business Practices; (5) Damage to Physical Assets; (6) Business Disruption and System Failures; and (7) Executive, Delivery and Process Management. As indicated earlier, IT is highly relevant to ORM, for example, shortcomings in access control systems can lead to internal and external fraud, while inadequate cyber-security can lead to system failures and virus outbreaks. In this study, we highlight the relationship between IT and ORM, and examine how organizations develop their managerial approach to addressing this risk. Accordingly, our literature review is structured in two parts: we concentrate first on the relevance of IT use and operational risk, and then we discuss two different approaches to ORM.

IT and operational risk

The rise of operational risk as a distinct field of knowledge is at least in part the outcome of heavy dependence on IT in the financial sector for the execution of transactions and the processing of authorizations (Power, 2005; Ciborra, 2006; Cummins and Embrechts, 2006). Sassen (2005), for example, explains that the combined power of sophisticated software and digital networks has vastly increased 'the number of transactions, the length of transaction chains (i.e., distance between instrument and underlying assets), and thereby the number of participants' (*ibid*: 19). This increasing reliance on IT has been accompanied by the growth in losses associated with the inappropriate or unintended use of IT-enabled privileges and with system failures. Examples of high-profile operational losses include the demise of Barings Bank as a result of failures in IT-enabled internal control, failures in incident recovery following the 9/11 attacks and the damage to IT infrastructure such as trading systems and networks, the system errors at the Tokyo Stock Exchange, and the huge losses at UBS in London resulting from ineffective internal fraud control. Nonetheless, Robertson (2011) contends that these operational risk incidents were mainly isolated and self-contained events, whereas the 2007–2009 financial crisis was the culmination of operational risk failures rooted in the extensive transaction chains of the digitized and globalized financial market. In other words, the financial crisis was a reflection of the risks implicit in complex financial products and the interconnectedness of the world's financial markets.

While the significance of operational risk has been acknowledged in the finance literature (Chavez-Demoulin *et al.*, 2006; Cummins *et al.*, 2006; Gillet *et al.*, 2010), Goldstein *et al.* (2011) argue that in the information system (IS) field, scant attention has been given to IT-related operational risk beyond discussing 'data-related' risks in the context of information security management. In particular, IS security research has focused on different risk management frameworks (Rainer *et al.*, 1991; Eloff, 1993; Bandyopadhyay, 1999; Karabacak, 2005; Baskerville, 2008; Mattord and Wiant, 2008), risk management as professional knowledge development (Baskerville, 1991a, b; Power, 2005), and on the risk management implementation process and its effectiveness (Straub, 1990; Straub and Nance, 1990; Dhillon and Backhouse, 1996; Straub and Welke, 1998). Concluding from their empirical investigation, Goldstein *et al.* (2011) stress the negative effects of IT-related operational risk events and call for empirical research aimed at understanding how financial organizations manage these different types of risks. Siponen and Willison (2007) find that there is a lack of theoretical development and empirical research in the field of security and risk management.

Research approaches to ORM

Another set of studies has examined the role of IT in supporting ORM. Researchers have identified other fields from which operational risk studies can draw inspiration: IS development (Ciborra, 2006), accounting control (Power, 2005) and information security management (Goldstein *et al.*, 2011). Much of the academic debate on ORM turns on the relative advantages and disadvantages of 'quantitative or hard' and 'qualitative or soft' approaches to data collection and risk measurement. Ciborra (2006) explains that the quantitative approach draws on the market risk discipline with a special focus on quantitative modelling and risk calculation, where the role of IT is especially valuable in collecting data and calculating risk for the purpose of deriving appropriate capital buffers to meet regulatory requirements. This approach is popular in the finance literature where studies examine techniques for estimating operational risk losses and for predicting risk distribution (Chavez-Demoulin *et al.*, 2006; Fontnouvelle *et al.*, 2006; Allen and Bali, 2007). Although this stream of research has value for estimating the capital requirement needed to comply with Basel II, a regulatory framework setting out the amount of capital that the banks must hold to cover operational risks, Ciborra (2006) argues that it disregards contextual elements important in risk definition, risk identification and the evaluation process.

In contrast, the qualitative approach considers the identification of risk drivers and focuses on behavioural aspects (Power, 2005). IT is considered both a tool for risk data collection, and also an enabler for implementing, controlling and monitoring ORM. For example, a database is useful in assisting managers to collect and organize historical loss data, and IT can be built in as part of the internal control mechanisms for the reporting and monitoring of operational risk events.

Overall, our assessment of the literature finds that while there is common agreement on the significance of ORM, studies on its adoption and institutionalization remain few and limited in scope. Setting aside financial analysis and modelling of operational risk events, we find that such ORM studies are primarily conceptual with little support from empirical research (Goodhart, 2001; Power, 2005; Ciborra, 2006). Research is required for: how organizations make sense of operational risk as well as how managers decide on which approach to take and what is the role of IT. We believe therefore that to address these issues, research needs to be broadened out beyond the present economic and finance tradition to include social and political approaches (Power, 2005), and that structuration theory (ST) offers a valuable analytical lens for explaining how ORM is developed in organizations. In the next section, we introduce the fundamental concepts of ST and discuss its relevance.

Theoretical framework

Since Giddens first began to develop ST (1976, 1979, 1981, 1984), a number of IS researchers have adopted it (Jones and Karsten, 2008), both as a meta-theory and as a theory to drive empirical research (Pozzebon and Pinsonneault, 2005). ST is unusual in that IS researchers have adopted it for both positivist research (Poole and DeSanctis, 2004) and interpretivist research (Orlikowski, 2000 and Walsham, 2002). As the theory is grounded in human action, it offers an appropriate framework for studying institutionalization and for understanding and how social practices subsequently decay and are replaced by new ones. It explains how practices, rules and norms are reproduced or institutionalized in an organizational setting.

We use ST for the analysis and description of ORM implementation and draw on its main constructs to analyse the phenomenon (Walsham, 1995). We have in this way selected a highly abstract theory in order to provide key conceptual guidance for an empirical study. The constructs of ST have been used to produce theoretical propositions arising directly from the specific phenomenon of ORM presented in the discussion section. Table 15.1 presents how we linked concepts, data and propositions. A core concept of ST maintains that social structures are both the product and medium of human action: the duality of structure. Structure consists of rules and resources while agency represents human action, capable of reinforcing norms and hence reproducing social

Table 15.1 Summary of findings and their relation to data and theory

ST concepts	Findings	Propositions
Social structure	• Regulatory context of Basel II • Business context of the importance of business continuity in the financial industry	**Proposition 1:** The regulatory context and technological development contribute to shaping the implementation of ORM in the financial sector
Modalities of structuration	• Facilities: the use of Excel as a tool at exploratory stage and the development of RCSA information system as a tool to embed the formal rule in the ORM policy • Interpretive schemes: aligning with the Basel II definition and gaining knowledge from the consulting firm to create common language of risk identification, mitigation and action plan • Norm: role and responsibility set out by the ORM policy, RCSA and action plan escalation procedures	**Proposition 2:** Implementing ORM is a process of reflexive monitoring and restructuring organizational practices in a financial institution **Proposition 3:** The role of IT in ORM is contingent on the extant organizational structure and on the choice of risk management approach
Reflexitivity and Restructuration	• Evolving understanding of the value of ORM programme via training and education programme • Evolving change in ORM programme via the self-reflexive monitoring promoted by the RCSA, for example, modification of risk categories and the transition from the excel to the RCSA information system • Expansion of ORM department and access to a greater organizational resources	**Proposition 2:** Implementing ORM is a process of reflexive monitoring and restructuring organizational practices in a financial institution **Proposition 3:** The role of IT in ORM is contingent on the extant organizational structure and on the choice of risk management approach

structures, but also of rejecting norms and hence transforming them. There are three dimensions of social structures: signification, domination and legitimation. Giddens (1984: 29) further identifies three associated modalities of structuration: *interpretive schemes, facility and norms*.

ST researchers argue that it is through structures and modalities that we can understand better how organizational practices are reinforced or transformed, and in our case these are instrumental for understanding the institutionalization of ORM. Indeed, although much of the research in the ORM literature has adopted a deterministic, economic approach in operational risk identification and assessment, Macintosh and Scapens (1990) argue that this positivistic perspective ignores social behaviour. Both Power (2005) and Ciborra (2006) stress the need to study the behavioural aspects of the risk management process, that is, the significance of human action. In the following paragraphs, we discuss each structure and its associated modality.

Signification structure relies on the modality of *interpretive schemes*, the cognitive schema that agents draw on to make sense of their activities in an organizational setting, thereby sustaining the signification structure in the organization. In the context of this study, members of an organization might not at first be able to understand the underlying meaning and definition of a number of elements in the ORM framework, such as the meaning of technology risk or business continuity risk. Furthermore, a managerial choice in favour of either a quantitative or a qualitative approach affects the meaning of the risk evaluation, understood as a precise monetary amount or as a value in a Likert scale (Baskerville, 2008). Thus, managers may create a mechanism to support the process of establishing, creating and communicating definitions, rules and policies, and by this means the signification structure is produced and reproduced through users reviewing and resetting many of their previous assumptions and beliefs: the use of such interpretation and shared knowledge sustains the signification structure in the organization.

The domination structure involves the exercise of power by controlling authoritative resources that arise from the control over the coordination of human actions, or allocation resources, which arise from the command over material artefacts (e.g., tools or databases) or other properties (e.g., operational procedures) in the environment. In an organizational context, the reporting structure can be understood as the form of power in the domination structure. In the process of distributing resources, the domination structure is drawn on and thereby reproduced during such deployments of resources. The powerful stakeholders can demonstrate their power through possession of, and allocation rights, over organizational knowledge and technologies. In this study, we hold the view of Orlikowski (2000) whose practice lens sees technology as part of the facility modality that mediates between action and structure.

The legitimation structure is concerned with social rules and there are important distinctions between informal and formal norms and the different levels of sanction associated with them (Giddens, 1984). Human agents can define what is allowed in a particular context and in so doing they reiterate the social structure of legitimation. In other words, the legitimation structure offers rules and moral conduct for agents to draw on when decisions are being made about whether to approve or disapprove of their actions in a social setting. It validates organizational obligations and norms, and makes agents accountable for their actions (Macintosh and Scapens, 1991). In addition, there are informal norms that form no part of any explicit policy but nevertheless are observed by the workforce. Informal norms abound in any social environment, even in the most highly regimented, and the case study organization was no exception. Informal norms are valuable because they provide employees with useful *modus operandi* in areas where there are no rules: they are important for establishing new conventions within emerging practice.

Formal and rule-based norms can be replaced by informal practices, which themselves in turn might be institutionalized and formalized over time. With both types of norms, formal and informal, there are two further issues that can be examined for their impact on practices and human action, namely, the level of sanction (high or low) and the certainty of sanction (certain or uncertain). In the case of ORM, formal norms are those that are issued as written policy and guidelines for behaviour, such as information policies. Examples can be found in the periodic meetings and production of reports for identifying and assessing the effectiveness of the controls put in place to manage risks, or the procedures for developing action plans to improve risk management practices. Policies might further state that the lack of compliance with these policies might lead to specific organizational sanctions. These particular issues have special resonance in recent IS risk and security literature, which has focused on the role of sanctions for achieving compliance with security policies (Boss *et al.*, 2009; D'Arcy and Herath, 2011).

Important features of ST and very pertinent to our research focus are the notions of agency and reflexivity. Reflexive monitoring refers to agents' knowledge and capability of monitoring their actions and the context of those actions (Giddens, 1984). As a result of such monitoring, agents transform the structures they produce by their actions. Monitoring figures is a core concept in risk management, which depends on continuous scrutiny of the risks and of the mitigants in place, whether technical, such as firewalls or intrusion detection systems, or managerial, such as security governance. Constantly reviewing their effectiveness provides organizational feedback and forms an essential part of the management of risk.

Taken all together, we consider that focusing on these structures and related modalities can help us to examine and conceptualize how ORM is institutionalized for the following reasons. First, a structurational perspective allows us to examine how interpretation, negotiation and discussion among organizational members shape the development of ORM. Through the three structures and modalities we can analyse the changes in certain interpretive schemes (such as organizational knowledge of risk), certain facilities (such as resources to access ORM risk data) and certain norms (such as ORM policies). Second, ST supports our understanding of how organizational practices, rules and norms are reproduced and institutionalized. In the context of ORM, the concepts of reflexivity and transformation of structure provide us with an analytical lens to understand the evolving risk definitions, the modifications in ORM policy and the development of the IS for ORM in a financial organization.

Research approach

We consider the interpretive approach (Walsham, 1993) suitable for conducting our investigation because of its emphasis on meanings and signification (Taylor, 1971). In using ST in an empirical setting, we agree with Macintosh and Scapens (1990) who call for an interpretive approach, particularly one based on case studies. They reason that:

> it [structuration theory] permits the researcher to explore the issues in specific time-space locations and to develop theories in relation to particular contexts ... Case studies are particularly suitable for this type of research as they allow the researcher to adopt a holistic orientation. (p. 469)

We use ST for interpreting the case, applying it retrospectively in the tradition of Barley (1986), Lyytinen and Ngwenyama (1992) and Karsten (1995).

Site, unit of analysis and timeline

The focus of this study is to examine the initiative by TUTIS (a pseudonym) to implement an enterprise-wide ORM programme over a 5-year timeframe; the unit of analysis is at the organizational level. TUTIS, headquartered in Northeast United States with over 2000 employees, provides financial services, such as custody and asset servicing, for a variety of financial instruments. After the year 2000, the company underwent a series of consolidations and integration and now runs its business through subsidiaries or joint ventures in the United States and overseas. It came to our attention as the winner of an industry award for its ORM implementation.

One of the researchers became interested in its ORM initiative after attending a 1-week corporate training programme at TUTIS in July 2004. Between 2004 and 2007, the researcher tracked the process of implementation and then discussed the matter with senior executives, the ORM department, consultants and other members of the organization both during company visits and at industry conferences. In addition to the 1-week visit in 2004, the same researcher spent a month in 2005 and a further week in 2007 at TUTIS. The exchanges and observations made during these visits gave the researcher insight into the organizational culture and attitudes relevant to the ORM programme. In December 2007, a formal request for conducting this empirical study was submitted and approved.

Data collection and analysis

From 2004 one of the researchers began the process of data collection. The primary sources for this study comprise documents ranging from internal newsletters, internal memoranda, ORM policies, internal presentation materials, risk event data as well as the internal employee handbook (see Appendix).

The earlier observation notes and our chosen theoretical framework proved good foundations for soliciting particular documents and materials. Different materials in our collection often recorded the same event or development, hence multiple documentary sources helped enrich and validate our interpretations (Taylor, 1971). If the statements in documents seemed contradictory or unclear, we would: (1) revisit the observation notes; (2) ask for more documentary information; and (3) use e-mail-based and phone interviews. Using the hermeneutic circle (Klein and Myers, 1999), we repeated this procedure until we arrived at a plausible interpretation.

After our initial document and field notes analysis, at the end of 2007, we further conducted four e-mail interviews with the manager of the ORM department and, additionally, six phone interviews (taking around half an hour each) with staff from the ORM department and various business units within TUTIS. The interviews were mostly with staff who were involved at the early stage of the ORM programme, and hence were able to provide insights regarding the changes in the organizational structure dating back to the initial rollout. Their input was of great value in validating the interpretations derived from the documentary analysis.

The data analysis was carried out in the following steps. The first step was to organize the data in chronological order and classify different documentary information (e.g., memoranda, employee handbooks and organizational policies). The combination of documents, observation notes and interviews gave us an initial interpretation of the implementation programme and allowed us to pinpoint the major events associated with the structuring of ORM at TUTIS. The second step was to interpret data in accordance with the concepts of the theoretical framework (see Table 15.1). The analysis consisted, as indicated above, in finding instances in the case that corresponded to the main concepts of the theoretical framework. Once we had done this, we inductively articulated the propositions presented in the discussion section. The third step of validating our analysis was to check our initial interpretations with those we had interviewed. Whenever possible, we incorporated their feedback that enriched and strengthened the final analysis.

The case study

The case concerns the development and implementation at TUTIS of an ORM programme over a period of 5 years. Our narrative starts with the introduction of operational risk regulations from the Basel Committee that sets the scene for ORM implementation in our organization, described below in three stages. The section, 'TUTIS: Establishing the ORM structure', describes the managerial decisions in defining operational risk and implementing an early stage ORM programme. A subsequent section, 'Risk and Control Self Assessment' (RCSA), explains the process by which managers and organizational members collect, redefine and evaluate various forms of operational risks at TUTIS. Finally, 'RCSA Information System' focuses on the role of IT at the outset of RCSA, and the consequent decision to develop the RCSA IS.

Basel II and ORM

In 1974, a group of central banks formed the Basel Committee on Banking Supervision to coordinate prudential banking supervision issues. In 1988, the Basel Committee introduced an approach to determining minimum regulatory capital requirements, known as the Basel Capital Accord or Basel I, for market and credit risk. The objective was to ensure banks would have adequate capital to cushion the effect of unexpected losses.

From the mid-1990s onwards operational risks became more significant. The Basel Committee (2001) stated that:

> Development such as the use of more highly automated technology, the growth of e-commerce, large-scale mergers and acquisitions that test the viability of newly integrated systems ... the increased prevalence of outsourcing and the greater use of financing techniques that reduce credit and market risk, but that create increased operational risk.

Against this background in 2004, the Committee revised its capital adequacy framework and published the revised standards as the Basel II Accord, introducing a minimum capital requirement (Pillar 1) for operational risk, a supervisory review process (Pillar 2) and market discipline (Pillar 3) to support the Pillar 1 implementation. National supervisory authorities were advised to review and monitor compliance with the minimum capital requirement.

In calculating the operational risk capital requirement for TUTIS, the most challenging task was to establish a mechanism for collecting and analysing historical internal loss data for the many possible operational risk events. These events ranged from business disruption and systems failures, internal fraud, execution delivery and process management across the various business lines. In accordance with the new regulations, many major financial institutions would embark on initiatives to establish ORM structures to identify, measure, monitor and control the institution-specific risks and to maintain an appropriate capital requirement.

TUTIS: establishing the ORM structure

TUTIS launched its own ORM function in the expectation that its US regulators would soon require alignment with the Basel II Accord. A senior executive commented on the relevance of IT and operational risk:

> One such change is the higher and more complex level of risk that now follows our business. Making certain that our systems can

continue to function even after some major disruption or catastrophic event has likewise become a great challenge.

The industry also faces increased criminal activity in the nations' cyber infrastructure with increasing assaults from viruses, phishing and similar online fraud.

With these two objectives, after the Basel Committee published a consultative document on the treatment of operational risk, TUTIS instituted in mid-2001 the organizational process to formalize and centralize the management of operational risk throughout the enterprise.

The ORM manager, with just two members of staff in the unit at first, was responsible to the Chief Risk Officer, who in turn reported to the Chair of the Board. As strategic governance, the company also established an ORM Steering Committee consisting of senior executives from the business lines, risk management and support functions.

The ORM department spent its first six months of existence gathering information, researching the Basel II accord and attending industry conferences. To secure even more expertise, an external consulting company was brought in. On completion of this first information-gathering exercise, the new team drew up a framework and multi-year business plan defining the risk categories, developing the risk assessment procedures, and establishing a company-wide risk database, as well as policies on how to communicate the new programme to employees.

Working with the external consultants, the ORM department set about the first stage by defining operational risk itself and the categories of risk:

the risk of loss, including reputational harm, resulting from inadequate or failed processes, people and systems, or from external events

By including reputation risk, 'the company's image in the industry, and with customers, the media and regulators', the bank effectively extended the Basel II definition. The major risk categories such as technology were identified and mapped to the Basel II 'risk buckets', along with a further 30 sub-risk categories. Within the technology category, for instance, the following sub-categories were determined: data integrity, security, hardware, software and communications equipment risk. These sub-categories and their respective definitions eventually formed the basis of a common risk language within the bank supporting analysis and reporting, as well as risk response, at both the corporate or individual line of business level.

To win support from the management of each division, in the roll-out phase presentations were given to the Internal Risk Management Committee and senior management. When asked in a phone interview about getting support, the ORM manager spoke of the bank's low risk tolerance culture:

> What really helped is the company culture. We have always been a highly controlled company, a lot of mitigants and expertises have already been built in the operations, BCP (business continuity planning) and technology. Thus, once the concept was explained to the executives as well as the fact that the regulatory communities began to talk about it, our senior management really set the tone at the top from day 1.

Risk and control self assessment

The RCSA is an important element in ORM, focusing especially on risk planning, risk assessment and evaluation. RCSA was one of the popular approaches developed for the financial sector for the purpose of risk identification and assessment of controls to mitigate risks. In order to ensure this approach could be implemented enterprise-wise, the ORM department decided before the rollout to pilot test the procedures. In an interview, the ORM manager commented on the reason for launching the RCSA so early in the ORM programme:

> We knew that there are pieces of puzzles needing to be put together. A lot of firms started with the collection of loss incidents. In our firm, because of the nature of the company, we did not have a lot of losses. So we did not think that was the best way to start. We decided to start with the RCSA component.

The decision not to start by collecting the quantitative data from operational loss incidents in effect led to the choice of a qualitative risk management approach. The ORM department considered selecting a qualitative approach because it allowed staff to concentrate on the identification and evaluation of operational risks and the counter-measures for managing them. At the same time as the pilot tests, there were other two major developments: the updating of the ORM policy and the publication of the guidelines. Both documents were distributed to all employees with the aim of enhancing employee awareness of operational risks and the policy for managing them.

As well as providing guidelines on the RCSA procedures to be adopted by the organization, the ORM policy set out the management reporting structure. The guidelines detailed the roles and responsibilities, risk category definitions and the action plan. The policy gave examples of risks, such as *authorized access to data is above what is necessary to execute responsibilities* or *inability to process transactions through normal channels due to unavailability of systems*. Most departments of TUTIS were expected to complete an RCSA at least annually, and their senior managers were obliged to review and approve the results.

In addition to the formal policy approach, the ORM department worked with Corporate Communications to develop employee education and awareness by more informal means. A special edition covering the ORM programme was published in the house magazine. It featured interviews with the Chairman and the ORM staff as well as a description of the entire RCSA process. A piece in the magazine reported on the learning that employees had gained from the pilot tests:

> I look at my job differently now, thinking about risk from a new perspective and questioning whether we have right controls in place. I also see that education can help reduce risk.

Another explained:

> This process helped us focus on risk more clearly and in a new way. By asking all the right questions, it enabled us to assess our issues and mitigants- and to make an informed decision about how we're managing risks.

An employee handbook on managing operational risk was distributed to all employees and the house magazine featured a story about this. As part of the campaign to improve awareness, Corporate Communications chose nine case studies arising from the RCSAs undertaken across the organization and compiled them into an internal publication distributed to all employees. The handbook featured business managers reporting on how the RCSAs had helped them to identify risks and the steps for mitigating them. For example, one story featured an assessment that had discovered errors in handling securities issues and as a result the department implemented an electronic processing system to reduce the possibility of errors and prevent financial loss for the company and customers. A senior manager reported:

> Without our risk management self-assessment, we would have gone through 'normal channels' to bring automation to our system (to reduce

errors inherent in manual processing), the fact that the automation effort was part of our RCSA action plan expedited the process.

Some of the key messages contained in the handbook were later used as themes for posters displayed throughout the organization. The senior manager of the Risk Management Division issued a circular to all employees about the displays.

As a result of the enterprise-wide RCSAs, the ORM department obtained feedback that was useful for updating its policies. Using the input from employees, ORM staff adjusted the RCSA templates adding two further sub-risk categories in the Business Continuity category. The names of some sub-risks were altered 'through the continuous loop-back improvement process' and 'to achieve a little more fine tuning'. In addition, to ensure a common and consistent understanding of the different operational risk categories, the risk definition document was updated in Years 4 and 5, changing some risk names and adding examples of where things could go wrong. For instance, examples added under the 'business continuity risk' category were the 'inability to recover data' and 'inadequate backup of important customer or corporate information'.

The bank realized it needed to maintain and monitor all the updates, the RCSA assessments and the implementation of action plans across all business units in the different subsidiaries. Consequently in Year 4 in each business unit TUTIS created posts to liaise with ORM department and thus have an important role in ensuring the continuity of the ORM programme. The senior manager of each department made appointments on the basis of the person's domain knowledge and leadership abilities. Once chosen, the appointees had to attend the regular orientation and training sessions about new developments in the ORM programme. The ORM manager underlined the benefits of this approach:

> The benefits of this initiative are not one-sided. The liaison role is viewed as a career development opportunity for employees. Managing directors are encouraged to include the role as an essential element of the coordinator's annual goals and development plans.

The main responsibility of the liaison post was to participate in the RCSAs in different roles. The person appointed had to work with at least one business unit with which he/she was closely associated, here having more involvement in the RCSA itself, but also with another unit acting mainly as facilitator. Several interviewees commented on how this initiative helped them to share knowledge at a higher level and one even saw it as a key operational risk mitigant:

> A knowledge-sharing culture ensures a broader, more solid base of knowledge, which makes us strong. If someone suddenly leaves their job, knowledge-sharing will mitigate that risk by ensuring someone else can quickly fill that person's shoes. At TUTIS, we put a high value on knowledge-sharing, and it shows.

RCSA information system

When conducting RCSAs, each business line had to document their identification and assessments of relevant risks, as well as the controls put in place to mitigate them. The initial documentation for the RCSAs was stored in Excel, Word and Access formats 'because there was no third-party software available in the market from a reliable and financially-sound vendor to house the information gathered from the RCSA process'. The ORM manager said that this technology was 'simple to use and allows us to work on risk categories and to collect risk information'. This method also allowed the ORM staff to modify the RCSA assessments on the basis of actual experience before committing to an IS. However, as the RCSAs proceeded and the amount of data grew, problems arose with the chosen software in retrieving and updating the risk information collected from the various business departments. At one point, the Excel spreadsheet contained close to 45,000 cells of data and ORM staff were also spending more and more time troubleshooting the Access database. None of the ORM staff was trained in Access. As two members from the ORM department recalled:

> Each time we uploaded data, we got more and more 'exceptions'. But nothing in Access identifies the particular problem that causes an exception. So the staff were literally tracking down extra spaces between words hoping to eliminate the errors and produce simple reports.

Moreover, because all the assessment data were recorded in Excel, Access and Word documents, before the submission of RCSA results, the manager and senior manager of each business unit had to review the paper copy to ensure the appropriateness of the action plan.

The inability of Excel and Access to support the management of operational risk data at TUTIS gradually became a significant issue, as revealed in the ORM department's own RCSA. Consequently, an action plan was launched to evaluate the two options of off-the-shelf products or those developed in-house. As it proved difficult to find a satisfactory off-the-shelf product to meet TUTIS's particular needs, the decision was made to go for an in-house system. The new system was expected to allow business users to update their assessment in real-time and generate reports in various formats. Thus, the development of this system was centred on a rule-based design incorporating most of the RCSA guidelines and the escalation notification procedures identified in the Chief Operating Officer's internal memo.

In a phone interview a business manager observed at the time that 'the system now drives the process'. The RCSA IS was seen to ensure efficiency and to enhance communications between business users and the ORM department. The senior manager of the technology development department explained the benefits of a rule-based system:

> As the RCSAs move through different stages, users know exactly what to do. Ensuring this was a big part of the design.

In December 2007, the RCSA IS was upgraded to allow authorized staff (i.e., ORM liaison persons, the ORM staff and managing directors of business units) to access it remotely, review risk data and action plans. The Chief Executive Officer underlined to us the company philosophy and leadership in managing risk:

> In 2006, we continued strengthening our highly sophisticated risk systems ... At the heart of our regulatory compliance programme is a commitment to employee awareness and personal responsibility, which is reinforced through training and ongoing communications.

In a phone interview, a business unit manager commented on how much the RCSA IS and the follow-up action plan had changed the routine in her business unit:

> RCSA is now more like DNA. We now look at our day to day processing, the risk assessment came into our mindset to make sure that we update our risk or include our mitigants. So yes, it has become a routine.

Case analysis

Using the three dimensions of social structures and modalities, our analysis breaks down the various elements of the whole ORM programme into its several parts. The introduction of the new procedures and systems into the organization to enable the RCSAs represented an attempt to restructure the bank into a risk-sensitive organization, which is able to spot the challenges of operational risk and to overcome them. To achieve this, the bank sought to integrate different modules of the ORM into routine bank practice. Each module, whether about planning for, identifying, analysing or responding to risk, was gradually written into the bank's rules and absorbed into practices over a period of 5 years. This path towards institutionalizing the ORM, whose analysis forms the core of our research objectives, is examined below using the structures and modalities of ST. We begin with interpretive schemes, then pass to facilities and finally norms.

Signification structure, interpretive schemes and ORM

The importance of interpretive schemes within the nascent ORM programme was made evident in several ways. In the early stages of the pilot test, the risk management vision still needed the support of experienced and well-disposed managers to sponsor the new development. We believe that this need also reflects the structure of domination insofar as power was critical at this early juncture to the growth of ORM. The fact of the high-level reporting line of the newly instituted ORM influenced attitudes throughout the bank and delivered a clear, unequivocal message of commitment from top management. The effectiveness of this may be apprehended by the case of the employee who spoke of seeing risk from a new perspective, and who saw education about managing operational risk as an important tool for reducing risk, indicative perhaps of how the interpretive schemes through which employees made sense of the new risk management systems and practices had been restructured.

The importance of signification can be seen in the development of a common language and semantic rules that were drawn on to create taxonomies and aid communication about risk. The definition and classification of operational risk from the Basel Committee was used as the foundation of the signification structure of ORM in the bank. The decision to engage individuals in the annual RCSAs facilitated the production and reproduction of the meanings of the many risk categories specifically in addressing the business context of risk at TUTIS. As such, the signification structure was continuously reconsidered by TUTIS and modified in a cyclical fashion.

We further saw the development of an IS to support the RCSAs. Given the fear of external regulatory sanctions for any non-compliance with

Basel II regulations, which reflected the structure of (external) domination, this development seemed normal but further research could investigate where the tipping point might be found in terms of sanction level and sanction certainty. To explain the success of the IS, we point to its enacted properties, that is, the sets of assumptions and beliefs drawn on in the adoption of the technology-based practices; the RCSA system would not function unless the beliefs and the practices of the organization had not themselves been restructured. Incidentally, there is a danger that the technology-based and formalized management of risk could become driven by form rather than substance – a matter of staff simply complying with rules and going through the motion – rather than having their risk 'antennae' fully alerted, and being fully risk aware.

This question of whether risk remains a conscious factor in the minds of employees or merely lies dormant in their consciousness is one that is touched on by the respondent cited above who, using the DNA metaphor, characterizes risk management as routine. Her observation epitomies the journey taken to institutionalize ORM, traversing from action to structure and back again until shaped as a routinized, formal process with technology surrounded by bureaucratic rules, yet built into the practices of the organization. As a result, we might say that senior management successfully modified the interpretive schemas of employees. The ability to rotate the risk liaison people also indicates success in institutionalizing the ORM programme, given that wider attitudes and beliefs had been adapted accordingly. Knowledge about the RCSA did not reside in just a few individuals but could be drawn upon and restructured repeatedly through different incumbents engaging with the new ORM systems and practices.

Domination structure, facility and ORM

As described in our theoretical framework section, the domination structure is concerned with the mediation through authoritative resources or allocative resources. In our case, we find that data collected from the RCSAs are important resources from the perspective of the domination structure. The allocative resources include such tools as the risk data collected, which then must be available and have to be managed, raising questions of access privilege (who can read, write, edit and delete which files/records). At the outset, each department could be considered as the powerful stakeholder as the knowledge and information of various operational risks is locally held. During the RCSAs, the ORM department began the process of collecting a wealth of data that both informs at a strategic level and supports local ORM functions. In so doing, the

ORM department began to gain power and become dominant in managing the overall ORM process. The iterative cycle of refining the categories of risk and the terminology between the ORM department and the other business departments at TUTIS can been viewed as a process of reflexive monitoring and transforming of the domination structure.

The institutionalization of ORM requires not just the database of risk events but also action plans, escalation procedures and the managing of various deadlines. As the ORM programme gradually bedded down, the RCSA system became the main repository of risk information within the bank. As the unique reference point for risk categories, for example, the RCSA system became the single authoritative taxonomy of risk within the bank. As a result, the visibility of the ORM department and its status within the bank rose sharply, consequently restructuring and reshaping the power hierarchy in the process: unsurprisingly ORM staff numbers increased in just a few years from 2 to 10 units with a concomitant increase in the resources commanded by the department. The modality of technology interacted with the modality of interpretive schemes here insofar as the definition and re-definition of the risk and sub-risk categories in the ORM programme engaged directly with user perceptions. Retuning the risk categories and adjusting their names altered how the risks were perceived, conceptualized and responded to.

From the perspective on technology of the structuration model, the RCSA IS can be interpreted as a means of enforcing the domination structure at TUTIS. First, the ORM department built the structures (such as escalation procedures and risk categories) within the technology. Upon its implementation, authorized staff such as liaison persons, ORM staff and managing directors of the bank divisions were authorized to access and review the risk data. In other words, the RCSA IS developed into a facility that these chosen staff could use to coordinate, monitor and control the operational risk activities of the bank. This iterative process hence reproduces, modifies and reinforces the ORM practices at TUTIS. In the context of the ORM, this system therefore became an authoritative resource within the bank to be implicated in the exercise of power.

Legitimation structure, norms and ORM

The legitimation structure arises in terms of the development and enforcement of formal and informal norms. The early stages of implementing the ORM are exploratory, with the stress on informality and open dialogue in order to involve as many employees as possible in the definition of risks, categories and the review of controls. The ORM department designed a strategy to provide the dominant values and norms through employee education and awareness programme. The publication of the special issue of the house magazine and the handbook strengthened the formal norms of conduct regarding the managing of operational risks. This strategy, which also served for eliciting requirements for the eventual technical system, was later followed by a gradual tightening up of the bureaucratic controls around the risk management process.

Formal norms were tightened noticeably in Year 4 when the Chief Operating Officer set out new rules and procedures. Sanctions were introduced for failing to perform RCSA exercises or to follow through on the changes that they necessitated in the action plan. The use of terminology such as 'escalation notification' marked the intention to raise the stakes and heralded the threat of a higher level of sanction for any non-compliance, echoing as mentioned above the recent literature on IS security compliance and the importance of level and certainty of sanction in achieving compliance. Many of the formal norms were deliberately inscribed into the ORM system itself, both with regard to the changes in procedures in Year 4 but also more generally as indicated by the remark that 'the system now drives the process'. Thus, the initial phases saw a 'loosening up' of the organization, in a creative mode, followed by a later gradual 'tightening up', where the transformations evidenced in the norms, interpretive schemes and ultimately in the technology bear witness to the reshaping of the organization.

Besides, through the design of employee education, RCSA sessions and IS, TUTIS undertook a restructuration process of ORM rules and procedures over the period of 5 years. Having set up the initial ORM structures, TUTIS routinely (and reflexively) monitored their performance and adjusted them accordingly, resulting in transformed structures. For example, the RCSA sessions allow the employees to describe risk data relevant to their daily work experiences. It helped reinforce the development of common understanding about operational risk across the organization. At the same time, it also contributed to the continuous refinement of risk classification and ORM policy at TUTIS.

Discussion

In this research, we investigated the institutionalization of ORM in a financial enterprise, examined the complex relationship between IT and operational risk and how an organization develops and refines structures that lead to successful implementation. We used ST to facilitate our understanding of how organizational members at TUTIS define, make sense of, and institutionalize ORM, paying particular attention to the role of IT in this process. In discussing the theoretical implications, we summarize our findings and their relation to data and theory, as depicted in Table 15.1, articulating three propositions derived from our findings and analysis. They are not formulations that attempt to predict how organizations behave, rather they are analytical generalizations (Lee and Baskerville, 2003), that is, generalizations aimed at contributing to the extant body of knowledge of IT and ORM.

> **Proposition 1:** The regulatory context and technological development contribute to shaping the implementation of ORM in the financial sector.

By concentrating on the notions of structure and agency action in risk management, our approach allowed us to gain a deeper understanding of how risk identification and assessment were conditioned by the regulatory initiative and by technological developments. This proposition highlights the influence of domination structures from the context. Moreover, our findings offer empirical evidence for the relationship between IT and operational risk suggested in the prior literature (Power, 2005; Ciborra, 2006). In this study, we find that the increasing reliance on IT for financial product development, transaction execution and processing brought to the attention of management the emerging importance of ORM.

Furthermore, our empirical study found evidence that the increasing complexity in the use of IT supporting business transactions also brought new risks that endanger organizational financial performance and reputation. Our proposition lends support to the notion that the adoption of IT to mitigate operational risk in turn paradoxically generates other forms of risks. Increasing risk emerged with electronic trading, with trades executed in real time. Not only was IT needed in respect of continuous electronic trading, but the regulators in any case insisted on its use for ORM in order to manage risks, identify insider trading and track other market abuse.

Hence, this study provides empirical evidence to show that an organization's practice is closely influenced by a wider external social structure, such as regulation and industry practices (Macintosh and Scapens, 1991). This is related not only to structures of domination, but also to structures of legitimation through what an organization sees as legitimate practices in other firms. This proposition is also linked to structures of signification as our case shows that the regulatory context of Basel II had a significant role in shaping management's understanding of the nature of operational risk by making it consider the internal definitions of such risks. The definition and guidelines published by the Basel Committee laid the foundation for TUTIS to acquire an early understanding of the nature and purpose of ORM and without this regulatory climate, it might have been difficult to force top management to commit meaningful resources in this area.

Proposition 2: Implementing ORM is a process of reflexive monitoring and restructuring of organizational practices in a financial institution.

One important premise in ST is that social structures and organizational practices are not static, but can be reproduced through the actions of the agents concerned. Agents are constantly and reflectively monitoring their own and others' actions and interactions, and searching for opportunities to change. Previous studies have stressed the need to incorporate both economic and objective perspectives as well as individual and subjective perspectives on organizational change and management processes (Macintosh and Scapens, 1990; Whittington, 1992; Jones *et al.*, 2000). Within the ORM literature discussed earlier, we also saw the debate between the dominant economic/quantitative approach and the alternative social/qualitative approach in identifying risk and deriving an appropriate capital charge (Ciborra, 2006). Nonetheless, as we pointed out in our literature review, there is a lack of empirical research into how an organization establishes which risk management approach to adopt and how to implement it.

In our case study, we show that the regulatory framework provided structure to the technical background and initial definition of operational risk, but through the workshops, users started to populate the risk data with detailed subjective interpretations derived from their experiences in their daily working environment. The manager of the ORM department began by focusing the RCSAs on detailed data collection about risk and its mitigants, that is, a qualitative risk management approach. This decision contrasted with common practice in other finance companies, which typically began with loss events for the purpose of quantification.

We found that the social interaction in the RCSA sessions and the internal publicity campaign enhanced the development of risk knowledge at TUTIS, and thus the reproduction of the signification structure surrounding the ORM programme. Proposition 2 conveys the structuration process in ST, in the sense of relating agency (the production of handbooks and magazine) with the reinforcement of norms (providing legitimacy to the ORM process). Moreover, we learnt that the employee education and awareness programme strengthened and reinforced the informal norms that employees draw on in terms of the legitimation structure. We realized that the participation and discussion outcomes emerging from the RCSA helped to refine procedures in the ORM policy, and thus the reproduction of the legitimation structure.

Our analysis of the domination structure also indicated that the creation of new roles and the assignment of responsibilities had a key part in exercising authority over other organizational members in institutionalizing ORM. We found that the employee awareness and policy reinforcement are particularly relevant in the context of the financial crisis. Robertson (2011) argues that in spite of the fact that subprime market participants already knew the operational risks associated with underwriting and property document evaluation, not enough attention was paid to the possible consequences. We contend that the institutionalization of an ORM programme can help banks, mortgage brokers and insurance companies to recognize and manage operational risks associated with various financial activities in the securitization market.

Goldstein *et al.* (2011) argues for more empirical research into the process of how a financial institution identifies, controls and monitors operational risks. We found that the development of an RCSA IS was an important step in the domination structure controlling the risk data and tools, and that the choice of risk management approach had to align with organizational work practices. Second, organizational members drew on the risk definition and evaluation of the Basel Committee for their early interpretations, but reflexive monitoring reshaped the risk definitions and assessments and ultimately reinforced them. Third, legitimation and domination have mainly concentrated on the use of sanctions to approve or disapprove of organizational practices. Indeed in our empirical case, the use of 'escalation notification' exemplifies the implementation of sanctions for enforcing compliance with ORM policy. However, we also find positive mechanisms for engendering compliance, such as its inclusion in the employee handbook and the creation of the new positions of ORM liaison. This could contribute to further study on the role of positive mechanisms or alternative managerial practices in risk management.

Proposition 3: The role of IT in ORM is contingent on the extant organizational structure and on the choice of risk management approach.

Our earlier review of approaches to managing operational risk referred to Ciborra's (2006) suggestion that the use and development of IT is contingent on the chosen approach. The empirical analysis for this study lent support to Ciborra's argument about the role of IT in a qualitative approach as a means of facilitating the collection of risk data and the implementation of monitoring mechanisms. In particular, the structural analysis in this study offers a rich description of the role of IT in the routinization of risk management practice. Technical capability was not the chief criterion for determining which technology to use, rather the choice was determined by how the organization designs its risk management programme. For example, the earlier approach of the ORM department had been to adopt a qualitative risk management approach focusing on building up the knowledge on which employees draw in respect of the signification structure. To facilitate this process, the ORM department manager considered Microsoft Excel and Access as the most suitable technologies at that time, because they were easy to use in the collection and modification of risk categories and data for RCSA. Thus, we believe that this structuration of technology and risks can be developed further to suggest that the success of risk management practice relies on the alignment between the IT strategy and the risk management strategy. As Orlikowski (2000) suggests:

> Through such a repeated interaction, certain of the technology's properties become implicated in an ongoing process of structuration. The resulting recurrent social practice produces and reproduces a particular structure of technology use. (p. 406)

Our analysis shows that the adoption of the Microsoft Excel database led to two organizational consequences for ORM. First, Excel became an allocation resource in the domination structure demonstrating the command of the ORM department over operational risk data within the organization. The Excel database was a valuable source on which the ORM department drew to refine risk categories at TUTIS. Second, our empirical findings illustrate how the use of IT in ORM could itself also generate unintended operational risks. As Microsoft Excel became appropriated by the ORM department, its use began to have unanticipated consequences arising from the growing amount of risk information being collected.

The development of the RCSA IS further illustrated how the use and development of IT aligns with the restructuration process of ORM. In our analysis of the social structures at TUTIS, we found that the

RCSA IS was the result of the routinization of signification, domination and legitimation structures, while at the same time it also served as the medium for these social structures. For instance, in the course of the RCSA the assumptions and beliefs surrounding the ORM programme were reshaped and restructured. Once this was done the development of the rule-based IS embodying the RCSA guidelines and escalation notification procedures could begin. Meanwhile, the appropriation of use by ORM department managers and liaison officers reinforced the significance of social structures in regulating and producing shared meaning for other organizational members.

Therefore, we see two theoretical implications with the respect to the role of IT. Our approach contributes an understanding of how IT becomes integrated into organizational practices. The process and temporal approach allows us to concentrate on the sequences of events and provide insightful analysis about how and why the process develops in certain direction (Mahring and Keil, 2008). Our case study demonstrates that the choice of technology was not determined by technological capability, but by the particular risk management approach that the organization decided to follow. Technology was first considered as the tool for risk data collection, but later was further developed to implement monitoring mechanisms. Moreover, our in-depth analysis of the interaction between IT and ORM offers theoretical insights into the appropriation of IT in the context of a qualitative risk management approach. Power (2005) argues that a qualitative approach to risk management focuses on behavioural aspects. Our findings reinforce this argument showing that the design and implementation of the RCSA IS facilitated the restructuration process of ORM. The rule-based system enabled the managers, and staff members, to coordinate and control the operational risk activities of the bank, such as the reporting procedures and escalation notification.

Limitations and further research

ST has been widely adopted and adapted by IS researchers in the last decade. One limitation of ST for this study has been in the lack of support from the theory about how to apply it. The problem is that ST as it stands does not support the analyst in how the constructs of signification, domination and legitimation should be applied to research data. Another limitation concerns the scope of this study. The essence of ST is that structuration is a continual process that describes how human agents condition and are conditioned by the structural properties of a social system: the stabilization of structure might be temporary and might be modified, altered and discarded at some time. In view of the need to limit scope, we confine ours to the cycle of structuration where the risk management practice is considered stabilized and institutionalized in the organization. Although we feel comfortable with the period of time that our study spanned, an area of future research would be to continue a longitudinal investigation to see how exogenous stimuli or reflexivity arise and lead to changes in the organization, and what role IT plays during this restructuration process. Furthermore, we acknowledge that ORM alone could not fully address the complexity of the financial crisis. There has been also a credit crisis related to the low confidence of investors and the withdrawal of their funds from the market, whereas this research attempts to shed light on just the ORM perspective. However, our empirical findings reveal how social interaction, employee participation and education can reinforce the development of the RCSA assessments and they highlight the organizational knowledge that is needed to manage financial risks better.

Conclusion

One of the motivations of this paper was to make a contribution to the under-researched but important area of the management of risk. We have contributed in two ways. First, we have provided an empirical piece that describes in detail the interplay of different organizational and contextual factors that contribute to the institutionalization of risk management. Our paper shows how regulation, business context and technology development combined to increase risk awareness and to achieve the eventual institutionalization of ORM in a financial organization. Second, our theoretical lens helps us to explain its gradual emergence and institutionalization. Our analysis illustrates how and why IT became the tangible core of risk management in the bank we studied. Finally, we have articulated three concrete theoretical propositions regarding the relationships among IT, risk management, organization structures and regulations. Although these propositions are not exhaustive, we believe they can serve as a starting point for conducting further research in this under-researched area.

References

Allen, L. and Bali, G. (2007). Cyclicality in Catastrophic and Operational Risk Measurements, *Journal of Banking & Finance* 31(4): 1191–1235.

Andersen, L., Hager, D., Maberg, S., Naess, M. and Tungland, M. (2012). The financial Crisis in an Operational Risk Management Context – A review of causes and influencing factors, *Reliability Engineering and System Safety* 105(5): 3–12.

Bandyopadhyay, K. (1999). A Framework for Integrated Risk Management in Information Technology, *Management Decision* 37(5): 437.

Barley, S.R. (1986). Technology as an Occasion for Structuring: Evidence from observations of CT scanners and the social order of radiology departments, *Administrative Science Quarterly* 31(1): 78–108.

Basel Committee on Banking Supervision (2001). Working Paper on the Regulatory Treatment of Operational Risk. Basel, Switzerland: Bank for International Settlement.

Basel Committee on Banking Supervision (2005). International Convergence of Capital Measurement and Capital Standards: A revised framework. Basel, Switzerland: Bank for International Settlements.

Baskerville, R. (1991a). Risk Analysis as a Source Of Professional Knowledge, *Computers & Security* 10(9): 749–764.

Baskerville, R. (1991b). Risk Analysis: An interpretive feasibility tool in justifying information systems security, *European Journal of Information Systems* 1(2): 121–130.

Baskerville, R. (2008). Strategic Information Security Risk Management, in D. Straub, S. Goodman and R. Baskerville (eds.) *Information Security Policies, Processes, and Practices*, Armonk, NY: M.E. Sharpe, pp. 112–122.

Boss, S., Kirsch, L., Angermeier, I., Shingler, R. and Boss, R. (2009). If Someone is Watching, I'll Do What I'm Asked: Manadatoriness, control, and information security, *European Journal of Information Systems* 18(2): 151–164.

Chavez-Demoulin, V., Embrechts, P. and Nešlehová, J. (2006). Quantitative Models for Operational Risk: Extremes, dependence and aggregation, *Journal of Banking & Finance* 30(10): 2635–2658.

Ciborra, C. (2006). Imbrication of Representations: Risk and digital technologies, *Journal of Management Studies* 43(6): 1339–1356.

Cummins, J.D. and Embrechts, P. (2006). Introduction: Special section on operational risk, *Journal of Banking & Finance* 30(10): 2599–2604.

Cummins, J., Lewis, C. and Wei, R. (2006). The Market Value Impact of Operational Loss Events for US Banks and Insurers, *Journal of Banking & Finance* 30(10): 2605–2634.

D'Arcy, J. and Herath, T. (2011). A Review and Analysis of Deterrence Theory in the is Security Literature: Making sense of the disparate findings, *European Journal of Information Systems* 20(6): 643–658.

Dhillon, G. and Backhouse, J. (1996). Risk in the Use of Information Technology within Organizations, *International Journal of Information Management* 16(1): 65–74.

Eloff, J. (1993). A Comparative Framework for Risk Analysis Methods, *Computers & Security* 12(6): 597–603.

Fontnouvelle, P., Dejesus-Rueff, V., Jordan, J. and Rosengren, E. (2006). Capital and Risk: New evidence on implications of large operational losses, *Journal of Money, Credit & Banking* 38(7): 1819–1846.

Giddens, A. (1976). *New Rules of Sociological Method: A Positive Critique of interpretative Sociologies*, London: Hutchinson.

Giddens, A. (1979). *Central Problems in Social Theory: Action, Structure and Contradiction in Social Analysis*, London: Palgrave Macmillan.

Giddens, A. (1981). *A Contemporary Critique of Historical Materialism*, London: Palgrave Macmillan.

Giddens, A. (1984). *The Constitution of Society*, Cambridge: Polity Press.

Gillet, R., Hubner, G. and Plunus, S. (2010). Operational Risk and Reputation in the Financial Industry, *Journal of Banking & Finance* 34(1): 224–235.

Goldstein, J., Chernobai, A. and Benaroch, M. (2011). An Event Study Analysis of the Economic Impact of IT Operational Risk and its Subscategories, *Journal of the Association for Information Systems* 12(9): 606–631.

Goodhart, C. (2001). Operational risk. *Financial Markets Group*, Special Paper 131, London: London School of Economics.

Jones, M. and Karsten, H. (2008). Review: Giddens's structuration theory and information systems research, *MIS Quarterly* 32(1): 127–157.

Jones, O., Edwards, T. and Beckinsale, M. (2000). Technology Management in a Mature Firm: Structuration theory and the innovation process, *Technology Analysis & Strategic Management* 12(2): 161–177.

Karabacak, B. (2005). ISRAM: Information security risk analysis method, *Computers & Security* 24(2): 147.

Karsten, H. (1995). Converging Paths to Notes: In search of computer-based information systems in a networked company, *Information Technology & People* 8(1): 7–34.

Klein, H. and Myers, M. (1999). A Set of Principles for Conducting and Evaluating Interpretive Field Studies in Information Systems, *MIS Quarterly* 23(1): 67–94.

Lee, A.S. and Baskerville, R. (2003). Generalizing Generalizability in Information Systems Research, *Information Systems Research* 14(3): 221–243.

Lyytinen, K.J. and Ngwenyama, O.K. (1992). What Does Computer Support for Cooperative Work Mean? A structurational analysis of computer supported cooperative work, *Accounting, Management and Information Technologies* 2(1): 19–37.

Macintosh, N. and Scapens, R. (1991). Management Accounting and Control Systems: A structuration theory analysis, *Journal of Management Accounting Research* 3(Fall): 131–158.

Macintosh, N.B. and Scapens, R. (1990). Structuration Theory in Management Accounting, *Accounting, Organizations and Society* 15(5): 455.

Mahring, M. and Keil, M. (2008). Information Technology Project Escalation: a process model, *Decision Science* 39(2): 239–272.

Mattord, H. and Wiant, T. (2008). Information System Risk Assessment and Documentation, in D. Straub, S. Goodman and R. Baskerville (eds.) *Information Security Policies, Processes, and Practices*, Armonk, NY: M.E. Sharpe, pp. 69–111.

Orlikowski, W. (2000). Using Technology and Constituting Structures: A practice lens for studying technology in organizations, *Organization Science* 11(4): 404–428.

Power, M. (2005). The Invention of Operational Risk, *Review of International Political Economy* 12(4): 577–599.

Poole, M. and DeSanctis, G. (2004). Structuration Theory in Information Systems Research: Methods and control, in M. Whitman and A. Woszcznski (eds.) *The Handbook of Information Systems Research*, Hershey, PA: Idea Group Publishing, pp. 206–249.

Pozzebon, M. and Pinsonneault, A. (2005). Challenges in Conducting Empirical Work Using Structuration Theory: Learning from IT research, *Organization Studies* 26(9): 1353–1376.

Rainer, J., Snyder, J. and Carr, H. (1991). Risk Analysis for Information Technology, *Journal of Management Information Systems* 8(1): 129.

Robertson, D. (2011). So that's Operational Risk. Office of the Comptroller of the Currency. Washington. OCC Economics Working Paper 2011–1, p. 52.

Sassen, S. (2005). The Embeddedness of Electronic Markets: The case of global capital markets, in K. Cetina and A. Preda (eds.) *The Sociology of Financial Markets,* Oxford: Oxford University Press, pp. 17–37.

Siponen, M. and Willison, R. (2007). A Critical Assessment of IS Security Research Between 1990–2004. 15th European Conference on Information Systems, St. Gallen, Switzerland.

Straub, D. (1990). Effective IS Security: An empirical study, *Information Systems Research* 1(3): 255–276.

Straub, D. and Nance, W. (1990). Discovering and Discipline Computer Abuse in Organizations: A field study, *MIS Quarterly* 14(1): 45–60.

Straub, D. and Welke, R.J. (1998). Coping with Systems Risk: Security planning models for management decision-making, *MIS Quarterly* 22(4): 441–469.

Taylor, C. (1971). Interpretation and the Sciences of Man, *Review of Metaphysics* 25(71): 3–51.

Walsham, G. (1993). *Interpreting Information Systems in Organizations,* Chichester: John Wiley & Sons.

Walsham, G. (1995). Interpretive Case Studies in IS Research: Nature and method, *European Journal of Information Systems* 4(2): 74–81.

Walsham, G. (2002). Cross-cultural Software Production and Use: A structurational analysis, *MIS Quarterly* 26(4): 359–380.

Whittington, R. (1992). Putting Giddens into Action: Social systems and managerial agency, *Journal of Management Studies* 29(6): 693–712.

Appendix

Table 15.A1 Documents and interviewees

Publication date	Document title/event	Document type
YEAR 1		
January	TUTIS–ORM initiative	Internal presentation slides
April	The magazine	Internal newsletter
November	Chairman speech	Public speech transcript
November	operational risk management policy	Management policy
YEAR 2		
January	Employee brochures	Staff handbook
January	The magazine	Internal newsletter

(*continued*)

Table 15.A1 Continued

Publication date	Document title/event	Document type
February	TUTIS Introduces new approach to managing operational risk	Newsletter for TUTIS customers
February	Business continuity planning	TUTIS report
May	Critical infrastructure protection in the financial services sector	Industry report
June	Managing risk and safeguarding TUTIS	Staff handbook
July	Presentation to an external financial institution	Internal presentation slides
September	How to rate inherent risk	Guidelines
September	Posters	Internal memorandum
September	Posters	Posters
YEAR 3		
January	The magazine	Internal newsletter
April	International business conference	External presentation slides
YEAR 4		
February	The magazine	Internal newsletter
March	Escalation procedures	Internal memorandum
June/July	The magazine	Internal newsletter
September	Operational risk management policy	Policy
September	RCSA guidelines	Guidelines
October	The magazine	Internal newsletter
October	Posters	Internal memorandum
YEAR 5		
March	ORM liaisons meeting	Internal presentation slides
June	Risk definition	Policy
June	Master initial RCSA default template	Assessment template
June	Master initial RCSA IT template	IT RCSA assessment
June	TUTIS annual report	Annual report
September	ORM liaisons meeting	Internal presentation slides
October	RCSA kickoff presentation	Internal presentation slides
October	International business forum	Internal presentation slides
November	ORM liaisons meeting	Internal presentation slides
November	ORM presentation to an external financial institution	External presentation slides

(*continued*)

Table 15.A1 Continued

Position	Role in ORM programme
Senior Manager, ORM department	Was involved as a user from business unit and later transferred to the ORM department to oversee the expansion and continuous development of the ORM programme at TUTIS
Senior Manager	Corporate information security reports to him. Is an approver of RCSA and a member of executive oversight committee, and has been involved in vetting technology scenarios in TUTIS major risk report
Manager, ORM department	Has been in charge of the design and implementation of the entire ORM programme since it started. Have participated in all RCSA pilot sessions. Act as the primary contact of this research project
Manager, business unit X	Has been actively involved on the business side with the TUTIS ORM programme for several years and was involved in two of internal ORM case studies
Senior Manager, business unit Y	Has been actively involved on the business side with the ORM programme for several years and is an ORM Coordinator and is involved in the Risk Incident Collection Pilot
Manager, business unit Z	Was involved in RCSA exercise and has been dealing with the technological risk at TUTIS

Section V
Action Research Approaches

16

A Critical Perspective on Action Research as a Method for Information Systems Research

Richard L. Baskerville[1] and A. Trevor Wood-Harper[2]
[1]*Copenhagen Business School, Denmark*
[2]*Information Research Centre, University of Salford, UK*

Introduction

The purpose of this paper is to review critically the origins, techniques and roles associated with a growing information systems (IS) research method known as 'action research'. This method is widely cited as an exemplar of a post-positivist social scientific research method, ideally suited to the study of technology in its human context. We seek to illuminate both the attractions and the detractions that this method holds for IS researchers.

The discipline of IS seems to be a very appropriate field for the use of action research methods. IS is a highly applied field, almost vocational in nature (Banville and Landry, 1989). Action research methods are highly clinical in nature, and place IS researchers in a 'helping-role' within the organizations that are being studied. (cf. Schein, 1987, p.11). It should not be surprising that action research is the 'touchstone of most good organizational development practice' and 'remains the primary methodology for the practice of organizational development' (Van Eynde and Bledsoe, 1990, p. 27). Action research merges research and praxis thus producing exceedingly relevant research findings. Such relevance is an important measure of the significance of IS research (Keen, 1991). However, the action research method has proved very unpopular with North American IS research. Action research articles in major

---

North American research publications are extremely rare. Orlikowski and Baroudi (1991) discovered only one action research article among the 155 major research publications between January 1983 and May 1988. Action research contributed only 0.6% of this research literature. Despite its overwhelming acceptance in organizational development, it is virtually non-existent among North American IS research.

Outside North America, action research has made more contributions to the literature of the IS research community. In particular, Checkland's soft systems methodology (Checkland, 1981; Checkland and Scholes, 1990) has influenced IS research by linking action research and systems development. This has increased the presence of action research in British, Scandinavian and Australian IS literature. However, action research is not a predominant IS research method even in those geographic areas. Given the conducive relationship between the vocational nature of the IS field and the clinical nature of action research, why is action research contributing so little to the IS research literature (particularly in North America)? Perhaps we are missing an understanding of the relationship between IS research domains and the features of action research.

This paper is organized as follows: first a philosophical viewpoint (is established) for the study. Following this introduction, the origins of the method are considered. The paper continues by briefly describing the method and then discussing its role in IS research. In conclusion the features of action research that present the IS researcher with problems and opportunities are clarified.

Critical reviewers have revealed serious doubts about the appropriateness of research into IS. Jarvenpaa *et al.* (1985) found that experimental IS research was lacking in task and measurement validity. Ives and Olson (1984) found that IS survey research suffered from poor instruments and lack of control. Baroudi and Orlikowski (1989) found a general lack of statistical power in IS research. Bembasat *et al.* (1987) noted that IS case study investigators had a history of ignoring methodological issues, and a failing to specify clear objectives. Cooper (1988) pointed to underlying problems in the natural sciences paradigm currently associated with IS research and suggested the adoption of methodological pluralism.

As the critical revelations of IS research problems continue, interest grows in alternative methods of discovery. No doubt interest will rise in post-positivist research methods such as grounded theory (Glaser and Straus, 1967), deconstruction (Rosenau, 1992) and action research. This latter method has a longer history and has attracted perhaps the largest following in certain geographic regions (such as

Northern Europe, England and Australia). Since the action research method involves the close collaboration of both researchers and practitioners, a thorough understanding of its techniques and implications may be essential to everyone in the field of IS during the final decade of the 1990s.

The philosophical issue

No accurate description of action research can avoid consideration of its philosophy. This is because its usage entails some assumptions about scientific knowledge that are not widely institutionalized. This is important for the scientists who apply the method, since some of their colleagues may earnestly question the findings on very fundamental grounds.

This difficulty is diminishing, however, as the field of IS enters a new stage in its maturity. Many scientists who have interests in the field are becoming more concerned with the social and psychological aspects of the introduction of technology into the human work place, rather than concentrating only on the technical aspects (Blackler, 1988). Some IS research is becoming more sophisticated (or perhaps esoteric) in its social science, and this is confronting IS scientists with the disparate philosophies of science that have haunted the social sciences for decades (Klein *et al*, 1991).

The present social scientific institutions are broadly based on the empirical tradition, and parallel the current philosophy of the natural sciences. In this, IS science is not an exception. The IS foundations in computer science and engineering imply an appreciation of mathematics and physics. Scientists can conduct research on this basis and be assured that the findings will be accepted by the widest majority of their colleagues. This means that IS research scientists presently can contribute meaningful research without understanding or participating in the philosophical turmoil at the sociological periphery of IS science.

These alternative philosophies endorse research methods that may not appear to be scientific to the scientist schooled only in the statistical tradition of Pearson, the nomothetic logical positivism of Hempel or the falsifiability of Popper (cf. Hirschheim, 1985). The consequences of this limited perspective are threefold: dismiss the findings of such methods as unscientific, accept such findings on good faith or the reputation of the author, or lodge a considerable investment in grappling with the philosophical literature. The latter course is not a short side trip for the busy scientist; it also will not be a totally happy experience. The threatening discovery that some views of science discredit the findings of traditional methods is reached quickly (commonly called 'positivist-bashing'). The more recent post-modern views of social science have altogether dismissed the idea of grand unifying scientific paradigms as an impedance (Rosenau, 1992).

Action research is a method that could be described as a paragon of the post-positivist research methods. It is empirical, yet interpretive. It is experimental, yet multivariate. It is observational, yet interventionist. Enticingly, the research subjects are often quite willing to pay the costs of being studied, especially since they may influence the outcomes of the project. To an arch positivist it should seem very unscientific. To the post-positivist, it seems ideal.

Origins of action research

The action research method developed when the calamities of World War II precipitated massive social changes in the research arena of the social sciences. Lewin (1951) is credited with developing the method at the Research Centre for Group Dynamics (University of Michigan) in order to study social psychology within the framework of field theory. However, another group working independently at the Tavistock Clinic (later the Tavistock Institute) developed a similar method as a sort of psychosocial equivalent of operational research (Trist, 1976).

The Tavistock Institute dealt with psychological and social disorders caused by battlefields and prisoner-of-war camps. Previous to this war, these psychological syndromes had not been identified in such a large population of patients. Scientists did not understand enough about the complex causes of such social illnesses to formulate confidence in any universal treatments. Each case appeared somehow 'different'. Hence, the idea of social action arose. Scientists intervened in each experimental case by changing some aspect of the patients' being or surroundings. Since scientist and therapist were one, the scientists were participants in their own research. The effects of the actions were recorded and studied. In this manner, a body of knowledge was developed about successful therapy for the illnesses (cf. Rapoport, 1970).

Lewin's work (1951) sought a general theory of how social change could be facilitated. His original model of action research included iteration of six phased stages, rather than the five now commonly assumed. The six stages were (1) analysis, (2) fact-finding, (3) conceptualization, (4) planning, (5) implementation of action, and (6) evaluation. While the level of abstraction is slightly different, the essential method is very similar to the later version described below.

Action research has been linked closely to systems theory from its inception, although Susman and Evered (1978) (and later Susman, 1983) made the most seminal connections. These ideas recognize that human activities are systematic, and that action researchers are intervening in social systems. Warmington (1980) explicitly described the implications of action research for the field of systems analysis.

At Lancaster University, Checkland's (1981) extensive use of action research in the methodology of systems development is a landmark for the technique in IS research. Checkland's view of human activity systems drew considerable IS attention to action research. Checkland not only used the approach extensively in developing the soft systems methodology, but action research concepts for gaining professional knowledge permeated the soft systems approach itself.

Despite the attention currently focused on action research in the IS research community, we must recognize that the technique never succeeded in procuring strong status in the main stream of social psychology or social science research (Sanford, 1976). Outside IS, widely published action research arises mostly in applied health fields, (e.g. Jowett, 1988; Israel *et al.*, 1989; Webb, 1989) and management research (e.g. Lukka, 1987). It seems to have been forced to the periphery of legitimate scientific methodologies today, perhaps because its postpositivist foundations frequently bring epistemological contention into the discussions of the research findings.

Clark (1972) cast action research as a methodological 'orphan' in post-World War II science. He attributed the failure of action research to 'get off the ground' in the 1950s and 1960s to the funding structure of social science research. He reasoned that research was being increasingly sponsored by public money. In response, leading researchers tended to seek projects that relied on 'hard' quantitative data: projects that sported the computer analysis that attracted government attention. This post-war emphasis on 'professionalism' and precise data collection methods led to a general decline in qualitative research skills.

Another factor is the relationship between action research and consulting. This should not be surprising, since the main stream of consulting literature can be traced back through Lippit and Lippit (1978) to Schein's *Process Consultation* (1969). Schein based process consultation on Lewin's action cycle and Gordon Lippit was Lewin's PhD student. The consulting literature and action research literature emerged among separate streams of thought from Lewin, and rarely reference each other. Still, observers may easily confuse these two intellectual cousins, requiring action researchers to defend their method against the challenge that 'this is nothing but consultancy!' (Jönsson, 1991, p. 393).

We see that IS research scientists considering the adoption of the action research method must recognize its tenuous stature as a scientific method. This is not a main stream social science technique being applied in the new field of IS. Rather it is an obscure, contentious method found on the periphery of main stream social science being transported into the IS field. Perhaps, as its proponents imply, this is the field within which it will finally flourish. However, it may alternatively continue to dwell on the periphery of IS research as it has in other branches of social science.

Description of the method

Action research is an interventionist approach to the acquisition of scientific knowledge that has sound foundations in the post-positivist tradition. Blum (1955) explained the essence of action research as a simple two stage process. First, the diagnostic stage involves a collaborative analysis of the social situation by the researcher and the subjects of the research. Hypotheses are formulated concerning the nature of the research domain. Second, the therapeutic stage involves collaborative change experiments. In this stage changes are introduced and the effects are studied.

However, in order to achieve scientific rigor, additional structure is usually imposed on action research. The most prevalent description (Susman and Evered, 1978) details a five phase, cyclical process which can be described as an 'ideal' exemplar of the original formulation of action research. In practice such methods often vary depending on the application. This ideal approach first requires the establishment of a client-system infrastructure or research environment. Then, five identifiable phases are iterated: (1) diagnosing (2) action planning, (3) action taking, (4) evaluating and (5) specifying learning. Figure 16.1 shows this action research structural cycle.

The client–system infrastructure is the specification and agreement that constitutes the research environment. It provides the authority, or sanctions, under which the researchers and host practitioners may specify actions and provides the legitimation of those actions as beneficial to the client or host organization. Considerations include the boundaries of the research domain, and the entry and exit of the scientists. It must also patently recognize the latitude of the researchers to disseminate the learning gained in the research. This infrastructure must define

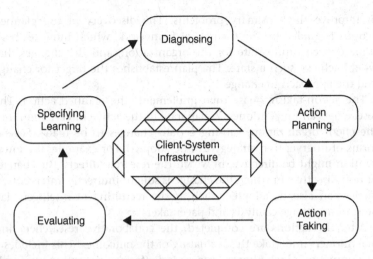

Figure 16.1 The action research cycle (Susman, 1983)

the responsibilities of the client and the researchers to each other. For example, the infrastructure will probably assume that the researchers will not purposely specify actions that are harmful to the organization.

A key aspect of the infrastructure is the collaborative nature of the undertaking. The research scientists work closely with practitioners located within the client-system. These individuals provide the subject system knowledge and insight necessary to understand the anomalies being studied. Clark described these practitioners:

> For convenience it is useful to think of the practitioner as part of a set of actors who are oriented to solution of practical problems, who are essentially organizational scientists rather than academic scientists (Clark, 1972, p. 65).

Diagnosing corresponds to the identification of the primary problems that are the underlying causes of the organization's desire for change. This involves self-interpretation of the complex organizational problem, not through reduction and simplification, but rather in a holistic fashion. This diagnosis will develop certain theoretical assumptions (i.e. a working hypothesis) about the nature of the organization and its problem domain.

Researchers and practitioners then collaborate in the next activity, action planning. This specifies organizational actions that should relieve or improve these primary problems. The discovery of the planned actions is guided by the theoretical framework, which indicates both some desired future state for the organization, and the changes that would achieve such a state. The plan establishes the target for change and the approach to change.

The action-taking phase then implements the planned action. The researchers and practitioners collaborate in the active intervention into the client organization, causing certain changes to be made. Several forms of intervention strategy can be adopted. For example, the intervention might be directive, in which the research 'directs' the change, or non-directive, in which the change is sought indirectly. Intervention tactics can also be adopted, such as the recruiting of intelligent lay persons as change catalysts and pacemakers.

After the actions are completed, the collaborative researchers and practitioners undertake the evaluating of the outcomes. This includes a determination of whether the theoretical effects of the action were realized, and whether these effects relieved the problems. Where the change is successful, the evaluation must critically question whether the undertaken action, among the myriad routine and non-routine organizational actions, was the sole cause of success. Where the change is unsuccessful, some framework for the next iteration of the action research cycle (including the adjustment of the hypotheses) should be established.

While the activity of specifying learning is formally undertaken last, it is usually an ongoing process. the knowledge gained in the action research (whether the action was successful or unsuccessful) can be directed to three audiences. First, what Argyris and Schön (1978) called 'double-loop learning', the restructuring of organizational norms to reflect the new knowledge gained by the organization during the research. Second, where the change was unsuccessful, the additional knowledge may provide foundations for diagnosing in preparation for further action research intervention. Finally, the success or failure of the theoretical framework will provide important knowledge to the scientific community faced with future research settings.

The action research cycle can continue, whether the action proved successful or not, to develop further knowledge about the organization and the validity of relevant theoretical assumptions. As a result of the studies, the organization thus learns more about its nature and environment, and the constellation of theoretical elements of the scientific community continues to benefit and evolve.

Hult and Lennung (1980) summarized this process with their meticulously developed definition of action research:

Action research simultaneously assists in practical problem-solving and expands scientific knowledge, as well as enhancing the competencies of the respective actors, being performed collaboratively in an immediate situation using data feed back in a cyclical process aiming at an increased understanding of a given social situation, primarily applicable for the understanding of change processes in social systems and undertaken within a mutually acceptable ethical framework.

Action research therefore attempts to link theory and practice, thinking and doing, achieving both practical and research objectives (Susman, 1983). The gaining of knowledge is seen as an active process, such that our beliefs are redefined in the light of the outcomes. A means for dealing with reality is more desirable than a representation of reality. Action research is a pragmatic approach which desires to 'come to terms' with the world.

Role of the method

Like any research method, action research is most valid within a domain of ideal research questions. Some research questions can be more effectively answered by other methods. Some research questions cannot be effectively answered by any other method. This section begins with the features of the known domain of ideal research questions within the IS field. Following this the features of this method that present the researcher with problems or opportunities are explored.

Domain of ideal use

The type of learning created by action research represents enhanced understanding of a complex problem. The researcher obtains information about a particular situation and a particular environment. This then, gives a contingent value to the truth learned. The researcher expects, however, to generate knowledge which will further enhance the development of models and theories. The aim is the understanding of the complex human process rather than a universal prescriptive truth.

Also, the mutually accepted ethical framework discussed above may cause some concerns. If the goals of the researcher and client differ drastically there is tension. The researcher has lost sight of the fact that he is to be of value to those whom he researches. Therefore, parties must negotiate their goals. Some method for satisfying all of their goals must be found (Warmington, 1980).

Finally, in the process of learning, an explicit, clear conceptual framework must exist which the researcher imposes on the situation. This must be acceptable to the researcher and the organizational actors in the action research study (Warmington, 1980). This is needed so that the explicit lessons will emerge from the research cycle.

The ideal domain of the action research method is therefore revealed in three distinctive characteristics of the method:

1. The researcher is actively involved, with expected benefit for both researcher and organization.
2. The knowledge obtained can be immediately applied. There is not the sense of the detached observer, but that of an active participant wishing to utilize any new knowledge based on an explicit, clear conceptual framework.
3. The research is a cyclical process linking theory and practice.

Checkland (1985) based the intellectual context on a simple model of the elements of any piece of research (see Figure 16.2). He referred to this as the 'organized use of rational thought'. The essential elements of this model are F, an intellectual framework of linked ideas – a theory; M, a methodology for using this framework; and A the area of application – research question. The ideal domain of a research method is one where M provides the richest scientific knowledge about F in the context of A. Considering action research within this model, Figure 16.3 depicts how

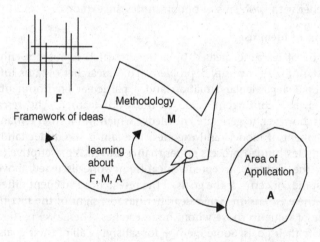

Figure 16.2   Organized use of rational thought (Checkland, 1985)

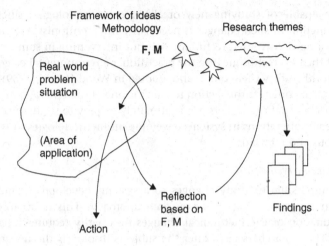

Figure 16.3 Cycle of action research (Checkland, 1991)

this method cycles the research themes of *F* and *M* through *A* to generate reflection, action and ultimately scientific findings (Checkland, 1991). From Checkland's perspective, action research is a cycle of continuous inquiry where theory interacts with practice. This continuous interaction of theory and practice is the major characteristic of the ideal domain of the action research method.

To claim that theory and practice interact where research is most closely focused on the techniques and principles of a vocation is tautological. Yet, if the field of study in IS is 'vocational in character', as Banville and Landry (1989, p. 58) suggest, then the ideal domain of action research (as characterized above) includes the very broadest range of IS research questions.

Within this domain, we can further identify at least one area of research which may be outside its ideal of the more common approaches. This area deals with new or changed systems development methodologies. Galliers and Land (1987) identified six general application areas in IS research: society, organization, small group, individuals, technology and methodology. They found that, out of the available research methods, mathematical modelling and laboratory experiments were inappropriate for research into methodologies. The complex, multivariate settings of systems development methodologies inevitably opens a validity question for any method that assumes abstracted causality. Case studies, under the characteristic constraint of non-intervention (Jenkins, 1985) are incapable of studying new or changed methodologies, since the introduction of such changes is necessarily interventionist. We cannot study a newly invented technique without intervening in some way to inject the new technique into the practitioner environment, i.e. 'go into the world and try them out' (Land, quoted in Wood-Harper, 1989). This leads us to conclude that action research is one of the few valid research approaches that researchers can legitimately employ to study the effects of specific alterations in systems development methodologies. It is both rigorous and relevant.

Rigorous intervention.

It is impossible to study changes to a systems development method within a rigorous case study research approach. This is because the introduction of the methodical changes necessarily requires intervention. The researchers must alter the subjects insofar as the researchers must suggest the changes in method and provide training or training materials, *i.e.* the method as a structure for behaviour must be changed in the research subject domain.

Relevance

Alternative research methods (to action research) must struggle to maintain relevance to the real world. Laboratory experiments and statistical models are necessarily abstracted from the richly multivariate circumstances in the real world. The empirics of action research require that it takes place fully within such multivariate real-world environments. Relevance is less of a problem.

The relevance of action research to systems development methodology has not been forcefully stated in the past. We suggest that action research, as a research method in the study of human methods, is the most scientifically legitimate approach available. Indeed, where a specific new methodology or an improvement to a methodologies is being studied, the action research method may be the only relevant research method presently available.

Problems and opportunities

Researchers who wish to apply action research will have several problems of concern. However these problems are more likely to be general difficulties with research in social science rather than problems peculiar to action research. For example:

1. The lack of impartiality of the researcher has led to rejection of the action research method by a number of researchers. However this is

not necessarily a problem singular to the action research method. It is rooted in the philosophical supremacy of the researchers. Philosophical supremacy refers to the refusal of scientists to accept any knowledge founded in any alternative philosophy of science other than their own (Baskerville, 1991). The same problem would confront a researcher who chooses to study new methods using opinion questionnaire survey methods. The lack of relevance would lead to the rejection of this knowledge by a number of researchers.

2. Some of the action research offered to the scientific community lacks rigor. This makes it difficult for the work to be assessed for the award of research degrees and for publication in academic journals. It also undermines credibility of the method with research funding agencies. [Unfortunately the lack of scientific discipline may be due – to a lack of scientific discipline.] Here we distinguish rigorous action research from liberal action research. Rigor relates to fitting the research methods to the problem in order to produce valid scientific explanations, and the use of multiple methods to produce valid research constructs (Straub, 1991). Liberal action research results when the researchers become so involved in the immediate practical effects of the research they neglect the scientific discipline. This loss can be a natural consequence of the researchers' concern for their subjects. Rapoport (1970) recognized this as the goal dilemma of action research. On the contrary, rigorous action research clings tenaciously to its disciplined constructs of cyclical theoretical infrastructure, data collection and evaluation: there is a clear cycle of activity; there is a premise; a pronounced theory (under test); there is empirical data collection (e.g. diaries). We note that the lack of scientific discipline is a reasonable complaint about liberal action research, but we also recognize there are similar complaints about other research methods (e.g. survey methods, cf. Baroudi and Orlikowski, 1989).

3. Action research is sometimes branded as 'consulting masquerading as research'. The historical reasons for this were discussed earlier. At least four factors clear differentiate action research and consulting (cf. Gummesson, 1988): (i) researchers require more rigorous documentary records than consultants; (ii) researchers require theoretical justifications and consultants require empirical justifications (iii) consultants operate under tighter time and budget constraints; (iv) the consultation is usually linear – engage, analyze, action, disengage – while the action research process is cyclical. These differentiations are not widely known and even seasoned action researchers sometimes have trouble delineating action research from consulting (Jönsson, 1991). Rapoport called this the role dilemma of action research.

Perhaps this too arises from sloppy action research, action research that loses its scientific threat and finally converts entirely into consulting. The researcher using this method often must remain particularly strong and loyal to their research rigor, since client interests tend to subjugate scientific necessities (Seashore, 1976).
4. Action research is context-bound, and not context-free. Therefore it is difficult to determine the cause of a particular effect that could be due to the environment, researcher or methodology. This means that action research produces narrow learning in its context because each situation is unique and cannot be repeated. Certainly action research is more deeply engulfed in any multivariate social experimental approach. But this is the nature of an idio-graphic method. It still has an underlying theory that is tested and either falsified or sustained. Because the theory arises from particular needs, action research is a fine theory discovery method. This is a very important characteristic of action research, since the theoretical progress of IS research is alarmingly slow (Alavi *et al.*, 1989). Like other scientific methods, further testing and even cross-method triangulation must generalize by confirming or falsifying any causal links suggested by action research theories. In this regard an action research study is no less effective and credible than most cross-sectional statistical survey methods.

These problems are actually general problems of social science research. In reality action research shares these problems with the other methods. Perhaps the distinguishing difficulties with action research are those of degree rather than taxonomy. Rapoport (1970) identified three dilemmas in action research: ethics – personal over-involvement with the research, goals – the two taskmasters in social research (subject and science) and initiatives – the practical pressures that interfere with the conduct of 'a disinterested pursuit of knowledge'. Scientists who employ other methods, even survey research, also know these three dilemmas. These are not peculiar to action research.

These dilemmas are much stronger in action research projects. Perhaps many, if not most, action researchers are trapped by these pitfalls. When they attempt to present their findings, the shortcomings of the projects are rightly discovered. If this is the case, then the difficulty with action research is not one of poor understanding of the method by those who review the research, but poor understanding of the method by those who conduct the research. The solution is better training for action researchers. Such training will help prepare action researchers for negotiating the dilemmas.

Characteristic strategies

In the preceding paragraphs, action research is shown to be no less credible as a social science research method than any of its alternatives. The action researcher, however, faces more challenges in maintaining rigour in the research. The social science research community has entertained enough liberal action research to confuse reviewers and examiners about the exact characteristics of proper action research. In this section some characteristic strategies are offered for researchers who demand scientific rigour while conducting action research. These quality guidelines will also be useful to those who must examine action research for graduate degrees, and those who must review action research for publications or grants.

Consideration for the paradigm shift

Action research does not occur in the traditional positivist philosophy of science and has its own domain of ideal research questions. Is action research appropriate for the question (e.g. immediately relevant methodology or theory-formulation)? Also, who composes the main body of scientists concerned with this research question? If this body chiefly contains scientists whose reference disciplines do not recognize methodological pluralism, then the action researchers must substantiate carefully the interpretive scientific foundations of their project in order to achieve credibility. Without credibility, the research will not spawn future follow-up work.

Establishment of a formal research agreement

The ethics of human subjects research discourage research without the 'informed consent' of the subject. This implies that conducting action research under the disguise of consulting would be unethical. Further, clients may welcome the research content of action research – pleased to learn that their problems are worthy of scientific interest. They may fund peripheral costs of the research such as data compilation and preparation of working papers. Further, the client may wish to review publications for public relations purposes. In return, the researcher may charge no fee, or discount consulting fees in return for an action research agreement.

The consent and disclosure agreement is only part of the client–system infrastructure. The researcher should prepare the subjects for the 'warrants' that will authorize the research team to initiate action within the organization. Researchers should clearly brief subjects concerning the experimental nature of the action-taking and the iterative nature of the learning cycle.

Provision of a theoretical problem statement

One of the most important differences between the diagnosis stage of an action research project and the advice stage of a consulting project is the careful theoretical foundation of diagnoses. The theoretical foundation must be present as a premise if the experiment (the intervention action) is to remain valid as research. Therefore the diagnosis document should include a scholarly statement of the theoretical underpinnings of the diagnosis. Understandably, iterations of the research cycle may lead to learning that adjusts the theory to keep it consistent with the observations. The mutations of this theory should be recorded carefully in the research notebooks.

Planned measurement methods

Action research is certainly empirical, although the collected data may be very unstructured. Rigorous action researchers plan methodical data collection methods. This is critical for credibility since it is ultimately impossible for the researchers to sustain claims of validity in their data analysis if the data cannot be produced for examination.

Argyris *et al.* (1985, p. 239) viewed 'Talk as data: a window onto the logic of action'. They suggested a range of reliable data collection techniques such as audiotaped observations, interviews, action experiments and participant-written cases. Action experiments entailed discussions with subjects 'on the spot' during action taking, while participant-written cases were the written recollections of the subject following action taking.

Outside the context of action research, Naur (1983) suggested the use of diaries as research data collections. Researchers may collect data by keeping diaries – and requiring their subjects to keep diaries. Teams can keep group diaries to reduce the volume and subjectivity of the data. Such diary activity alone is a serious intervention since there is evidence that diary-keeping can improve the management of IS development projects (Jepsen *et al.*, 1989). Formal, detailed diaries pose serious difficulties for data analysis, considering the volume and unstructured nature of the data. The researchers can impose some organized structure to the diaries that will aid in data analysis.

Data validity is a problem with these techniques, partially because of the interpretive nature of the data but also because of the intersubjectivity of data capture. The researchers inevitably influence their subjects and vice-versa. The presence of a disassociated 'watcher' a monitor, may improve validity somewhat. The monitor is an independent, knowledgeable individual who seeks to validate the research. The monitor attends interviews, reviews diaries or other data collections, and proofreads working papers. The role of the monitor is to discover inadvertently misguided research assumptions caused by the close personal involvement of the primary researcher.

Regardless of the data collection method, rigorous action researchers design and specify the measurement techniques clearly when setting up research infrastructure. Above all, rigorous researchers clearly pronounce the measurement approach before undertaking the intervention.

Maintain collaboration and subject learning

Another characteristic strategy of rigorous action research is the careful nurturing of collaboration with subjects. The subjects may well have key knowledge that is critical to the discovery of important aspects of the theory under test. Rigorous action researchers avoid dominating the diagnosis and action planning phases (i.e. assuming the authoritative role of the external consultant).

The cycle of subject learning is also critical for developing the knowledge necessary to claim any idiographic usefulness for the theory under test in the action research project. During the learning cycle, the subjects acquire learning about the immediate problem situation. This leads to imperative modification of action-taking and sustains the action research cycle. Without subject learning, the action research cycle ends prematurely.

Promote iterations

Action research is also characteristically cyclical. The research data should record the repetitive planning, taking and evaluating of organizational actions. In this environment action failures (in terms of the immediate problem situation) are as important as action successes. Rigorous action research cannot disguise negative effects of some actions, as these may provide richer learning than the positive effects. The cycles will continue until the immediate problem situation is relieved. Unfortunately this sometimes occurs before adequate data is collected to resolve conflicts within the theory. That is, in some cases, an action research project may not generate enough data to support adequate analysis of a generated theory – even idiographically.

Restrained generalization

Action research, being naturally idiographic, presents researchers with a serious conflict regarding any generalization from the project findings. As mentioned earlier, only the most tentative causal links can be claimed owing to the multivariate nature of the study. Yet for a vocationally-oriented field like IS, it is the promise of generalizability that interests the majority of scientists. It is generalization that makes theories relevant. Some scientists believe such relevance is as important as rigour in the achievement of important IS research (Keen, 1991).

For the action research, the traditional foundation of generalization, diachronic reliability, is problematic. This is the traditional repeatability criterion underlying many positivist methods. An action research project, by nature of its intervention into a unique organizational setting, can never be repeated. Kirk and Miller (1986) suggested that synchronic reliability was more useful in qualitative research. This form of reliability is based on the consistency of observations within the same time period. These observations represent alternate forms of data (e.g. two researchers) relating to the same phenomenon. These data would never be identical but should be consistent with the theory under test.

Some authorities dismiss reliability altogether as a necessary premise of generalizability. Gummesson (1988) argued that validity (the degree to which the research accomplished its intended goals within its scientific paradigm) was a sounder criterion for generalization. Generalization based on the validity of action research, although lacking any substantial proof of reliability, is no less acceptable than generalization from statistical samples based on reliability but lacking substantial proof of validity.

> It no longer seems so 'obvious' that a limited number of observations cannot be used as a basis for generalization. Nor does it appear to be 'obvious' any longer that properly devised statistical studies based on large numbers of observations will lead to meaningful generalizations.
>
> Evart Gummesson (1988), p. 78

Action researchers can legitimately generalize their findings on the basis of the validity of their research. In addition, action researchers can design synchronic reliability into the structure of their research project. However they must exercise restraint in their conclusions since these must be reported from a limited number of observations. This, of course, implies another characteristic of rigorous action research: circulation of the results to the scientific community. Thus the theory will evolve under the pressure of further study and correction.

Conclusion

Action research is regarded by many as the ideal post-positivist social scientific research method for IS research. The present scientific institutions in IS, however, broadly favour the current philosophy of the natural sciences. Further, action research rose from problems experienced in the field of social psychology, yet never succeeded in procuring major status in the main stream of social psychology or social science research. This suggests that action researchers in IS assume certain risks that their findings will be rejected on philosophical grounds.

The features and characteristics of the approach define a domain of ideal use for the method. Within this domain, perhaps the study of IS development methodology is most critical to our field. A number of problems confront the action researcher such as lack of impartiality, lack of discipline, confusion with consulting and its context-bound nature. However these problems confront researchers using alternative methods as well. The difficulty with action research may be a matter of degree, and the easy loss of scientific rigour.

Action researchers can achieve scientific rigour through a number of characteristic strategies. First they must establish an ethical client-system infrastructure and research environment. They must plan their data collection carefully. They must observe iterative phases that formulate theory, plan action, take action, and evaluate the action. Through this process they must promote collaboration by the subjects and support their subjects' learning cycles. Despite the idiographic nature of the study, the researcher may imply certain generalizations based on the theory and learning. Reports of the research must disseminate the scientific knowledge achieved by the study to allow future work that can confirm or refute any causal suggestions or claims of generalized theory.

The origins and techniques of action research have yet to draw a large following in the main stream of social science. Altogether, the features of the domain of ideal use, the features of the method that create problems and opportunities, and the strategies for applying the method represent the major characteristics of the role of this method for IS researchers. A critical review of these reveals that this research approach could appropriately assume a growing role in main stream IS research and practice.

Acknowledgement

The authors have adopted a certain specific phraseology suggested by an unknown reviewer's comments which we found to be much clearer than our own. Our thanks to this reviewer.

References

Alavi, M., Carlson, P. and Brook, G. (1989) The ecology of MIS research: a twenty-year status review, in *Proceedings of the Tenth International Conference on Information Systems*, Boston, 4–6 December Baltimore: ACM Press, pp. 363–71.

Argyris, C. and Schôn, D. (1978) *Organizational Learning: A Theory of Action Perspective* (Addison-Wesley, Reading).

Argyris, C. Putnam, R. and Smith, D. (1985) *Action Science* (Jossey-Bass, San Fransisco, CA).

Banville, C. and Landry, M. (1989) Can the field of MIS be disciplined? *Communications of the ACM*, **32**, 48–61.

Baroudi, J. and Orlikowski, W. (1989) The problem of statistical power in MIS research, *MIS Quarterly*, **13**, 87–106.

Baskerville, R. (1991) Philosophical bias of methods and tools, *Information Systems Research Arena of the 90s*, Nissen, H.E., Klein, H. and Hirschheim, R. (eds).

Benbasat, I., Goldstein, D. and Mead, M. (1987) The case research strategy in studies of information systems, *MIS Quarterly* **11**(3), 368–86.

Blackler, F. (1988) Information technologies and organizations: lessons from the 1980s and issues for the 1990s, *Journal of Occupational Psychology*, **61**, 113–27.

Blum, F. (1955) Action research – a scientific approach? *Philosophy of Science*, **22**, 1–7.

Checkland, P. (1981) *Systems Thinking, Systems Practice* (J. Wiley, Chichester).

Checkland, P. (1985) From optimizing to learning: a development of systems thinking for the 1990s, *Journal of the Operational Research Society*, **36** (9), 757–67.

Checkland, P. (1991) From framework through experience to learning: the essential nature of action research, in *Information Systems Research: Contemporary Approaches and Emergent Traditions* (Nissen, H.E., Klein, H.K. and Hirschheim, R. (eds) North-Holland, Amsterdam) pp. 397–403.

Checkland, P. and Scholes, J. (1990) *Soft Systems Methodology in Practice*, (J. Wiley, Chichester).

Clark, A. (1972) *Action Research and Organizational Change* (Harper and Row, London).

Cooper, R. (1988) Review of management information systems research: a management support emphasis, *Information Processing and Management*, **24** (1), 73–102.

Galliers, R. and Land, F. (1987) Choosing appropriate information systems research methodologies, *Communications of the ACM*, **30**, 900–2.

Glaser, B.G. and Straus, A.L. (1967) *The Discovery of Grounded Theory, Strategies for Qualitative Research* (Aldine, Chicago).

Gummesson, E. (1988) *Qualitative Methods in Management Research* (Chartwell-Bratt, Bickley, Bromley).

Hirschheim, R. (1985) Information systems epistemology: an historical perspective, in *Research Methods In Information Systems*, (Mumford, E., Hurshheim, R., Fitzgerald, G. and Wood Harper, T. (eds) North-Holland, Amsterdam).

Hult, M. and Lennung, S.-Å. (1980) Towards a definition of action research: a note and bibliography, *Journal of Management Studies* **17**, 241–50.

Israel, B., Schurman, S. and House, J. (1989) Action research on occupational stress: involving workers as researchers, *International Journal of Health Services*, **19** (1), 135–55.

Ives, B. and Olson, M. (1984) User involvement and MIS success: a review of research, *Management Science*, **30** (5), 586–603.

Jarvenpaa, S., Dickson, G. and DeSanctis, G. (1985) Methodological issues in experimental IS research: experiences and recommendations, *MIS Quarterly*, 141–56.

Jenkins, M. (1985) Research methodologies and MIS research, in *Research Methods in Information Systems*, Mumford, E., Hirschheim, R., Fitzgerald, G. and Wood-Harper, T. (eds) (North-Holland, Amsterdam) pp. 103–17.

Jepsen, L., Mathiassen, L. and Nielsen, P. (1989) Back to the thinking mode: diaries for the management of information systems development projects, *Behaviour and Information Technology* 8 (3), 207–17.

Jönsson, S. (1991) Action research, in *Information Systems Research: Contemporary Approaches and Emergent Traditions*, Nissen, H.-E., Klein, H.K. and Hirschheim, R. (eds) (North-Holland, Amsterdam) pp. 371–96.

Jowett, S. (1988) Hospital and community liaison links in nursing: the role of the liaison nurse, *Journal of Advanced Nursing*, **13**, 579–87.

Keen, P. (1991) Relevance and rigour in information systems research, in *Information Systems Research: Contemporary Approaches and Emergent Traditions* L. Nissen, H.-E., Klein, H.K. and Hirschheim, R. (eds) (North-Holland, Amsterdam) pp. 27–50.

Kirk, J. and Miller, M. (1986) *Reliability and Validity in Qualitative Research* (Sage, Newbury Park).

Klein, H. Hirschheim, R. and Nissen, H.-E. (1991) A pluralist perspective of the information systems research arena, in *Information Systems Research: Contemporary Approaches and Emergent Traditions*, Nissen, H.-E., Klein, H.K. and Hirschheim, R. (eds) (North-Holland, Amsterdam) pp. 1–20.

Lewin, K. (1951) *Field Theory in Social Science* (Harper & Bros, New York).

Lippit, G. and Lippit. R. (1978) *The Consulting Process in Action* (University Associates, San Diego, CA).

Lukka, K. (1987) Budgetary biasing in organizations: theoretical framework and empirical evidence, *Accounting Organizations and Society*, **13** (3), 281–301.

Naur, P. (1983) Program development studies based on diaries, in *Psychology of Computer Use*, Green, T., Payne S. and Van der Veer, G. (eds) (Academic Press, London) pp. 159–70.

Orlikowski, W. and Baroudi, J. (1991) Studying information technology in organizations: research approaches and assumptions, *Information Systems Research*, **2** (1), 1–28.

Rapoport, R. (1970) Three dilemmas of action research, *Human Relations* **23**, 499–513.

Rosenau, P. (1992) *Post-Modernism and the Social Sciences: Insights, Inroads, and Intrusions* (Princeton University Press, Princeton, NJ).

Sanford, N. (1976) Whatever happened to action research? in *Experimenting with Organizational Life: The Action Research Approach*, Clark, A. (Compiler) (Plenum, New York).

Schein, E. (1969) *Process Consultation: Its Role in Organizational Development* (Addison-Wesley, Reading, MA).

Schein, E. (1987) *The Clinical Perspective in Fieldwork* (Sage, Newbury Park, CA).

Seashore, S. (1976) The design of action research, in *Experimenting with Organizational Life: The Action Research Approach*, (Clarke, A. (Comp.) (Plenum, New York) pp. 103–17.

Straub, D. (1991) Session of 'Rigor in information systems research: a discussion of the session papers', In *Information Systems Research: Contemporary Approaches and Emergent Traditions*, Nissen, H.-E., Klein, H.K. and Hirschheim, R. (North-Holland, Amsterdam) pp. 103–6.

Susman, G. (1983) Action research: a sociotechnical systems perspective, in *Beyond Method: Strategies for Social Research*, Morgan, G. (ed) (Sage, Newbury Park) pp. 95–113.

Susman, G. and Evered, R. (1978) An assessment of the scientific merits of action research, *Administrative Science Quarterly*, **23**, 582–603.

Trist, E. (1976) Engaging with large-scale systems, in *Experimenting with Organizational Life: The Action Research Approach*, Clark, A. (Comp.) (Plenum, New York).

Van Eynde, D. and Bledsoe, J. (1990) The changing practice of organization development, *Leadership and Organization Development Journal*, **11** (2), 25–30.

Warmington, A. (1980) Action research: its method and its implications, *Journal of Applied Systems Analysis*, **7**, 23–39.

Webb, C. (1989) Action research: philosophy, methods and personal experiences, *Journal of Advanced Nursing*, **14**, 403–10.

Wood-Harper, T. (1989) *Comparison of information systems definition methodologies: an action research multiview perspective*. PhD Thesis, University of East Anglia.

17
The Rise of the Phoenix: Methodological Innovation as a Discourse of Renewal

David G. Wastell[1], Tom McMaster[2] and Peter Kawalek[3]
[1]*Nottingham University Business School, UK;*
[2]*Information Systems Institute, Salford University, UK;*
[3]*Manchester Business School, UK*

Introduction

Every 500 years (or 540, 1000, 1461, even 12,994, depending on the cultural context!), the legendary and beautifully plumaged Phoenix[1] self-cremates in its nest of cinnamon twigs, rising again to embalm its predecessor in an egg of myrrh. Something of a Jungian archetype, the Phoenix symbolizes the universal cycle of birth, death and re-birth, figuring widely in religious and secular imagery, and in classical and popular culture. Renewal is the theme of this paper, but in the more mundane context of organizational resilience. Resilience is a cosmopolitan idea, encountered in many disparate domains, ranging from ecological policy (e.g. Folke *et al.*, 2002) to child welfare (Newman and Blackburn, 2002). Although its definition is elusive (Cho *et al.*, 2006) and its utility contested (even in seemingly well-entrenched terrain),[2] the concept has gained recent prominence in the management literature, especially among the enthusiasts of 'positive psychology' (Luthans, 2002). Its proselytizers see resilience as an organizational capacity that can be designed and fostered as a protective shield against the apocalyptic turbulence and uncertainty of the contemporary business environment (Mallik, 1998; Hamel and Välikangas, 2003; Sheffi, 2005). Resilience is 'the key skill for surviving in the multitude of changes as we move into the digital economy ... [leaders] must cultivate

Reprinted from "The rise of the phoenix: methodological innovation as a discourse of renewal," by D.G. Wastell, T. McMaster and P. Kawalek in *Journal of Information Technology*, 22, 2007, pp. 59–68. With kind permission from the Association for Information Technology Trust. All rights reserved.

the resilience of the workforce and create appropriate systems. If an organization does not create new strategies and systems that enhance organizational resilience, it will not adapt' (Pulley, 1997).

The International Resilience Project (Grotberg, 1997) provides a useful and widely quoted generic definition of resilience as: 'a universal capacity which allows a person, group or community to prevent, minimise, or overcome the damaging effects of adversity … resilient behavior may be in the form of maintenance or normal development despite the adversity, or a promoter of growth beyond the present level of functioning'. Champions of organizational resilience emphasize its positive nature as an active coping response to threats, crises and major disruptions (Riolli and Savicki, 2003). A constellation of desirable dispositions is invoked: the need for a constructive outlook; for flexibility, experimentation and bricolage; and the determination to innovate and to learn from experience (e.g. Mallik, 1998). This stress on positive development moves resilience beyond the idea of 'simple adaptation' (Luthans, 2002). The potential for renewal is a resonant theme:

> 'to thrive in turbulent times, organisations must become as efficient at renewal as they are at producing today's products and services. Renewal must be the natural consequence of an organization's innate resilience' (Hamel and Välikangas, 2003).

Like the Phoenix, organizational entities may rise again from their metaphorical ashes to better meet the exigencies of a changing world. This potentiality is the theme of this paper.

Much of the writing on resilience is partisan, normative, and rhetorical. It exudes an instrumental rationality that implicitly privileges the top–down agency of senior management (or proxies such as HR experts) to create and nurture resilience as a designed capacity. In this paper, we take a different tack, focusing our narrative on its unplanned, endogenous manifestation in the meso-regions of the organizational hierarchy. This is made possible by our sustained, ethnographic engagement with one beleaguered group, the IT department in a large public sector bureaucracy. The case is of particular relevance in the context of IFIP WG8.6, as the development of an innovative IS methodology was the key to survival and renewal. As we know only too well, innovation in IS practice is a problematic endeavour: new methods and tools commonly face substantial resistance and frequent rejection (Orlikowski, 1993; Iivari, 1996; Hardgrave *et al.*, 2003). The critical studies of Kautz and McMaster (1994) and Wastell (1996) narrate the vicissitudes of implementing structured methods and Fitzgerald *et al.* (2002) comment generally on the widely reported low level of method use.[3]

Innovation and the IS function

In general, these are 'interesting times' for the IS/IT function. As organizations come to rely more and more on technology to deliver strategy and drive performance, the pressures on IT departments have steadily intensified (Fitzgerald *et al.*, 2002). The threat of outsourcing looms large, serving to 'encourage' those who might falter or fail. A challenging world indeed for the traditional IT department, immured in the basement of the organization. The imperatives for organizational change are at least as pressing in today's public sector as in the commercial sphere. The injunctions to reform and modernize public services are strident and ubiquitous, encapsulated in the global mantras of the New Public Management (Wastell, 2006). Technology is integral to this change agenda. The vocabulary of e-Government depicts ICT, in language bordering on the evangelical, as the talismanic enabler of transformation (Kawalek and Wastell, 2005).[4] Here, the IT/ IS function in a metropolitan local authority recognized that it was becoming increasingly marginal to the operations of the organization as a whole. It did not provide the capability required to support an ambitious programme of strategic change that had been articulated in the authority's business strategy, or to respond to the ever-pressing injunctions of the external modernization agenda. Faced with this crisis, rather than adopting a defensive stance, they demonstrated impressive resilience, embarking upon a proactive process of reform in order to re-position themselves in the strategic vanguard of the organization. At the heart of this was a new methodological approach to the development of information systems embodying a more business and customer-oriented ethos.

The dominant theoretical approach for the study of innovation in our field draws on the classical diffusionist framework of Rogers (1995), which has spawned the influential Technology Adoption Model (Davis *et al.*, 1989).[5] In essence, Rogers (1995) portrays innovation as a decision-making process in which individual adopters decide whether to embrace a new technology or not. The limitations of Rogers for understanding the social and temporal complexities of organizational innovation have been addressed, *inter alia,* by Van de Ven (1995) and Lundblad (2003). Here, we frame innovation as a process of organizational change, rather than individualistic adoption decisions. Change processes in organizations involve complex interactions between groups and levels that evolve dialectically through time (Pettigrew, 1990).

Intensive, longitudinal studies are required to tease out the underlying socio-political dynamics, focusing in particular on the occurrence of supervening events, critical 'turning points', which provide the necessary impetus to punctuate the natural inertia that would otherwise prevail (Gersick, 1991; Newman and Robey, 1992). Such crises may arise from many sources (Kovoor-Misra *et al.*, 2001): from technological disasters and from declining performance, but equally from growth too (developmental crises). Crises may evoke defensive reactions that include the state of paralysis described as 'threat-rigidity' (Barnett and Pratt, 2000), but they may provide innovatory opportunities too: to deal with problems, to unfreeze old behaviours, to develop new ways of understanding and acting (Kovoor-Misra *et al.*, 2001). Seeger *et al.* (2005) refer to this resilient orientation as a *discourse of renewal*, its hallmark being a practical, prospective orientation to the future rather than an exculpatory and defensive attitude to the past. When methodological innovation forms part of a resilient, progressive response to an impending threat, the auguries are good, but without this clarity of purpose and the keenly felt need to change, the attempt to innovate is likely to founder. This may well explain the high prevalence of failed IS innovation.

The paper will cover the following broad areas. It will first describe the local context and the change process within the field setting, and briefly describe the research methodology. A detailed historical narrative will then be provided describing the vicissitudes of the IT department over the critical time period, highlighting the development of the new methodology and the role it played. We will conclude by reflecting on what has been learned regarding the nature of resilience and of methodological innovation as a process of organizational change.

Antecedent context and methodology

The setting for the project is Salford City Council (SCC), a local government institution in the north west of England. Salford is a medium-sized city of around 250,000 inhabitants, and one of 10 local authorities making up the Greater Manchester conurbation. Like most local authorities in Britain, SCC is organized around key service areas, such as housing, social services, education, etc. There is a central IT services department (ITSD) staffed (at the outset of the story) by around 20 professionals organized in a number of specialist teams (e.g. software development, PC support, maintenance).

The story begins in the summer of 1999, shortly after the 'failure' of a project known as CAPELLA. This initiative, supported by European funding, had begun in mid-1997, its aim being to implement an integrated set of software engineering tools (CASE)[6] in ITSD in order to improve the department's software productivity and quality. The project was a collaborative one involving academic partners in local universities and one European research institution. This antecedent failure is significant and will be returned to in the Discussion. In short, CAPELLA foundered because key stakeholders (practitioners especially) were uncommitted to the use of the CASE tool-kit, which became seen as increasingly marginal to the urgent, practical problems facing ITSD (e.g. Y2K, legacy system maintenance). Of particular salience here was the clarion call in CAPELLA's final report for 'strong alignment of the introduction of new technologies [with] short term demands [and] long term business goals'. The Report went on to recommend the adoption of a new systems development methodology. The need for a more business-oriented approach had also been articulated in the City's Information Society Strategy, published earlier that year. The Strategy's aim was to harness the potential of IT to improve the social and economic well-being of the people of Salford. It was recognized that a Business Process Reengineering (BPR) approach was required to implement the strategy, focusing on the innovative use of IT to realize radical business change. Quoting again from the CAPELLA report:

A new strategic role is emerging, facilitating change within the City Council. The Council is not a strategic animal, services are driven by operational needs. It's hard for IT to provide business benefits in this context. We need to be seen as a critical lever for change ... revolutionising public services.

The miscarriage of CAPELLA and the publication of the Information Society Strategy form key antecedent features of the local context. It is also important to consider change events in the wider environment of the sector as a whole (Meyer *et al.*, 1995). Here, the most potent forces relate to the emergence of e-Government in the UK, which may be traced back to the publication of central government's 1999 white paper, *Modernizing Government*. This challenged all public sector organizations (including local government) to deliver efficient and responsive 'citizen-centred services', and IT was seen as critical to achieving these aims. The ambitiousness of the agenda was reflected in the target to 'electronically enable' 100% of relevant services, initially by 2008, but subsequently accelerated to 2005. Various national initiatives subsequently lent force to the modernization programme. A so-called 'Pathfinder' initiative was launched in 2001, whereby significant new funding was set aside for local authorities able to demonstrate a leading position in relation to some aspect of e-Government.

Rather than adopting an external methodology, ITSD took the decision to develop its own in collaboration with its academic partners. This decision to a large degree reflected the prior failure to implement the CASE tool, and was reinforced by the strong collaborative relationships that had been forged during CAPELLA despite its ultimate miscarriage. Following an action research (AR) approach,[7] work commenced in July 1999, spearheaded by a small team led by the Head of ITSD. The team also comprised two of the local academics from CAPELLA and several of ITSD's software developers, including one section leader. The remit of the academics was to bring to bear their prior knowledge of IS methodology, to document the emerging framework (to be known as SPRINT), to support its use and to facilitate its further development. The role of the practitioners was to co-develop the methodology, contributing to its progressive refinement, applying it in practice and reflecting on its strengths and weaknesses. The practical means of developing the framework was that of collaborative working and reflection, with all members of the team working closely together on a series of projects, using this shared experience as the basis for developing and refining the methodology. Much of this reflection was embedded in the work itself, during project meetings, informal discussions, etc., supplemented by *ad hoc* brainstorming sessions to capture key ideas and experiences. More formal workshops were also held off-site to discuss major developments to the methodology.

The following section will describe the history of the project. Table 17.1 provides a project time-line to support the narrative. It summarizes the main events that took place, in terms of internal developments and in the external environment (locally and nationally) that materially impinged on the work. The account has been constructed from the collective reflections of the AR team, corroborated where possible by contemporaneous documentation (e.g. workshop minutes, internal reports, policy documents). All three authors have been directly involved in the collaboration with SCC,[8] and the coherence and validity of the narrative derive from this direct engagement. Formal interviews with key practitioners were carried out in the summer of 2004 to provide further reflection, corroboration and to fill in any lacunae. Quotations in the text below were extracted from these interviews.

Table 17.1 SPRINT time line

Dates	Internal event (to BPR team)	External event
July 1999	SPRINT project commences	
Oct 1999	Draft SPRINT framework published. BPR programme and team given formal approval, initial pilot project launched	Analysis of telephone calls to SCC's Treasury dept. reveals 90% unanswered
Jan/Feb 2000	SPRINT report produced for pilot project. Projects in Housing and Treasury launched	Benefits Fraud Inspectorate review awards Treasury 0 grading for benefits process
April/May 2000	Treasury project completes with detailed analysis and reengineering proposals. Contact Centre main recommendation	Customer Services (CS) dept. created with corporate role
June/July 2000	Revision of SPRINT to address call centre requirements. Housing report delivered	Outsourcing threat comes to fore. Think-tank set up to consider options, with Manchester Business School (MBS)
Aug–Oct 2000	Planning for second wave of BPR projects as part of rolling BPR programme	Contact Centre brought into full operation
Jan/Feb 2001	Work on further SPRINT projects (Registrar and Job applications) commences	National e-Government Pathfinder scheme announced, £25 m new funding. Salford Pathfinder bid successful
July 2001	Completion of the above projects. First formal SPRINT workshop	Creation of Salford Advance
Sept–Dec 2001	Detailed mapping of all customer transactions commences, part of e-Government compliance & planned expansion of Contact Centre	MBS report published in Dec. Outsourcing finally recedes as threat
Mar–Jun 2002	Projects in Education and Social Services complete	Stall at national Pathfinder conference in London to disseminate outputs of work
July 2002	Second SPRINT workshop, and review of BPR programme	
Sept 2002	Projects completed in Licensing and Economic Development. Transaction mapping completes	

(*continued*)

Table 17.1   Continued

Dates	Internal event (to BPR team)	External event
Oct–Dec 2002	Review of SPRINT instigated	National Strategy for local e-Government published
Jan/Feb 2003	Fully revised version (3.0) of SPRINT produced	Benefits service awarded a 4 star rating and Charter Mark for excellence

The SPRINT chronicles

Episode 1: The birth of SPRINT and early experiences (1999–2001)

As noted, the project was formally launched in July 1999, its aim being to develop a home-grown methodology for carrying out BPR projects and hence for implementing the City's ambitious Information Society Strategy. Interviewed in 2004, the Head of ITSD reflected on the motivation for the project, intimating the sense of alienation felt at the time.

> We were largely a traditional, technically orientated IT department; our people were predominantly technology people. We did try to understand the Council's strategic agenda but our alignment was vague. We were seen as people who built software, put PCs on desks and installed networks rather than adding strategic value.

Another senior officer in ITSD, subsequently to head up the BPR team, described the situation in somewhat bleaker terms.

> We went through a strange phase in the olden days. Departments increasingly thought they could do things for themselves, they could buy their own system and didn't need ITSD. This was leading us to stagnation in the way we were moving, we had no role or identity. Y2K also diverted us. We were hardly involved in the SAP procurement, we were too busy on Y2K. We were feeling very marginal at the time.

In the eyes of the Head, the aim of the project was bold and radical, nothing less than to re-position IT as a 'true enabler of business transformation'. Work began based on prior BPR work by the academics, largely in the commercial sector (Wastell and White, 1993). This was reviewed by the AR team and a draft methodology produced in early October 1999, which was christened SPRINT (Salford Process Reengineering Involving New Technology). In mid-October, a paper was presented by the Head of ITSD to SCC's senior management team, recommending adoption of SPRINT and its deployment on a comprehensive programme of BPR projects. Significantly, no additional resource was requested in order to carry out this ambitious initiative; it would be done within the existing IT budget. The recommendation was accepted and an internal BPR team was constituted to carry forward the work, in conjunction with the academics. In effect, this formalized the AR team. The first project carried out was crucial in proving and refining the methodology. It focused on the administrative team supporting the committee-based decision-making structures operational within the Council at that time. Work began in late October, and concluded in January 2000 with the production of a set of radical proposals. Far from mere office automation of the clerical function (as had been originally envisaged), the proposals focused on the need to support the role of elected representatives in decision-making through the creation of a new Information Management function. More details of this inaugural project, including its evaluation, may be found in Kawalek and Wastell (2005).

Two further projects were quickly instigated early in 2000 in the housing and treasury departments, respectively. The second of these was a notable success. A key problem facing Treasury was the high number of unanswered telephone queries, identified in a report the previous autumn. The department had also performed very poorly in an external audit of its housing benefits process, having been awarded the bottom grade by the Housing Benefits fraud inspectorate. Users participated fully and vigorously in the BPR process, including carrying out a comprehensive process mapping exercise, largely unaided by the BPR experts. Workshops were held on a regular basis, and the work was enthusiastically led by a senior user. The main reengineering recommendation was to create a dedicated 'Customer Contact' centre for Treasury, which went live in October 2000. The transformation in Treasury's housing benefit service effected by the Centre was ultimately reflected in the award of 4-star rating (Table 17.1). Two further BPR projects were launched over the summer of 2000 and adaptations made to SPRINT to add new tools, including tailoring its use for customer-centred analysis and Contact Centre design.

Three external developments were influential over the ensuing 12 months. First was the appearance of a serious threat to outsource the IT function. To forestall this, ITSD proposed setting up a think-tank to examine the implications fully, and an independent assessment was also commissioned from Manchester Business School (MBS). SPRINT itself was important in deflecting the threat. The Head of ITSD commented: 'SPRINT allowed me to say to senior management that we're repositioning ourselves, we're addressing our weaknesses, that he should trust the in-house service'. Although the outsourcing threat persisted for over a year, ITSD's dogged resistance prevailed and by the time the MBS report was published, the threat had receded. The second important development was the announcement of the national Pathfinder initiative (see previous section) in early 2001. SCC were one of the successful contenders, with SPRINT featuring centrally in their bid. Substantial funding (£0.5m) was obtained to accelerate SCC's BPR programme, to 'commodify' the SPRINT methodology into a resource for the local government community as a whole, and to mentor other local authorities in IT-enabled business change. The final development was the success of the embryonic Contact Centre, which came to be seen as a model for SCC as a whole to improve its customer relations. It was established as corporate facility, with plans to extend the range of services to be transferred into the Centre.

Episode 2: Review and subsequent developments (2001–2004)

A formal workshop was held in July 2001 to review these early experiences with SPRINT, to update and refine the methodology accordingly, and to plan the Pathfinder activities in detail. It was attended by all, the AR team, as well as several other IT staff. The meeting was positive and constructive. Many aspects of SPRINT were felt to be particularly valuable: e.g. the emphasis on process mapping and the value of direct observation ('light ethnography') in actual work settings. Several action points resulted, including the need to develop some new components. Mood had lifted. The head of the BPR team reflected:

Things came together nicely. SPRINT arrived at the right time, and there were also areas in the authority that needed major change. We saw the situation as an opportunity to flex our muscles. SPRINT helped to crystallize our new role. We were lucky that we decided to do BPR, and then the crises came in Council Tax and Housing Benefits, and then e-Government. There was a lot of change going on at the time ... *we were needed.*

A radical re-organization of IT services was instituted in the summer of 2001. The more routine activities of legacy system maintenance and PC support were split off into separate sections, and a new organizational entity was created, emblematically christened 'Salford Advance' to emphasize its progressive role. Salford Advance subsumed the BPR team, a small R&D Group and training. It was a clear step towards realizing the Head's vision of more strategic role for IT, and also helped in creating focus and dedicated resource for the Pathfinder work.

Over the following year, SPRINT was internally deployed on a further 12 projects and most of the enhancements identified at the first workshop were implemented. Externally, over 40 other local authorities were mentored as part of the Pathfinder work. A second SPRINT workshop was held in July 2002, to review progress and identify areas for development. Several major new SPRINT features were proposed, by *both* practitioners and academics. The relationships between SPRINT, e-Government, and other change initiatives, such as 'Best Value' (Boyne *et al.*, 2002), were also much discussed. An independent evaluation was subsequently instigated of all on-going and completed projects. The Evaluation Report documented 14 projects, 10 completed and four in progress. All had produced SPRINT outputs, and four had been implemented in full or to a significant degree. Three of these had resolved into call centre implementations, reflecting alignment with the emergent corporate plan alluded to above. The other six completed projects had reached the end of phase 1, with useful analysis having been produced, but no decision to move into implementation. In part, the Evaluation Report attributed these areas of blockage to the presence of a complex and fluid agenda of change within SCC, with a range of initiatives (Best Value, e-Government) competing for resources and attention.

Regarding SPRINT itself, the Report commented favourably as follows:

> The BPR team followed the methodology closely and deeply. The mapping of business processes was seen as a useful way of engaging the users and checking whether the BPR team had understood the process as it existed. The methodology does offer a series of tasks and tools that are valued by those who use them. By being 'road-tested' within an actual organisation, the methodology has gone beyond its academic origins. If it has been found wanting it is mainly in its larger ambitions. The 'real world' of organisations puts very strict limits on how a methodology can create change – it is competing with too many other things that are not easily factored into methodological design.

The Report made several recommendations for the further development of SPRINT including reorganizing the material in a user-friendly way, simplifying the language, and explicitly relating SPRINT to parallel initiatives. As a result, SPRINT was thoroughly revised, with the new version completed in January 2003. It was rewritten to be more accessible and was given an explicit e-Government cast. A number of new features were introduced and phase 3 replaced by a 'hand-over step' at the end of phase 2. At this point in time, the AR project had largely completed its work. The prime purpose had been to generate an effective BPR methodology and SPRINT, representing the collaborative efforts of practitioners and academics alike, was the product of this work. Appendix provides a brief overview of SPRINT, including its underlying philosophy; further details and a full description are publicly available on various web-sites (see below).

The detailed history thus closes here, and we will end with a brief summary of how matters have moved on since. A steady stream of new BPR projects has flowed, and by the summer of 2004, a cumulative total of 22 projects had been carried out. A further review of the methodology was carried out in mid-2004, strengthening its customer orientation and enhancing the visual appeal of the documentation; this new version was published later that year on a dedicated 'gov.uk' web-site.[9] External interest in SPRINT, inspired by the Pathfinder work, has continued to grow, and a User Group has been formed, which held its inaugural meeting in April 2004. The Group is chaired by a senior practitioner. At the time of writing, there are around 280 individual members, representing over 90 different organizations. The interview with the Head of ITSD in 2004, eloquently expressed how the fortunes of ITSD had turned around since the dark days of 1999. The Head commented on the role of SPRINT within this transformation as follows:

> SPRINT helped profoundly to re-position IT as a *true enabler of business transformation*. We're now on the top table. The Chief Exec now recognizes that BPR is key to achieving strategic aims and objectives. It's put us on the strategic change management map. As an example, we were central in developing a new business model for council services, called 'Think Customer'. It's all about joined up service delivery. We're even on the treasurer's radar now. The Council is constantly seeking substantial budget savings and we're seen as the 'ghost-busters', the ones that can fill the hole. We now make a real difference to delivering the Council's agenda.

Discussion

Let us begin by re-invoking our archetype, in the guise of Robert Aldrich's 1965 movie 'The Flight of the Phoenix'. At the height of the drama, the following snippets of dialogue take place in the blistering desert sun, beside the wreckage of the crashed plane, as the cast come to terms with the receding possibility of rescue. They contemplate an improbable plan to save themselves, by cannibalizing a new plane from the wreckage of the old, to bring off an audacious escape. Towns (the world-weary pilot) first addresses Dorfmann (the young German engineer); following an interjection from Renaud, the French doctor; there is a further exchange between Towns and Lew, his alcoholic navigator.

> **Towns:** Your theory's fine. But you get this: that engine's rated 2000 horsepower, and if I was ever fool enough to let it get started, it'd shake your pile of junk into a 1000 pieces and cut us up into mincemeat with the propeller ....
> **Renaud:** Excuse me captain but perhaps there is one other thing. The way it is now, some of these men may not last as long as the water. But they need to believe there is hope for them. I don't know Mr. Towns but maybe to build a thing like this could be a lot of help.
> **Towns:** ... I've lost five men Lew ... are you asking me to kill the rest of them trying to get that death-trap off the ground. I can't do it Lew, it won't work, it just can't work!
> **Lew:** All right, it can't. Maybe it can't and we'll all be killed. But if there's just one chance in thousand that he's got something, boy I'd rather take it than just sit around here, waiting to die.

Just as these maroons took fate into their own hands, choosing action over resignation, so too did a 'discourse of renewal' take hold in ITSD. Likewise, benighted at the outset of our narrative, key staff-members also chose not to 'sit around here, waiting to die'. Showing a spirit of resilience just as stirring in its own way, they fashioned SPRINT from the ashes of the ill-starred CAPELLA era, reinventing themselves as a potent, strategic force, with the methodology providing the vehicle for accomplishing their new role and identity. A dedicated BPR team now spearheads SPRINT's deployment on a large portfolio of projects, and has done so for more than 5 years. The seat at the organization's 'top table' has at last been secured.

The aim of this paper was to briefly introduce the SPRINT methodology, emphasizing the process of its production, and to use the case to reflect both on the nature of organizational resilience and the much-bruited troubles of methodological innovation. Let us begin our analysis with the latter. How then may we account for ITSD's accomplishment of successful innovation against the usual grain? From a conventional stand point, two familiar 'success factors' immediately stand out. We know only too well from the sad litany of failed IS projects (Laudon and Laudon, 2005) that the commitment of senior managers and the willing participation of staff are vital to the success of any change initiative. Both these key conditions were clearly met here. The project was led passionately by the head of ITSD, who operated throughout as a 'transformational leader', fully committed to bringing off the required changes (Bass, 1985). The adoption of an AR approach is also significant. It has been argued that public sector organizations are more conservative than their private sector counterparts (MacIntosh, 2003). Given its intrinsically participative nature, AR would seem particularly appropriate as a change methodology in such a context where there is a long-established culture of consensus and collegiality. Mustonen-Ollila and Lyytinen (2003) have found that the majority of IS process innovations originate from within the organization. Here, a core group of practitioners were engaged throughout SPRINT's development; the methodology was not imposed from without, but developed endogenously by the practitioners and the academics working in close collaboration. The AR methodology, with all key actants involved in the cyclical learning process that drove its development, meant all internal stakeholders were naturally drawn into the innovation process and held in place, with SPRINT at the centre of this strengthening network. Over time and a sustained series of deployments, this led to its ultimate congealment as a 'black box' (Latour, 1987), a fully accepted, organic part of the life of the department.

But this analysis is only part of the story. Other key factors were clearly at work. We argued in the Introduction that the turning point of any organizational innovation process is the presence of a threatening stimulus and that renewal is the hall-mark of resilient behaviour in critical situations. Without a sense of crisis, inertia will tend to prevail, and any mobilization for change (at whatever level) will quickly peter out. Crises need not be abrupt, cataclysmic events; they may emerge slowly, with growing force, as the adaptive relationship between the organization and its environment steadily breaks down over a period of time (Kovoor-Misra *et al.*, 2001). Moreover, crises may not necessarily represent direct, imminent threats. Barnett and Pratt (2000) introduce the concept of an autogenic crisis to refer to a latent threat, created or amplified by managers in order to concentrate minds, to develop solidarity and engender motivation for change. In contrast to CAPELLA, there was a much stronger sense of the need for radical change at the outset of the SPRINT era. The Information Society Strategy and the broader e-Government imperatives presented a powerful challenge to ITSD to develop its role, to take a more central place in the City's strategic agenda. This was later combined with a sustained outsourcing threat, against which the development of new capacities was a convenient tactical counter. To a degree, the crisis facing ITSD at the end of the 1990s was still theoretical. There were clear symptoms but at that point the crisis was implicit, the threat of outsourcing was yet to come, and the e-Government agenda still embryonic. Nonetheless, times were clearly a-changing, with ITSD's traditional, technology-focused paradigm perceptibly 'out of joint' with the brave new world of modernized public services.

A challenging new role at the centre of the business was thus slowly taking shape, in prospect at least. The impending crisis could have been resisted: there was no acute necessity to embrace the need for change and a defensive process of denial could have set in, with ITSD ignoring the emerging imperatives. Alternatively, the challenges could be viewed positively, as a developmental opportunity (Kovoor-Misra *et al.*, 2001; Seeger *et al.*, 2005). Such a resilient response prevailed; a proactive opportunity for growth and an expanded role was perceived. The sense of latent crisis prevailing at the project's outset produced a decisive alignment of all key internal actors within ITSD, both management and staff, around the need for change, and held them in place over a sustained period of transition, during which the latent threats translated into real ones, and waxed in their power. Within the initial 'problematization' (Latour, 1987), a discourse of renewal took shape, operationalized in the development of new methodology. Seeger *et al.* (2005) identify several characteristic features of such discourse: a positive orientation to the future rather than defensive rumination; a focus on constructing new technical faculties, methods and procedures; and an improvizational pragmatism emphasizing expediency and flexibility, rather than rational, top–down planning. The role of the leader is critical. Organizational change is *par excellence* an act of sensemaking (Weick, 1995): basic assumptions about role and identity must be reframed and reinterpreted. The leader's prerogative is to provide this new interpretive schema, not only to inspire through passion, but to create new meaning during times of uncertainty, to make sense of the world for those in doubt and confusion. The clear vision of the head of ITSD around the need for change and for the development of a BPR capability were decisive. He was the prime orator of the renewal rhetoric.

Improvization and resourcefulness are also distinctive ingredients of resilient behavior (Mallik, 1998; Hamel and Välikangas, 2003), the determination to persevere and to succeed, expediently using whatever is to hand. How vividly Aldrich's film depicts human ingenuity in the chutzpah to extemporize an entirely new plane from the shattered remnants of the old, a plane that flew against all odds and due scepticism. Much innovation, as in ITSD, is unmandated, arising spontaneously from the middle and lower levels of organizations (Borins, 2002). Change at the meso level requires special leadership characteristics. Resources are scarce and formal authority limited (Borins, 2002) with leadership as much about improvization and expediency (bricolage) as inspiration and vision: 'the main function of any leader is to draw organisation out of the raw materials of life by using ingeniously whatever is at hand' (Weick, 1995). The middle manager who would be innovator, rather than apparatchik, must have something of the subtlety and agility of the trickster about him (Hyde, 1998). Examples abound here of opportunism and improvization in the leadership provided by the Head of ITSD, at least matching his visionary rhetoric. These include: his shrewdness in exploiting crises (including for autogenic effect), the tactical alignment of SPRINT with the emergent Customer Contact centre, the artful deflection of the outsourcing threat, and the audacity to conjure from 'slack resource' both a BPR capacity and a major change programme.

CODA

In this paper, we have linked two phenomena not at first sight correlated, organizational resilience and methodological innovation, through the common concept of organizational crisis. We have seen how 'renewal discourse' is integral to resilience; how the survival of ITSD depended on the determination of its staff to reinvent themselves, to take up the challenge of a new and enlarged role, a role only they foresaw with any clarity. In contrast to the tacit managerialism of mainstream scholarship, the resilience encountered here is spontaneous and emergent, the antithesis of a designed-in capacity. Indeed, to the extent that ITSD pursued its own agenda without explicit senior authorization, the story of its ascendancy highlights the limits of hierarchical power and has a subversive edge. A critical counterpoint is added to the mainstream theme, destabilizing the conceit that resiliency can be designed top–down as the prerogative of senior managers and their proxies. The heroes in both our stories (film and real-life) are ordinary mortals, the accomplishments their own. A less promising team of quarrelsome misfits marooned in the desert can hardly be envisaged. Yet, despite the fissile relationships and flawed personalities, the 'team' ultimately triumphed. Its dysfunctions were the key to its success, but surely no group would have been designed this way *a priori*! In a similar vein, the development of Salford's BPR capability sprang from a unique configuration of chance, historical contingency and human virtuosity. The emergence of SPRINT exemplifies innovation thriving on hardship, and the resilience of ITSD is the product of this same adversity. Had there been a conscious, top–down initiative in 'to build capacity', the outcome might well have been very different, with the additional bureaucracy and resources engendering sclerosis and rigidity rather than innovation and entrepreneurship. Any such external intervention might well have been resisted anyway.

In general, we have noted that IS innovations often fail to take root, rapidly falling into desuetude, if indeed they are ever used in earnest. Through our direct engagement in a project running against the normal grain, we have been able to construct the micro-political causal narrative underpinning one instance of successful innovation. Lacking ethnographic grounding, such granularity of detail and understanding is necessarily absent in the high-level conceptual models that typify much theory in our discipline. Generalizing cautiously, we contend that the outcome of innovation efforts will critically depend on the alignment between the novel artefact (tool, methodology or work-practice) and the resolution of some impending threat, real or indeed latent. Where the artefact forms the active ingredient of a positive, resilient response, the prospects are auspicious; otherwise, the prognosis is less hopeful. The success of the SPRINT project shows that participative, incremental change can be highly effective, especially when driven by a strong sense of purpose and guided by artful leadership. These are modest generalizations, hedged by obvious caveats and contingencies; no necessary truth claims or predictive guarantees are intended. We stress that SPRINT itself (the product not the project) is not a portable commodity: its efflorescence in Salford is inseparable from the unique historical processes of its development there; simply transplanting it would not, in itself, replicate the same capability (McMaster and Wastell, 2005).

Notes

1. Firebird, Benu, Fenghuang, Ho-oo, or Yel according to ancient Russian, Egyptian, Chinese, Japanese, and Native Americans, respectively. As a symbol of renewal, examples are easily found, including the flags of Atlanta and San Francisco, both depicting the Phoenix surmounting a wreath of flames, an emblem of renaissance from human and natural disaster. This paper itself is a Phoenix, reincarnated from the ruins of so many earlier versions!

2. In reviewing the research literature relating to child welfare, Newman and Blackburn (2002: 9) observe: 'Many resilience promoting interventions do not appear notably different from interventions that simply seek to promote positive child development. When attempts are made to apply resilience theory, practitioners may recognise its value but find it hard to distinguish its implications from strategies they may already be using'.

3. These authors provide a useful framework for understanding the technical and political rationalities of 'methods-in-action', and of the barriers that militate against the adoption of formalized approaches (e.g. the messiness and contingencies of real-world practice). Significantly, they highlight the political role played by formalized methods in professionalizing and legitimizing IS practice, paving the way for a more proactive role of IS in strategy formulation. The comfort/confidence factor is also emphasized, recalling the tendency of developers to 'fetishize' methods, as recounted in Wastell (1996).

4. The recently published National IT Strategy, for instance, is emblematically entitled 'Transformational government enabled by technology' (Cabinet Office, 2005). E-government (in the UK) is seemingly passé; t-government's the thing!

5. Recent papers applying TAM to methodological change include Templeton and Byrd (2003) and Hardgrave *et al.* (2003).

6. CASE is an acronym for Computer Assisted Software Engineering. The CASE tool-kit in question was Oracle's Designer 2000 (D2K). More details of CAPELLA with an analysis of its miscarriage may be found in McMaster and Wastell (2004).

7. Greenwood and Levin (1998) define AR as research carried out by a team of professional researchers in collaboration with members of an organization or community, to support action leading to a more satisfying situation for the stakeholders. Given its applied nature, the discipline of IS has long been seen as a natural application domain for AR (Baskerville and Wood-Harper, 1998), typically to develop new systems (e.g. Simon, 2000; Davison, 2001). Mathiassen (2002) also uses an AR-like approach to support and improve IS development practices, though he refers to his mode of enquiry as *collaborative practice research*.

8. DW throughout both CAPELLA and SPRINT, TM during CAPELLA only, and PK throughout SPRINT and the latter phase of CAPELLA.

9. See: www.sprint.gov.uk. Earlier versions may be inspected on www.wastell.org/SPRINT1 and www.wastell.org/SPRINT3 (both accessed, August 2006).

References

Avison, D., Wood-Harper, A., Vidgen, R.T. and Wood, J.R.G. (1998). A Further Exploration in to Information Systems Development: The evolution of multiview 2, *Information Technology & People* 11(2): 124–139.

Barnett, C.K. and Pratt, M. (2000). From Threat-Rigidity to Flexibility: Toward a learning model of autogenic crisis on organisations, *Journal of Organizational Change* 13(1): 74–88.

Baskerville, R. and Wood-Harper, A.T. (1998). Diversity of Information Systems Action Research Methods, *European Journal of Information Systems* 7(2): 90–107.

Bass, B.M. (1985). *Leadership and Performance Beyond Expectations*, New York: Free Press.

Borins, S. (2002). Leadership and Innovation in the Public Sector, *Learning and Organisational Development Journal* 23(8): 467–476.

Boyne, G., Day, P. and Walker, R. (2002). The Evaluation of Public Service Inspection: A theoretical framework, *Urban Studies* 39(7): 1197–1212.

Cabinet Office (2005). *Transformation Government Enabled by Technology*, Norwich: HMSO.

Cho, S., Mathiassen, L. and Robey, D. (2006). The Dialectics of Resilience: A multilevel analysis of a telehealth innovation, in B. Donnelan *et al.* (eds.) *The Transfer and Diffusion of Information Technology for Organizational Resilience*, New York: Springer, pp. 339–357.

Davenport, T. (1992). *Process Innovation: Reengineering Work Through Information Technology*, Cambridge: Harvard Business School Press.

Davis, F.D., Bagozzi, R. and Warshaw, P. (1989). User Acceptance of Technology: A comparison of two theoretical models, *Management Science* 35(8): 982–1003.

Davison, R. (2001). GSS and Action Research in the Hong Kong Police, *Information Technology and People* 14(1): 60–77.

Fitzgerald, B., Russo, N. and Stolterman, E. (2002). *Information Systems Development: Methods in Action*, New York: McGraw-Hill.

Folke, C., Carpenter, S., Elmqvist, T., Gunderson, L., Holling, C.S., Walker, B., Bengtsson, J., Berkes, F., Colding, J., Danell, K., Falkenmark, M., Gordon, L., Kasperson, R., Kautsky, N., Kinzig, A., Levin, S., Mäler, K.-G., Moberg, F., Ohlsson, L., Olsson, P., Ostrom, E., Reid, W., Rockström, J., Savenije, H. and Svedin, U. (2002). Resilience and Sustainable Development: Building adaptive capacity in a world of transformations, Swedish Advisory Council [WWW document]http://www.sou.gov.se/mvb/pdf/resiliens.pdf(accessed August 2006).

Gersick, C. (1991). Revolutionary Change Theories: A multi-level exploration of the punctuated equilibrium paradigm, *Academy of Management Review* 16(1): 10–36.

Greenwood, D.J. and Levin, M. (1998). *Introduction to Action Research: Social Research for Social Change*, London: Sage.

Grotberg, E. (1997). The International Resilience Project: Findings from the research and the effectiveness of interventions, in B. Bain, *et al.* (eds.) *Psychology and Education in the 21st Century*, Edmonton: IC Press, pp. 118–128.

Hamel, G. and Välikangas (2003). The Quest for Resilience, *Harvard Business Review* 81(9): 52–63.

Hammer, M. (1990). Reengineering Work: Don't automate, obliterate, *Harvard Business Review*, July–August 68(4): 104–112.

Hardgrave, B.C., Davis, F. and Riemenschneider, C.K. (2003). Investigating Determinants of Software Developers' Intentions to Follow Methodologies, *Journal of Management Information Systems* 20(1): 123–151.

Hyde, L. (1998). *Trickster Makes This World*, New York: North Point Press.

Iivari, J. (1996). Why are CASE Tools not Used? *Communications of the ACM* 39(10): 94–103.

Kautz, K. and McMaster, T. (1994). The Failure to Introduce System Development Methods: A factor-based analysis, in L. Levine (ed.) *Diffusion, Transfer and Implementation of Information Technology*, Amsterdam: Elsevier/North-Holland, pp. 275–287.

Kawalek, P. and Wastell, D. (2005). Pursuing Radical Transformation in Information Age Government: Case studies using the SPRINT methodology, *Journal of Global Information Management* 13(1): 79–101.

Kovoor-Misra, S., Clair, J.A. and Bettenhausen, K.L. (2001). Clarifying the Attributes of Organizational Crises, *Technology Forecasting and Social Change* 67(1): 77–91.

Latour, B. (1987). *Science in Action*, Boston: Harvard Press.

Laudon, J. and Laudon, K. (2005). *Management Information Systems*, New Jersey: Prentice-Hall.

Lundblad, J. (2003). A Review and Critique of Rogers' Diffusion of Innovation Theory as it Applies to Organisations, *Organisational Development Journal* 21(4): 50–64.

Luthans, F. (2002). The Need for and Meaning of Positive Organizational Behavior, *Journal of Organizational Behavior* 23: 695–706.

MacIntosh, R. (2003). BPR: Alive and Well in the Public Sector, *International Journal of Operations and Production Management* 23(3): 327–344.

Mallik, L. (1998). Putting Organizational Resilience to Work, *Industrial Management* 40(6): 8–13.

Mathiassen, L. (2002). Collaborative Practice Research, *Information Technology and People* 15(4): 321–345.

McMaster, T. and Wastell, D.G. (2004). Success and Failure Revisited in the Implementation of New Technology: Some reflections on the CAPELLA project, in B. Fitzgerald and E. Wynn (eds.) *Innovation for Adaptability and Competitiveness*, Boston: Kluwer.

McMaster, T. and Wastell, D.G. (2005). Diffusion or Delusion? Challenging an IS research tradition, *Information Technology and People* 18(4): 383–404.

Meyer, A.D., Goes, J. and Brooks, G.R. (1995). Organisations Reacting to Hyperturbulence, in G. Huber and W. Glick (eds.) *Organisational change and redesign*, Oxford University Press: New York, pp. 66–111.

Mustonen-Ollila, E. and Lyytinen, K. (2003). How Organizations Adopt Information System Process Innovations: A longitudinal analysis, *European Journal of Information Systems* 13(3): 35–51.

Newman, M. and Robey, D. (1992). A Social Process of User–Analyst Relationships, *MIS Quarterly* 16(2): 249–266.

Newman, T. and Blackburn, S. (2002). *Transitions in the Lives of Child and Young People; Resilience Factors*, Scottish Executive Education Department.

Orlikowski, W. (1993). CASE Tools as Organizational Change: Investigating incremental and radical changes in system development, *MIS Quarterly* 17(3): 309–340.

Pettigrew, A. (1990). Longitudinal Field Research on Change: Theory and practice, *Organisational Science* 1(3): 267–292.

Pulley, M.L. (1997). Leading Resilient Organizations, *Leadership in Action* 17(4): 1–5.

Riolli, L. and Savicki, V. (2003). Information System Organizational Resilience, *Omega* 31(3): 227–233.

Rogers, E.M. (1995). *The Diffusion of Innovations*, New York: the Free Press.

Seeger, M.W., Ulmer, R.R., Novak, J.M. and Sellnow, T. (2005). Post-Crisis Discourse and Organisational Change, Failure and Renewal, *Journal of Organizational Change* 18(1): 78–95.

Sheffi, Y. (2005). *The Resilient Enterprise: Overcoming Vulnerability or Competitive Advantage*, Newbury Park: Sage.

Simon, S.J. (2000). The Reorganisation of the Information Systems of the US Naval Construction Forces: An action research project, *European Journal of Information Systems* 9(3): 148–162.

Sullivan, H. and Skelcher, C. (2002). *Working Across Boundaries: Collaboration in the Public Services*, Basingstoke: Palgrave Macmillan.

Templeton, G.F. and Byrd, T.A. (2003). Determinants of the Relative Advantage of a Structured SDM During the Adoption Stage of Implementation, *Information Technology and Management* 4(4): 409–428.

Van de Ven, A.H. (1995). Managing the Process of Organizational Innovation, in G. Huber and W. Glick (eds.) *Organisational Change and Redesign*, Oxford: Oxford University Press, pp. 269–294.

Wastell, D.G. (1996). The Fetish of Technique: Methodology as a social defence, *Information Systems Journal* 6(1): 25–40.

Wastell, D.G. (1999). Learning Dysfunctions in Information Systems Development: Overcoming the social defences with transitional objects, *MIS Quarterly* 23(4): 581–600.

Wastell, D.G. (2006). Information Systems and Evidence-Based Policy in Multi-Agency Networks: The micro-political contingencies of situated innovation, *Journal of Strategic Information Systems* 15(3): 197–217.

Wastell, D.G. and White, P. (1993). Using Process Technology to Support Cooperative Work: Prospects and design issues, in D. Diaper and C. Sanger (eds.) *CSCW in practice*, London: Springer-Verlag, pp. 105–126.

Weick, K. (1995). *Sense-Making in Organizations.*, Thousand Oakes, CA: Sage.

Appendix: SPRINT headlines

SPRINT is a BPR methodology which attempts to bring together elements of good practice, drawing on the previous experience of its academic authors and the research literature, within a single framework. Key precepts are shown below. There are three main phases, each defined in terms of a set of aims and tasks. Phase 1 is essentially one of analysis, aimed at fully understanding the business context by considering all relevant perspectives, and analysing the effectiveness of current processes. The emphasis on context is crucial, forcing the SPRINT team to 'zoom out' from the original remit, which may focus too narrowly on a particular process. Two tasks are key: building formal process models using *Role Activity Diagramming* and *Critical Goal Analysis*. All strands of enquiry are focused on two pivotal questions: what are the relevant business goals and how well are they supported? The aim of phase two is to devise a set of reengineering proposals, based on a panoramic 'business vision', which guides subsequent design work in which innovative reengineering opportunities are sought. The third phase of SPRINT is concerned with implementation, through training, detailed process design and the development of any new IT infrastructure.

SPRINT recommends two levels of governance: a Steering Group and the BPR team. Senior management commitment is critical, and the former should therefore include representation at director level or similar. The BPR Team should comprise a senior user as Project Manager, together with BPR Consultants, other experts, and representative end-users.

SPRINT precepts	Comments, rationale
Breadth of vision	The methodology seeks to identify the full range of stakeholders in a BPR project. SPRINT has been influenced by other methodologies, most notably Multiview (Avison *et al.*, 1998) which acknowledge the complexity of organizational contexts and the presence of multiple perspectives
Depth of understanding	The development of a detailed understanding of processes through rigorous empirical study (including ethnography) is vital. Accounts of work given away from the scene embodied in manuals typically afford idealized representations, problematically related to actual practice (Wastell and White, 1993)
Radicalism	SPRINT embraces Hammer's (1990) injunction to exploit the full potential of IT to enable radical innovation. Although radical in vision, SPRINT is incremental in implementation, recognizing the inherent conservatism and collegiality of public sector organizations
Rigorous assessment	Evaluation is important to assess benefits and facilitate organizational learning. It should follow the principles of theory-based evaluation (Sullivan and Skelcher, 2002), involving the collection of quantitative and qualitative data, complemented by appropriate contextual detail, to build a causal narrative
Flexibility	To avoid ritualistic behaviour, SPRINT is neither detailed nor prescriptive; it is best described as a tool-kit providing a semi-structured learning environment, or 'transitional space' (Wastell, 1999). Case studies are provided rather than detailed step-by-step prescriptions. Users are strongly encouraged to adapt the framework, including the addition of new tools
Socio-technical philosophy	Despite the opprobrious reputation since acquired by BPR, socio-technical thinking informed early approaches such as Davenport (1992). SPRINT embodies this same human-centred outlook, emphasizing the non-Tayloristic use of technology to empower and augment the role of humans, not to automate and replace them

18

Systems Development as a Research Act

Jim Hughes[1] and Trevor Wood-Harper[1,2]
[1]*Information Systems Research Centre, University of Salford, UK*
[2]*School of Information Systems, University of South Australia, South Australia*

Introduction

The authors maintain that there is a weakness in many of the methods employed in information systems development and particularly in the requirements determination phase since this is the most organizationally dependent (Flynn, 1992). The weakness is that although the methods may have an underpinning philosophical basis, they are not explicitly embedded within any social scientific perspective. Such a perspective would enable methods or methodologies to address the organizational contexts in which their use may be envisaged (Hughes, 1998a). This would require systems developers to engage with social actors in order to find out about their social situations. This engagement may be considered to be as much interpretive research as it is practical systems development. Indeed it may be possible to extend the spectrum proposed by Nandhakumar and Jones (1997) in Figure 18.1 to include practical systems development within 'Consultancy'. In the figure they propose that it may be possible to consider the main methods of interpretive research as existing on a spectrum which spans from those which have most distance between researcher and subject to those in which the researcher is most engaged with the subject. They point to Gummesson's (1991) argument that in paid consultancy 'the engagement of the actors is tested by their willingness to pay' and that the effectiveness of the researcher 'can be assessed by the [social] actors'

```
┌─────────────────────────────────────────────────────────────────────┐
│ Distance                                                  Engagement │
│                                                                       │
│   • Analysis of published data                                        │
│       • Textual analysis                                              │
│           • Survey                                                    │
│               • Interview (structured > semi > unstructured)          │
│                   • Passive observation (and lab experiments)         │
│                       • Participant observation                       │
│                           • Action research                           │
│                               • Consultancy                           │
│                                                                       │
└─────────────────────────────────────────────────────────────────────┘
```

Figure 18.1 Distance and engagement between researcher and subject with different data gathering methods (Nandhakumar and Jones, 1997, p. 113)

willingness to offer them further contracts'. There are problems with this if consultancy can be considered to be research by satisfying these two criteria (Jönsson, 1991). Primary amongst these problems is that researchers require theoretical justifications whilst consultants require empirical justifications (Baskerville and Wood-Harper, 1996). It would seem reasonable then if practical systems development can be considered as interpretive research that there should be some conceptual or inquiring framework within which the work is performed and there should also be reflection, learning and an articulation of that learning. Clearly the articulation of learning about the conceptual framework would be different from say practical systems analysis reports. This difference is well expressed by Sandberg (1982, quoted in Gummesson, 1991, p. 106) who distinguishes between 'reflection' and 'dialogue and action'. In reflection the researcher maintains a distance from the project in order to analyse it with respect to some conceptual framework or theories. In dialogue and action the researcher is involved in dialogue with the organization and takes action in intervening in the domain. Importantly there is *always* an interaction between the researcher's reflection and his/her work for the client. The distinguishing characteristic is that for dialogue and action it is the requirements of the organization that are uppermost.

In order to explore the IS practitioner as researcher argument the paper is divided into two main sections. The first section considers a piece of research, which illustrates the argument. The research concerns two action case studies in which a conceptual framework was used in practical requirements determination contexts as the basis of intervention. The second section discusses systems development as research act and uses lessons from the illustrative piece of research to draw conclusions.

The action cases – an illustration of systems development as a research act

In this section the authors present a conceptual framework for use by practising systems developers in the determination of requirements and introduce the reader to the action cases and the learning outcomes. A fuller explication of the framework and the action case studies, which follow, can be found in Hughes (1998a).

The conceptual framework

The development of the conceptual framework was driven by a concern for the use of methods in the requirements elicitation phase of information systems development. The reason for the concern was that many of the methods traditionally employed in this most organizationally context-sensitive area pay little or no attention to organizational concerns from an explicit sociological viewpoint. The authors maintain that in order to find out what is happening in an organizational setting then it is not only desirable but also essential that the method of inquiry used includes a sociological perspective. Developers have traditionally used methods based on a technological rather than a sociological paradigm and this may pose a threat to any serious progress in eliciting requirements in situations which are explicitly sociological. This may apparently be more true for methods associated with requirements engineering, in which requirements are considered to be almost exclusively formal and hence are said to be able to be 'captured'. However there is also a failing amongst the more human centred or situationally centred methodologies such as Soft Systems Methodology (Checkland, 1981; Checkland and Scholes, 1990) that have no explicit sociological underpinning (Brown, 1992).

The framework uses ethnomethodology (Garfinkel, 1967) as the paradigm of inquiry since it is concerned with descriptions of everyday life expressed in the words of those organizational members (actors) involved. Ethnomethodology therefore can be considered to be useful in providing good quality data. However since the elicitation of requirements preempts the design of an information system some tenable method is required to analyse the good quality data that has been collected. In this framework Grounded Theory (Glaser and Strauss, 1967) is the basis of such a method since as a method of inductive analysis it allows categories concerning the data to emerge and be abstracted such that an account of the organization can be produced. This account is both written and depicted graphically in a hierarchical diagram of categories. A third conjunction of the framework includes the use of action case as the basis of reflection on both the practical intervention and on the conceptual framework. Each of these elements is described below.

Ethnomethodology — a paradigm of inquiry

Schutz (1964) introduced a set of tenets to the discipline of sociology that provides the basis for much of the later phenomenological, eth-nomethodological and constructionist theory and empirical studies. He argued that the social sciences should focus on the ways that the 'life world', or the world that everyone experiences and takes for granted, is produced and experienced by members (actors). This subjective orienta-tion led Schutz to examine what he called the 'common-sense' knowl-edge and the practical reasoning that members use to objectify its social forms. He maintained that individuals approach the life world with a 'stock of knowledge' which is composed of common-sense constructs and categories that are social, and that these constructs and categories are applied to aspects of experience which makes them meaningful. The numerous phenomena of everyday life are subsumed under a more limited number of shared constructs. The shared constructs become the means by which members understand and interpret experience since language is the central medium for transmitting meaning (Schutz, 1967). Thus social phenomenology is based on the tenet that social interaction *constructs* as much as *conveys* meaning. As a strategy of inquiry his aim was a social science which would 'interpret and explain human action and thought'. This focused on how objects and experi-ence are meaningfully constituted and communicated in the world of everyday life.

Garfinkel's ethnomethodology (Garfinkel, 1967) was not just an extension of Schutz's work but much more an alternative to the Parsons' (1966) theory of action in which he maintained that social order was made possible through institutionalized systems of norms, rules and values. Garfinkel felt that this cast social actors as 'judgmental dopes' responding to external factors and motivated by internalized directives. His response was based on similar lines to Schutz (1964) that individuals had language-based and interaction-based 'competencies'. It is through these competencies that the observable orderly features of everyday life are produced. Garfinkel's (1967) ethnomethodology differs from Schutz's (1964) social phenomenology in that the topic of study was the everyday procedures (methods) that social actors (ethno) used for creating, sustaining and managing a sense of reality. Ethnomethodological study focuses therefore on how actors accomplish, manage and reproduce a 'sense' of social structure. Ethnomethodologists focus on folk (common) methods and common sense reasoning. Garfinkel (1967) refers to this as

> the investigation of the rational properties of indexical expressions and other practical actions as contingent ongoing accomplishments of organized artful practices of everyday life. (Garfinkel, 1967, p. 11)

Since reality is produced by way of actors' interpretive procedures then the ethnomethodologists maintain that the actors' social circumstances are 'self-generating' which implies two important properties. First that meanings are essentially *indexical*, that is they depend on context and therefore it is only in the situated use in talk and interaction that objects and events become meaningful. Secondly that social realities are *reflexive* which is to say that interpretive activities are both in and also about the social settings that they describe. Thus the focus for ethnomethodological research is the treatment of talk and interaction as topics for analysis rather than merely as a means of communicating some underlying phenomena. Waters (1994) proposes that for ethnomethodologists the only way in which sociologists can reveal the 'facticity' of social experience is to approach it as would an anthropologist

> That is, the sociologist must seek to understand situations, in the terms in which participants give accounts of them, by calling to our attention the reflexive or accounting practices themselves. Sociologists must somehow induce participants to give accounts and thus to reveal the contextually rational properties of their social arrangements. (Waters, 1994, p. 38)

Indeed the social anthropologist Erving Goffman is often associated with ethnomethodology. Goffman (1959) expresses social action in a dramaturgical sense and as such assigns roles to individuals who perform these roles in order that they present a particular impression of themselves. He differs from ethnomethodologists such as Garfinkel since he considers the accounts that actors give as being too narrow a description preferring to include a wide range of other expressions such as body language, dress and so on.

Garfinkel however, maintained the value of the account and proposed methods which explicitly sought to disrupt the continuity of reflexive behaviour in order to demonstrate that the stable social order is a constructed and fragile reality to which we all conspire and which may be undone. One example of this disruptive inquiry noted by Waters (1994) included field work in which the investigators acted like lodgers when living with their own families, and another in which the investigators attempted to overpay for shop purchases. Once the required 'confusion' has been produced in the participant then they are required to give an account of the natural facts. Whilst this disruptive action may appear extreme Denzin (1971) argues that ethnomethodology offers very real insights into the ways in which organizations work. He identifies those especially which process people, since comparable organizations differ in the way that they classify similar events and even in the ways in which they attribute meaning to particular words or phrases.

In the action cases presented here, ethnomethodology provides the means of collecting high quality data using semi-structured interviews to tape, which were then transcribed verbatim. One further aspect of the ethnomethodological approach was to recognize Goffman's concern given above, that in social situations communication is not only described through verbal accounts. Thus the researcher/practitioner was also sensitive to other aspects of communication which undoubtedly had an influence on the collection and later analysis of the results. This is not surprising since this is the expected situation in interpretive research.

Grounded theory – procedures for data analysis

Grounded Theory or as it was originally titled 'The Discovery of Grounded Theory' (Glaser and Strauss, 1967) is a method for the collection and analysis of qualitative data. It was derived as a means of formalizing the operation of the principles of analytic induction first suggested by Znaniecki (1934) and later elaborated by others such as Robinson (1951) and Denzin (1970). In this method conceptual properties and categories may be 'discovered' or generated from the qualitative data by following a number of guidelines and procedures. The two critical stages of Grounded Theory identified by Glaser and Strauss (1967) are first that of constant comparative analysis, a procedure for the idetification of conceptual categories and their properties which may be embedded in the data and secondly theoretical sampling which is a category-enriching procedure. The procedures revolve around the coding of transcripts and the development of categories, which lead to the emerging theory.

Glaser and Strauss' (1967) original work had three main purposes. To offer the rationale for theory that was 'grounded', that is to say generated and developed through the inductive analysis of data collected during research projects. At that time this departure from traditional functionalist (Parsons, 1964, 1966) and structuralist (Merton, 1963) theories which were largely deductive was a radical shift. The second aim was to suggest the procedures and the reasons for them and the third aim was to propose legitimacy for careful qualitative research. Interestingly the final aim has been achieved to the extent that Grounded Theory underpins many models of qualitative research (Dey, 1993).

The main application areas of Grounded Theory were most notably in Glaser and Strauss' own research into 'status passage' (Glaser and Strauss, 1970). They were also used in a number of other, usually medical or nursing related, areas such as experiences with chronic illness (Charmaz, 1990) and homecoming (Hall, 1992). Additionally much work has been done with respect to guidance on the use of method. Most notable amongst them include Charmaz (1983); Turner (1983); Martin and Turner (1986); Strauss (1987); Strauss and Corbin (1990).

Grounded Theory differs from other approaches to the analysis of qualitative data because of its emphasis on theory. Strauss and Corbin (1994) maintain that theory consists of

> plausible relationships proposed among concepts and sets of concepts . . . Researchers are interested in patterns of action and interaction between and among various types of social units (i.e. actors) . . . They are also much concerned with discovering process – not necessarily in the sense of stages or phases, but in reciprocal changes in patterns of action/interaction and in relationship with changes of conditions either internal or external to the process itself. (Strauss and Corbin, 1994, p. 274)

In reply to criticism that their definition of theory may be too austere or formal they note two important aspects of Grounded Theory,

> First, theories are always traceable to the data that gave rise to them . . . Second grounded theories are very 'fluid' because they embrace the interaction of multiple actors, and because they emphasise temporality and process. (Strauss and Corbin, 1994, p. 276)

They stress that grounded theories are interpretive in their nature. This point will be referred to later in this section.

The method of Grounded Theory has spread to many other disciplines including research in information systems. However Strauss and Corbin (1994) regret that the methodology now 'runs the risk of becoming fashionable'. They identify the main risks of this diffusion of the method being the lack of conceptual development of processes. They attribute much of this diffusion of method to the overemphasis in the original (Glaser and Strauss, 1967) work on the inductive aspects of the method rather than the significance of grounded theories and on the importance of theoretically sensitized and trained researchers.

However the proponents of 'pure' Grounded Theory may consider that since the divisions amongst the original coauthors are so great, then the differences in the use of the method by others is only to be expected. This schism between Glaser and Strauss (Glaser, 1992) as to the focus of Grounded Theory is presented as a personal attack by Glaser. Unfortunately this distorts the academic argument which simply put, criticizes the Strauss and Corbin's (1990) version of Grounded Theory as discarding emerging theory which is the basis for induction and replacing it with *forcing* theory from predetermined frameworks. For the purpose of this paper it is the Strauss and Corbin writings that are taken as the latest 'version'.

Returning to the earlier point regarding the interpretive nature of Grounded Theory there is some debate regarding this stance. Whilst Grounded Theory points to its roots in the interactionist tradition and the influences of Mead (1934) and Blumer (1962; 1969) it may be considered to be positivist rather than interpretivist. This is particularly evident in the emphasis placed in more recent writings on the scientific criteria, such as repeatability, that must be applied to Grounded Theory research in order to validate the research process (Corbin and Strauss, 1990; Strauss and Corbin, 1990). However Denzin (1994) maintains that more accurately, Grounded Theory can be considered as postpositivist since although its proponents emphasize the 'good science' model it continues to fit itself to more interpretive styles. The authors consider Grounded Theory in this way given their concern for meaning induced from users' spoken words. They therefore agree with Miles and Huberman (1994) who consider the post-positivist perspective to place an emphasis on multiple realities and researcher interpretation. Thus the use of Grounded Theory and the results produced may be said to be contingent upon the situation or domain under study. This is more in line with the constructivist criteria for quality of research. These criteria rely upon the richness or authenticity of the learning that is achieved and an understanding of the constructions of others, and on the ontological authenticity in terms of the development of the researcher's personal constructs (Guba and Lincoln, 1994).

The use of Grounded Theory techniques is already established in information systems research (Calloway and Ariav, 1991; Pries-Heje, 1991; Toraskar, 1991, Baskerville and Pries-Heje, 1998) and has been used practically in knowledge elicitation (Oliphant and Blockley, 1991; Pidgeon *et al.* 1991). A major concern amongst all authors is the time taken to perform the analysis, which tends to preclude it from practical systems analysis activities. For the action cases described below the problems of time constraint were mitigated by the use of a software package, QSR NUD-IST (Richards and Richards, 1991), for coding indexing and sorting categories. The use of computers in qualitative analysis may be open to the criticism that for interpretive research the software may lead the research. Yet as Kelle (1995) points out much of this hostility has dissipated with the increased use of sophisticated software packages designed specifically to aid text structuring, indexing and storage.

Baskerville and Pries-Heje (1998) have considered the specific use of Grounded Theory in action research projects. They show how the theory development portion of action research can be made more rigorous by merging some of the techniques of Grounded Theory with the steps in action research; particularly those associated with theory formulation. In this paper the conjunction is considered with respect to action cases as discussed below.

Action case

The use of the term action case in this paper follows from Vidgen and Braa (1997) who approach action case as arising from 'soft' case study which is essentially a method for *understanding* in which there may also be some limited *intervention*, which causes change. It is used here from an alternative perspective in which intervention is planned and from which some understanding is gained about the conceptual framework in order that learning can take place. The term is also intended to convey that the learning may be achieved in a limited number of interventions. Indeed a single intervention for a practitioner should be sufficient to reflect and learn about some project. In terms of action research the term action case may be characterized as 'reflective action research' as discussed by Baskerville and Wood-Harper (1998) in which they maintain that the critical element 'is the actors' discovery of where their behaviour is unexplained by their own understanding'. They note that within reflective action research 'iteration is no longer an end in itself'.

This is clearly important for the practitioner since even within a *single* IS development project he/she may focus on the distinction between what was suggested by the theoretical framework versus what actually happened in practice. A consequence of this is the learning about the theoretical framework and the *process* of development.

Furthermore, action case as used in the illustrative research presented here has a strong resonance with the concept of 'double loop learning' as expressed by Argyris and Schon (1978). They consider double loop learning to mean that following some intervention in an organization it is possible to learn about the domain – they refer to this as single loop learning. However the learning may also challenge the 'norms' or framework which were the basis of the intervention. They suggest that this could cause some conflict amongst managers who established the norms. They refer to double loop learning as a resolution of the conflict. Indeed as Reason (1994) notes double loop learning is critical, since without the refection on the 'governing variables', or theoretical framework, then it is possible for individuals to produce self-fulfilling systems of action which may lead to escalating errors. We return to this critical issue in the action cases where practical considerations take precedence over the canonical use of methods as noted also by Baskerville and Pries-Heje (1998). Refection on this is central to learning in the practical situation and to the research outcomes.

Together then, the conceptual framework comprised the conjunction of ethnomethodology as a paradigm of inquiry, Grounded Theory as a method for data analysis and action case as the research strategy for reflection on the domains. The two action cases are given briefly below.

The action cases

The HVP study – domain

The first action case domain was a three site veterinary practice in a city in the East Midlands, which we shall call HVP. One site is in the city centre and the others are situated 5 miles south and 5 miles Northwest of the city centre in large village locations. The Practice is a mixed practice in that it does both small animal and farm animal veterinary work. The Practice is a partnership with four equal share veterinary Partners, one salaried Partner, four full-time veterinary assistants and two part-time veterinary assistants. There are thirteen practice receptionists including a reception supervisor at each site and eleven nurses including a nurse supervisor for each site. Additionally the Practice employs out-of-hours telephone receptionists who usually are the life partners of the vet on call. The general management of the Practice is through the Partners assisted by a full time Practice Manager and a Practice Accountant both of whom sit on the Practice management team. One accounts clerk and one administrative assistant provide additional administrative support for the Farm Office.

The HVP study – intervention

The nature of the intervention was to help the management team better understand its information needs prior to considering any investment in an IT infrastructure. They expected an outcome of the study to be an audit or evaluation of current work practices and recommendations for change, which would accommodate the introduction of computerized information systems. During the initial talks with the management team the developer made explicit the nature of the intervention methodology and the reasons for it. It was also established and agreed that the work would also have research outcomes. The team agreed that the outcomes of the research and the outcomes that they expected from the study were not in conflict.

The rationale for the study was linked to the management team's agreed strategy, which was presented through discussion rather than being formally documented. The management team in the last three years had seen an increase in the pressure on the city-centre site in terms of an increasing client base and the lack of appropriate accommodation to meet the increased demand. This led to the decision to open a new site, W, which would take some of the client numbers and also enable the practice to offer a purpose-built Farm Office and centre for farmers to visit to purchase veterinary products. The financial profile was such that finding the new premises was viable and the expectation was that the income from the new site would in the long term provide financial stability for the Practice. At the time of the study the management team realized that the growth in business since the opening of the W site had exceeded expectations and were considering ways to stabilize their client base such that a further site would not be required in the future. The management team broadly agreed that the move to a three-site practice had put, and would put, demands on their existing systems, procedures and management and staff.

The research/consultancy proceeded by establishing 'seed categories' for the interviews. Although a departure from the procedures of Grounded Theory, Miles and Huberman (1994) consider this a legitimate way to give initial focus for the interview questions. The three seed categories were understanding of job roles and responsibilities, decision-making processes and communication between the three sites. The first interviews were followed up with individuals and with groups in order to fill out emerging categories until the major categories were saturated. Saturation is achieved when transcript coding no longer adds to the dimensions or properties of the categories. This was followed in the analysis by the identification of the core category, which is the most abstract representation of the data.

Figure 18.2 illustrates how the highest level of categories relate to a core category. From the written accounts (known as memos in Grounded Theory) of each of these categories an understanding of the domain emerged which was grounded in the organization. The written accounts are given in full in Hughes (1998a).

The HVP study – the practical outcomes

For the HVP management team a number of practical recommendations were made in the form of a report. The report was a distillation of the rich account produced by the use of the analysis method into a relatively thin document that largely ignored the process and context issues, which had led the consultant to make the recommendations. Briefly the recommendations were: to restructure the role of the practice manager; to specify management roles in autonomous sites; to address formal communication systems such as day book and work rotas; to introduce computerized record keeping for client records in the first instance. The management team was pleased with the recommendations and has subsequently acted on all of them to their satisfaction.

The HVP study – the research outcomes

For the researcher one of the important lessons was to consider this distillation into thin descriptions for the management to be a part of

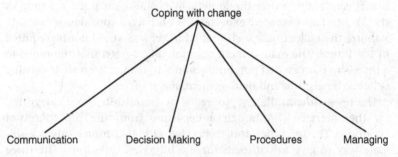

Figure 18.2   Core category and major categories from the HVP action case

the methodology for future interventions. Other research outcomes included the excessive time taken to interview, transcribe, code and categorize the use of seed categories and the adaptation of the original methods into a practical context. What emerged was a revised framework. This revised framework was part of the action cycle and informed future work. The second action case used the adapted framework and methodology.

The FP UK study – domain

The second action case concerns a small manufacturing company, which we shall call FP UK, based in Northeast Wales. It is part of the FP Group consisting of three private limited companies, which are financially independent. The parent company FP A/S was registered in Denmark in 1952 to produce iron dust cores, ferrites and ceramic capacitors. FP UK offers a manufacturing capability for the production of most types of high quality inductors and transformers. Transformers are produced as custom designs and also in standard ranges. A highly flexible production facility ensures short lead times on custom designs as well as standard products. A small amount of business is with factored products (selling Danish manufactured products). Over the years the FP Group has forged strong links with technical institutions and other companies in the UK and the EU and is currently involved in several joint research and development projects with academic and commercial concerns within the EU. FP UK specifically has a design alliance with a German manufacturer and outlets for sales in both Italy and Germany. FP UK employs 18 full time salaried staff who work in administrative or management roles and an additional 20 who are production line workers.

The FP UK study – intervention

FP UK faced two major decisions with respect to the future of the organization. The first was to determine whether the future for FP UK lies either in manufacturing or in sales. The second and related decision was to determine an investment strategy in IT/IS linked to business objectives. The intervention was an audit to establish an IS investment strategy that would enable FP UK to make the decision regarding their future direction.

As with the action case given above, initial discussions included an explicit discussion of the research as well as the practical outcomes. In this case two seed categories were used since these had proved useful in the first case. These were understanding job roles and responsibilities and the impact of IT on work. A change suggested by the learning from the first case was to cut the time taken for transcribing, coding and cate-gorizing. This was particularly important in the FP UK case because of the tighter deadline set by the sponsors. This was achieved by exploiting the NUD·IST software package and by not fully transcribing all inter-views. Using the NUD·IST package it was possible to listen to the taped interviews, transcribe the relevant passage, which would range from a couple of sentences to two or three paragraphs and augment existing categories or create new ones directly and therefore avoid the full tran-scription step. Because this seemed such a departure from the method, the taped interviews that were not fully transcribed were usually those where categories were being saturated; that is to say they were second or third interviews with the same person. A core category was identified, 'demarcation' and both a full account from the coding was produced in addition to a management report.

The FP UK study – the practical outcomes

For FP UK the practical outcomes were an identification of an existing situation that showed a lack of a common understanding in the use of a variety of information systems and their relation to each other. Also a conflict between organizational goals, expressed by the managing direc-tor, and the goals of particular functional areas. The report, which was well received, recommended a single network infrastructure, internal IT integration, exploitation of external IT links, staff awareness issues, the appointment of an IT support manager and the inclusion of IS strategy as part of the business planning cycle.

The FP UK study – the research outcomes

Although the study was a departure from the original procedures for data analysis described by Glaser and Strauss (1967) it should be remembered that the original authors and users of the methods had no recourse to the use of such powerful software tools. In the original paper-based method great emphasis was placed on transcription since the transcribed document was also the physical medium for coding. That is to say margin notes in the form of codes were critical to the success of the method. However the introduction of the software pack-age as the medium reduced the importance of the transcript except as evidence. (It is accepted that the tape itself is evidence but it is much less accessible than paper.) Hence the sequence 'tape–transcribe–code' becomes 'tape–partial transcribe–code'. The difficulty with this is that when the developer needs to compare new documents with existing documents then only the codes or categories or partial transcript are available and therefore the taped interviews have to be listened to again. A further difficulty with this practical adaptation is the auditability of the method since although categories can be traced to the source document, the document itself is not a full account of the interview. Another consideration on this point is that the paradigm of inquiry for the method, ethnomethodology, is concerned with transcripts being in the interviewees' own words. Whilst the adaptation is true to this in terms of the partial transcript, it clearly does not contain *all* of the interviewees' own words and therefore may not be in keeping with the ethnomethodological perspective. However as with the HVP action case, and as noted in the introduction, this dilemma between practical outcome within time constraints and theoretical rigour whilst of interest to the developer, must be resolved in favour of the practical outcomes. Other research outcomes included the favourable use of the software package in time critical situations and the need for initial seed categories.

Discussion

In this the second section of the paper we discuss the issues of system development as a research act drawing upon the illustrative action cases given above. The action cases presented a theoretical framework that was the basis of practical intervention. For the interpretive researcher reflection on the framework and articulation of that reflection can help to inform future interventions. For the practitioner it must be practical concerns that are uppermost. The major areas for concern arising from this are first the role of the practitioner/researcher and secondly the adaptation of, in this instance, social science research methods into the practical (real world) situation.

The role of the researcher/practitioner

The authors maintain that roles need to be considered for the systems developer, which move beyond the traditional notion of expert and indeed beyond the emergent role of facilitator. That role has been variously expressed as moral agent (Walsham, 1993) or reflective practitioner (Schon, 1983) and considered in the problem solving context (Jayaratna, 1994) where the emphasis is not exclusively on technical skill sets or interpersonal skills but on the thinking skills of the developer. Interestingly, this coincides with the view of the researcher as proposed by Lincoln and Denzin (1994). They would say the researcher, and in the context of this study the systems developer, may be considered to be the ultimate 'bricoleur' (or Jack of all trades). But more than simply the Jack of all trades, they are also the inventors

they know they have few tools and little by way of appropriate parts and so become inventors (Lincoln and Denzin, 1994, p. 584)

This is a deeper understanding of the limits of methods and openness to learning and adaptation. If applied to information systems methods it opens the door for methodology-in-action and the analysis of our experiences and making explicit learning with fellow analysts and sharing also with those who are affected, that is, 'users'. It is the methodological pluralism (Klein *et al.*, 1991) based on reflexivity, which is context, and the people (agents) in context. This role of developer as bricoleur broadens rather than narrows the scope of action for the systems developer. It challenges methodological purity in action, where dogmatism is at the fore. The bricoleur role also avoids the pitfall of treating the selection of methods and indeed methodologies as one might select a tool from a tool box since the role incorporates the reflective (thinking) aspect.

In the action cases above the use of methods from the social sciences and the explicit understanding and sharing of the ethnomethodology perspective help define the developer's role. However the learning from the action cases shows that this is not restrictive in terms of how the methods must be applied nor does it imply precedence of research outcomes over practical outcomes. In the action cases a paradigm of inquiry and methods of analysis have been used which have produced a written account – this is essentially a *research* outcome. The other research outcomes are expressed as an articulation of the learning that took place about the framework and the methodology for the intervention. For the practitioner however it is insufficient to have produced the account. The sponsors of a study expect also to have recommendations for future action, which they may consider, and then where appropriate act. Although the sponsors and other actors participate in the study they look to the researcher/consultant for what they may term 'expert' guidance – that is what they paid for! (Gummesson, 1991). There is therefore an expectation of a *practical* outcome. In the action cases the practical outcomes expected were achieved by re-presenting the thick descriptions formed from the textual account and the hierarchical accounts as thin descriptions that largely ignored process and context and achieved instead a distillation which was acceptable to sponsors. Rapoport (1970) refers this to as one of the three 'dilemmas' of action research where the practical pressures interfere with the research process. For the practitioner him or herself it is clearly important to distinguish between the practical pressures and the research process. This can be achieved by critically reflecting on the process and on the research framework.

Indeed, the reflective developer adapts the methodology and makes judgements based on the context. This strengthens rather than weakens the developer's position. Further to this the developer in the cases given actively engaged the users through the validation of interim accounts and hence shared the problems and ultimately gave ownership of future solutions to the users. It may thus be argued that the dilemma receded in the action cases with respect to the researcher/practitioner and it may be more constructive to re-cast the dilemma in terms of the systems developer engaging in interpretive research.

A criticism may be that the learning that takes place in this action case model is almost exclusively internal to the researcher. More commonly this may be expressed by the phrases 'you learn by your mistakes' and 'just put it down to experience'. It would be damaging to leave the situation there. It is the *articulation* of the learning that is powerful, since that is the means by which one person's practical experiences become the shared learning of a community.

There is clearly an implication for training and education of systems developers if this is to be a new role. Although outside of the scope of this paper the authors would point to Walsham's (1993) call for an education based on critical self-reflection. Also the work by Mathiassen *et al.* (1997) who provide an interesting training programme for developing skills in IT organizations which supports critical reflection and organizational learning.

Adaptation of research methods into practical systems development

The second learning point concerns bringing research methods into practical systems development. In the two action case studies the original tenets of both ethnomethodology and Grounded Theory were challenged by practical considerations and adapted accordingly. The authors would maintain that the procedures retain the essential principles of analytic induction within the Grounded Theory approach. However in order to avoid confusion it may be better to rename this set of procedures as grounding information systems rather than to suggest it is the same as the original Glaser and Strauss work. However as noted earlier even the original coauthors can no longer agree about the substantive theoretical basis of the methods. This departure from prescribed method is perhaps to be expected and as Baskerville and Pries-Heje (1998) note the use of action research will usually change the role of Grounded Theory's elements. This is not uncommon when considering the use of information systems methodologies which differ greatly in practice from their written theoretical form (Hughes, 1998b). The adaptation is indeed not only possible but also worthy. Fitzgerald (1996) notes

> In practice, situations will inevitably arise where the developer needs to step outside the methodology, but formalized methodologies often serve to impose a considerable inertia on the development process. (Fitzgerald, 1996, p. 19).

With respect to ethnomethodology in the action cases the movement away from 'pure' ethnomethodological principles was noted in the learning from the FP UK action case. What then remains may be said to be the essence or indeed spirit of ethnomethodology. That is to say that the concern remains with agency and actors and the construction of meaning by the words they use. As Button and Sharrock (1994) noted, when practical priorities become dominant features in the use of methodology it is the fact that the methodology 'instantiated ethnomethodological themes' that is of paramount concern. The action cases presented here adhere to that. This may be an expected outcome of *any* reflective action research since as Baskerville and Wood-Harper (1998) note

> The important characteristic of reflective IS action research is its focus on the distinction between theory-in-use *versus* espoused theory. (Baskerville and Wood-Harper, 1998, p. 100 – their emphasis)

The adaptation of methods or theories is entirely acceptable for the consultant engaged in the use of social science research methods. What is critically important is that the adaptation must be the result of reflection on what happened in practice against what theoretically may have been the expected outcome.

Conclusion

The argument presented here is not to persuade practitioners in IS to use and adapt the framework that has been described. It has been described for illustrative purposes only. The conjunction of ethnomethodology, Grounded Theory and action case provides but one means of intervention in, and understanding of organizational life. The authors' concern is for those IS practitioners who actively engage in organizational life. We would maintain that critical reflection and articulation of learning based on some state theoretical or conceptual framework should be the basis of their intervention. In that way they act both as researcher and practitioner and the results consequently inform both theory and practice. In information systems there is a very close relationship between research *for* systems development and research *into* systems development. The role of action case and an inquiring framework is important in this regard as they provide first a basis for understanding and improving practice and secondly insight for researchers. The onus for proceeding in understanding these issues lies equally with researchers as it does with reflective practitioners.

References

Argyris, C. and Schon, D. (1978) *Organizational Learning: A Theory of Action Perspective* (Addison-Wesley, Reading).

Baskerville, R. and Pries-Heje, J. (1998) Grounding action research. *Journal of Accounting, Management and Information Technologies* (forthcoming).

Baskerville, R. and Wood-Harper, A.T. (1996) A critical perspective on action research as a method for information systems research. *Journal of Information Technology.* 11(3), 235–46.

Baskerville, R. and Wood-Harper, A.T. (1998) Diversity in information systems action research methods. *European Journal of Information Systems,* 7(2), 90–107.

Blumer, H. (1962) Society as symbolic interaction, in *Human Behaviour and Social Processes,* Rose, A.M. (ed) (Houghton Mifflin, Boston) pp. 179–92.

Blumer, H. (1969) *Symbolic Interactionism: Perspective and Method* (Prentice Hall, Englewood Cliffs, New Jersey).

Brown, A. (1992) Grounding soft systems research. *European Journal of Information Systems,* 1(6), 387–95.

Button, G. and Sharrock, W. (1994) Occasioned practices in the work of software engineers, in *Requirements Engineering: Social and Technical Issues,* Jirotka, M. and Goguen, J.A. (eds) (Academic Press, London), pp. 217–40.

Calloway, L.J. and Ariav, G. (1991) Developing and using a qualitative methodology to study relationships among designers and tools, in *Information Systems Research: Contemporary Approaches and Emergent Traditions,* Nissen, H.-E., Klein, H.K. and Hirschheim, R. (eds) (North Holland, Amsterdam) pp. 175–93.

Charmaz, K. (1983) The grounded theory method: an explication and interpretation, in *Contemporary Field Research,* Emerson, R.M. (ed) (Waveland Press Inc., Illinois, USA) pp. 109–26.

Charmaz, K. (1990) 'Discovering' chronic illness: using grounded theory. *Social Science in Medicine,* 30(11), 1161–72.

Checkland, P.B. (1981) *Systems Thinking, Systems Practice* (John Wiley and Sons Ltd, Chichester).

Checkland, P.B. and Scholes, S. (1990) *Soft Systems Methodology in Action* (John Wiley and Sons Ltd, Chichester)

Corbin, J. and Strauss, A. (1990) Grounded theory research: procedures, canons, and evaluative criteria. *Qualitative Sociology,* **13**(1), 3–21.

Denzin, N. (1970) *The Research Act* (Butterworths, London).

Denzin, N. (1971) Symbolic interactionism and ethnomethodology, in *Understanding Everyday Life,* Douglas, J. (ed) (Routledge, London) pp. 259–84.

Denzin, N. (1994) The art and politics of interpretation, in *Handbook of Qualitative Research,* Denzin, N.K. and Lincoln, Y.S. (eds) (Sage, London) pp. 500–15.

Dey, I. (1993) *Qualitative Data Analysis: A User-Friendly Guide for Social Scientists* (Routledge, London).

Fitzgerald, B. (1996) Formalized systems development methodologies: a critical perspective. *Information Systems Journal,* **6**(1), 3–23.

Flynn, D.J. (1992) *Information Systems Requirements: Determination and Analysis* (McGraw-Hill, Maidenhead, UK).

Garfinkle, H. (1967) *Studies in Ethnomethodology* (Prentice Hall, Englewood Cliffs, NJ).

Glaser, B. (1992) *Emergence vs. Forcing: Basics of Grounded Theory* (Sociology Press, Mill Valley CA).

Glaser, B. and Strauss, A.L. (1967) *The Discovery of Grounded Theory: Strategies for Qualitative Research* (Aldine, Chicago).

Glaser, B. and Strauss, A.L. (1970) *Status Passage* (Aldine, Chicago).

Goffman, E. (1959) *The Presentation of Self in Everyday Life* (Allen Lane, London).

Guba, E.G. and Lincoln, Y.S. (1994) Competing paradigms in qualitative research, in *Handbook of Qualitative Research,* Denzin, N.K. and Lincoln, Y.S. (eds) (Sage, London) pp. 105–17.

Gummesson, E. (1991) *Qualitative Methods in Management Research* (Sage, London).

Hall, C. (1992) *Homecoming: the self at home,* unpublished doctoral thesis, University of California, Department of Social and Behavioural Sciences.

Hughes, J. (1998a) *The development of the GIST (Grounding Information SysTems) methodology: determining situated requirements in information systems analysis,* Unpublished PhD thesis, Information Systems Research Centre, University of Salford, Salford, UK.

Hughes, J. (1998b) Selection and evaluation of information system methodologies: the gap between theory and practice. *IEE Proceedings: Software* (Special issue – Information Systems, N. Jayaratna (ed.)), **145**(4), 1–5.

Jayaratna, N. (1994) *Understanding and Evaluating Methodologies* (McGraw Hill, London).

Jönsson, S. (1991) Action research, in *Information Systems Research: Contemporary Approaches and Emergent Traditions,* Nissen, H.-E., Klein, H.K. and Hirschheim, R. (eds) (North Holland, Amsterdam) pp. 371–96.

Kelle, U. (ed.) (1995) *Computer-Aided Qualitative Data Analysis: Theory, Methods and Practice,* (Sage, London).

Klein, H.K., Hirschheim, R. and Nissen, H-E. (1991) A pluralist perspective of the information systems research arena, in *Information Systems Research: Contemporary Approaches and Emergent Traditions,* Nissen, H.-E., Klein, H.K. and Hirschheim, R. (eds) (North Holland, Amsterdam) pp. 1–20.

Lincoln, Y.S. and Denzin, N.K. (1994) The fifth moment, in *Handbook of Qualitative Research,* Denzin, N.K. and Lincoln, Y.S. (eds) (Sage, London) pp. 575–86.

Martin, P.Y. and Turner, B.A. (1986) Grounded theory and organizational research. *Journal of Applied Behavioural Science*, **22**(2), 141–57.

Mathiassen, L., Borum, F. and Pederson, J.S. (1997) Developing managerial skills in IT organisations – a case study based on action learning, in *Proceedings of the 20th Information Systems Research Seminar in Scandinavia (IRIS 20)*, Oslo, Norway, pp. 849–65.

Mead, G. (1934) *Mind, Self and Society* (University of Chicago Press, Chicago).

Merton, R.K. (1963) *Society Theory and Social Structure* (Free Press, Glencoe).

Miles, M.B. and Huberman, A.M. (1994) *Qualitative Data Analysis*, Second Edn (Sage, London).

Nandhakumar, J. and Jones, M. (1997) Distance and engagement in IS research. *Information Systems Journal*, **7**(2), 109–31.

Oliphant, J. and Blockley, D.I. (1991) Knowledge-based system: advisory on the earth retaining structures. *Computers and Structures*, **40**(1), 173–83.

Parsons, T. (1964) Evolutionary universals in society. *American Sociological Review*, **29**(3), 339–57.

Parsons, T. (1966) *Societies: Evolutionary and Comparative Perspectives* (Prentice-Hall, Englewood Cliffs).

Pidgeon N.F., Turner, B.A. and Blockley, D.I. (1991) The use of Grounded Theory for conceptual analysis in knowledge elicitation. *International Journal of Man-Machine Studies*, **35**(2), 151–73.

Pries-Heje, J. (1991) Three barriers for continuing use of computer-based tools in information systems development: a grounded theory approach. *Scandinavian Journal of Information Systems*, **3**, 119–36.

Rapoport, R. (1970) Three dilemmas of action research. *Human Relations*, **23**(6), 499–513.

Reason, P. (1994) Three approaches to participative inquiry, in *Handbook of Qualitative Research*, Denzin, N.K. and Lincoln, Y.S. (eds) (Sage, London) pp. 324–39.

Richards, T. and Richards, L. (1991) The NUD·IST qualitative data analysis system. *Qualitative Sociology*, 14(4/2 winter), pp. 307–24.

Robinson, W.S. (1951) The logical structure of analytic induction. *American Sociological Review*, **16**(6), 812–18.

Schon, D.A. (1983) *The Reflective Practitioner. How Professionals Think in Action.* (Basic Books, New York, USA).

Sandberg, A. (1982) Fran aktionsforskning till praxisforskning. *Sociologisk Forskning.*

Schutz, A. (1964) *Studies in Social Theory* (Martinus Nijhoff, The Hague).

Schutz, A. (1967) *The Phenomenology of the Social World* (Northwestern University Press, Evanston, IL).

Strauss, A.L. (1987) *Qualitative Analysis for Social Scientists* (Cambridge University Press, Cambridge).

Strauss, A.L. and Corbin, J. (1990) *Basics of Qualitative Research: Grounded Theory Procedures and Techniques* (Sage, Beverly Hills, CA).

Strauss, A. and Corbin, J. (1994) Grounded theory methodology: an overview, in *Handbook of Qualitative Research*, Denzin, N.K. and Lincoln, Y.S. (eds) (Sage, London) pp. 273–85.

Toraskar, K.V. (1991) How managerial users develop their decision support?: a grounded theory approach, in *Information Systems Research: Contemporary Approaches and Emergent Traditions*, Nissen, H.-E., Klein, H.K. and Hirschheim, R. (eds) (Elsevier Science Publishers B.V, North-Holland) pp. 195–225.

Vidgen, R. and Braa, K. (1997) Balancing interpretation and intervention in information systems research: the 'action case' approach, in *Proceedings of the IFIP WG8.2 International Conference on Information Systems and Qualitative research*, Lee, A., Liebenau, J. and DeGross, J. (eds) pp. 524–41 (Philadelphia, USA).

Walsham, G. (1993) Ethical issues in information systems development – the analyst as moral agent, in *Human, Organizational and Social Dimensions of Information Systems Development*, Avison, D., Kendall, J.E. and DeGross, J.I. (eds) (North Holland, Amsterdam) pp. 281–94.

Waters, M. (1994) *Modern Sociological Theory* (Sage, London, UK).

Znaniecki, F. (1934) *The Method of Sociology* (Farrer and Rinehart, New York).

Printed in the United States
By Bookmasters